Looting Spiro Mounds

Looting Spiro Mounds

An American King Tut's Tomb

David La Vere

UNIVERSITY OF OKLAHOMA PRESS : NORMAN

Also by David La Vere

The Caddo Chiefdoms: Caddo Economics and Politics, 700 to 1835 (Lincoln, Nebr., 1998)

Life among the Texas Indians: The WPA Narratives (College Station, Tex., 1998)

Contrary Neighbors: Southern Plains and Removed Indians in Indian Territory (Norman, 2000)

The Texas Indians (College Station, Tex., 2004)

Library of Congress Cataloging-in-Publication Data

La Vere, David.
  Looting Spiro Mounds : an American King Tut's tomb / David La Vere.
     p.   cm.
  Includes bibliographical references and index.
  ISBN 0-8061-3813-0 (pbk. : alk. paper)
  ISBN 978-0-8061-3813-8
  1. Spiro Mounds Archaeological State Park (Okla.) 2. Indians of North America—Oklahoma—Le Flore County—Antiquities. 3. Archaeological thefts—Oklahoma—Le Flore County. 4. Excavations (Archaeology)—Oklahoma—Le Flore County. 5. Indians of North America—Antiquities—Collectors and collecting. 6. Indians of North America—Antiquities—Collection and preservation. 7. Le Flore County (Okla.)—Antiquities. I. Title.

  E78.O45L3 2007
  976.6'79—dc22

                                                            2006050078

The paper in this book meets the guidelines for permanence and durability of the Committee on Production Guidelines for Book Longevity of the Council on Library Resources, Inc. ∞

1   2   3   4   5   6   7   8   9   10

For Caryn Mills La Vere

Contents

Illustrations

Photos

Maps

Looting Spiro Mounds

Prologue

They crouched at the far end of the tunnel, the cramped space made closer by everyone pressing forward to get a look. A few wiped sweat from their eyes because the tunnel entrance was some twenty feet behind them, and what ventilation it provided was mainly eastern Oklahoma summertime heat and humidity. Still, the excitement was as thick as the air, and each man's pulse clicked up a beat or two. In the gloom of their miner's lamps they could tell they had hit something different. Here the dirt formed a wall, a shell harder and paler than the brown fill they had been tunneling through.

Maybe if they had thought about it, or if they had known what they were going to find, or even if their minds had worked that way, they would have taken a head count and known who was there and who was not, or at least how many of them were there. Probably three, certainly no more than six, but afterwards, no one could remember. Accurate memories faded fast in the light of all the claims and accusations that were about to barrel down on them, but none of the members of the Pocola Mining Company knew that at the time. Only a lucky few know when they're about to make one of the great finds of the century and have the presence of mind to take notes and come up with something smart to say. John Hobbs, Guinn Cooper, and the boys weren't all that lucky.

Taking a deep breath, one of the miners, no one could remember exactly who, lifted his pick and jabbed it into the dirt wall. The point cracked through a thin crust and into a sealed chamber beyond. Air hissed into the hole and pushed out a dead, musty stench. Someone pointed a lamp into the blackness. What its dim light illuminated would change the face of archaeology and come to be considered America's own King Tut's tomb.

1

The Mounds

1934

The American Indian curio market suddenly started ticking, the excitement level ratcheting up a level or two. Almost overnight and seemingly out of nowhere, a trickle of unusual and spectacular Indian artifacts had begun showing up on the relic circuit: a large stone pipe about two feet long; a few T-shaped clay pipes, some with stems eighteen inches long; two beautiful, white flint spear points about seventeen inches long; some ear spools; a few copper needles; and some beads and arrowheads. Not a lot, just enough to get people talking, and word sped from curio dealers to artifact collectors and beyond. Although 1934 was one of the worst years of the Great Depression, for Indian relic dealers, there was always the chance that a small investment in some points or pipes might bring amazing returns.[1]

Carl Guthe, chair of the National Research Council Committee on State Archaeological Surveys, kept a close eye on the curio market. Any newfound relics being sold off meant that somewhere someone had found an archaeological site and dug into it. It was his job to notice things like that, so he immediately picked up on the small For Sale ads in the back of *Hobbies* magazine, hawking the Indian artifacts.[2]

Hobbies: The Magazine for Collectors, a high-quality monthly magazine, was the bible for collectors of any stripe. Whether it was stamps, coins, antique guns or toys, or Chinese glassware, *Hobbies* had a section for each. The editors published stories and columns, offered tips, ran a classified ad section, and generally tried to bring together sellers and buyers. By the 1930s, collecting American Indian artifacts was enormously popular in the United States and Europe, so *Hobbies* dedicated a section to stories about collecting Indian artifacts. A regular column titled Around the Mounds discussed recent archaeological finds among the many American Indian burial and temple mounds scattered across the United States. In the magazine's classified ads, Indian relic dealers peddled their artifacts: bird points, two for twenty-five cents; an ancient slate ax, sixty cents; flint knives, spears, and drills, twenty-five cents each; and "rare incrusted hematite hoes" for a dollar. You could even buy an Indian skull for about two bucks, or finger bones for a few pennies.[3]

To the novice, the ads in *Hobbies* seemed a treasure trove of ancient Indian artwork. But to the experienced collector or the professional artifact dealer, someone who knew what was out there, the *Hobbies* ads in the early 1930s were disappointing. The problem was that most Indian relics listed were the same old stuff that had been circulating and recirculating for years. Major archaeological discoveries came only now and then, and if university-trained archaeologists made them, any artifacts went directly into the museums and would never see the print of a *Hobbies* ad. The only finds that made their way onto the curio market were those made by "pot hunters," what professional archaeologists called the unlicensed, untrained folks who dug up Indian burials to get at the grave goods.

And there were a lot of pot hunters out there. Some dug for the thrill of finding a bit of history. For others, it was pure business, and they hoped to sell what they found.[4] To professional archaeologists, "pot hunter" was not a term of endearment; it was the equivalent of "grave robber." Fresh artifacts always caught the eyes of private collectors and professional archaeologists, and these were quickly bought up and taken out of circulation. In 1934, it had been a few years since any new and exotic relics had shown up, and for Guthe and other academic archaeologists, no news was good news. These newly discovered artifacts meant that somewhere pot hunters had cracked open another ancient burial and were looting it of grave goods.

Whether one was an academic or a pot hunter, the American Indian curio market in the 1930s, while extensive, wasn't all that large. Anyone could deal in Indian artifacts. All one had to do was find something, maybe an unusual arrowhead or piece of pottery, and get someone to buy it. Still, there were a few full-time relic dealers, people who regularly advertised in *Hobbies*, such as Goodrich E. Pilquist, H. T. Daniel, and Joe W. Balloun, all of Dardanelle, Arkansas; Glen Groves of Chicago; Donald Boudeman of Kalamazoo, Michigan; and others scattered across the country.[5] These men knew where the relics were being found, even where they *might* be found, and they were first on the scene, shelling out cash to the pot hunters for items coming directly out of the ground. They would then contact their regular customers or advertise their purchases in *Hobbies*.

Buying from the dealers were the collectors. Theoretically, anyone could also be a collector. After all, every boy and girl in rural America probably had a few arrowheads tucked away in a cigar box somewhere. Still, there were some serious artifact collectors out there, men like Harry Trowbridge and John Braecklein, both of Kansas City; Edward Payne of Springfield, Illinois; and Colonel Fain White King of Wickliffe, Kentucky. These were well-read men who knew Indian relics. Though not university trained, they were about as well versed in Indian artifacts as were most academics of the day. For whatever reason, though, these men had a collector's bent.

They wanted to own and to possess artifacts and so were regular buyers. Always on the lookout for something fresh and exotic, they boasted a widespread network of dealer contacts as well as their own extensive collections of Indian artifacts. Braecklein, an architect credited with building the first skyscraper in Kansas City, had at one time a collection numbering over one hundred thousand artifacts. He later donated sixty thousand of them to the Boy Scouts of America.[6] Trowbridge, a friend of Braecklein's, had a standing order with Joe Balloun, one of the relic dealers in Arkansas, to let him know if Joe came across anything unusual.[7]

Once in a while, a collector decided to sell off some of his collection, or he died and his heirs didn't know what to do with a hundred thousand Indian artifacts. These might be bought intact by some wealthy collector or museum, or advertised in *Hobbies* and sold off piecemeal. Life wasn't bad for dealers because the supply of people who wanted to buy artifacts seemed endless. Some of these buyers aspired to become collectors; others wanted to become dealers in their own right. For some, purchasing artifacts was an investment hedge, a way of protecting their money at a time when stocks and bonds had tanked and real estate was depreciating. Others were just city kids who wanted arrowheads for their very own.[8]

Circling above it all and exercising a considerable economic pull were the museums—university museums, state natural history museums, art museums, private museums, and even the two giants: the Heye Museum of the American Indian in New York City and the Smithsonian Institution in Washington D.C. They all wanted and were willing to compete for the best artifacts. Some of this competition was economic, because a great find sold tickets, brought in donations, and increased funding to sponsor more excavations or purchase more artifacts. Some of it was a true search for knowledge, because an extraordinary artifact in a university or state museum's display case might well shed some light on America's ancient past. A great find also validated archaeology and its parent discipline, anthropology, and so helped rationalize digging into Indian burial mounds. Wealthy folks got in on the game because they wanted to create or fill their own museums. To have the best, most important Indian artifacts could put a museum on the map. And professional digs generated valuable scholarly records and a growing number of items for study. In reality, though, much of the archaeology up to the 1930s consisted of digging up prize artifacts and putting them on display, even if that meant ignoring the protests of the Indian people to whom they belonged.

So the demand for Indian artifacts was there, which in itself was remarkable because only fifty years earlier, the United States had gone out of its way to rub out just about everything Indian. Those Indians not killed off were by the late 1880s herded onto reservations where the "civilization" process began in earnest. Children were sent to schools to have the Indianness taught out of them. Missionaries fanned out to eradicate Indian religion. Traditional clothing was banned, long hair cut, speaking English insisted upon. Anything and everything Indian was downplayed and dismissed. Reformers who called themselves friends of the Indians believed that Indian society and culture offered nothing of value and so should be discarded in the trash bin of history. All this was done in the name of saving Indians, and in white Americans' minds, it seemed to be working. By the early twentieth century, most Americans believed Indians were a vanishing race—a people and way of life certain to dissolve into the American mainstream. If Indians were dying out, the value of their traditional artwork would only increase. Best to get it while you could, cheap.

The problem was production. The only artifacts that mattered to most collectors and museums were those made before the Indians were sent to the reservations. Even better was anything made before Europeans arrived in America. So traditional things were demanded, the older the better, but the really old objects were underground, buried in ancient graves or beneath centuries-old earthen mounds. There were only two ways to get at them. One was pot hunting; the other, an official archaeological dig headed up by a professional archaeologist, usually associated with and sponsored by a university or museum, maybe by a wealthy patron. Archaeological digs took money, something many institutions lacked during the Great Depression, but if an academic dig could be put together, then anything discovered this way would go directly to the museums. The small private collectors, such as Trowbridge and Braecklein, would be left out in the cold.

Most dealers and collectors, even some universities and museums, acquired many of their artifacts from the pot hunters who fanned out across the countryside in search of old Indian sites. Few pot hunters made a full-time living at it. It was mostly something they did in their spare time: a farmer during the season between harvest and planting, or a townie on a weekend walk in the woods. Kids were some of the best at it. Usually pot hunters would stroll along streams or the bluffs above them, anyplace that looked like a spot where Indian people might have camped. The hunters would take a long metal rod and poke deep into the ground. If the rod punched through something and gave way a little, they'd know they'd hit a pot or a skull and would begin digging.[9] It was a destructive way of finding Indian relics, but a pot with a hole in its side was still worth something. And there was always the chance that other items were down there as well. Less destructive pot hunters tried divining rods. Some claimed to be able to find a burial site by the color of the earth. Still, in the long run, and no matter how a relic was found—by official university-backed archaeology or entrepreneurial pot hunting—it all came down to breaking open an old Indian burial and taking away the goods that had been interred with the body. They often took the body as well.[10]

In the early 1920s, there was an artifact rush when pottery began turning up in Carden Bottoms in central Arkansas, between Petit Jean Creek and the Arkansas River. A sharecropper's plow dug into some old Indian graves, pulled up a pot, and the spree was on. With crops failing and no money, farmers in the area had nothing but time on their hands, so they and their wives and children turned out with iron rods and began poking and prodding the countryside. They found "wagonloads" of pots, bowls, jars, bottles, and pipes, as well as "animal and human effigies." Many of these were painted red, white, or black. Dardanelle artifact dealer and *Hobbies* advertiser Goodrich Pilquist quickly arrived on the scene and began buying up the relics. Wanting all he could get, he sponsored searches in other areas.[11]

Pilquist may have been a country boy, but he knew how to market a product. Validation by a professional only added to an artifact's value, so he contacted M. R. Harrington of the Heye Museum in New York City and told him what he had. Harrington raced down to Arkansas and announced that the relics were several hundred years old and made by Caddoans, an Indian people who'd once called that part of the country home. But Harrington was shocked by the destruction of the site. "It was sickening to an archeologist to see the skeletons chopped to pieces with hoes and dragged ruthlessly forth to be crushed under foot by the vandals—who were interested only in finding something to sell, caring nothing for the history of a vanished people. . . . What could I do? . . . So I made the best of it, and bought from the diggers, and from those who had financed them, such of the artifacts as I thought we needed."¹² What Harrington didn't buy, Pilquist did and later sold to museums across the country.¹³

In the spring of 1934, almost a decade after the Carden Bottoms finds, it seemed someone else had uncovered a large burial. Having spotted the artifacts on the curio market, Guthe tried tracing them to their source. Like Harrington at the Heye, Guthe was an academic and didn't approve of pot hunters, their techniques, or the open sale of artifacts. To him, relics were windows to the past that could tell about life in Indian America. They should remain in place until they could be properly photographed and recorded. Only then could they be removed to the safe lockers of a university warehouse. There they could be protected, studied in greater detail, maybe even put on display for the public to marvel at. Every archaeologist out there was bothered by the loss to the body of knowledge whenever artifacts were removed and sold by get-rich-quick dealers. But, like Harrington, Guthe could do nothing about it.

Nevertheless, the fact that a pot hunter had made a discovery did not mean it wasn't important. That's why museums and archaeologists, though they hated doing it, often bought from dealers. And Guthe knew that if an artifact was worth saving, he'd have to bid against private collectors, other universities, museums, and the wealthy patrons as well. Still, Guthe hoped to prevent another run of destruction like what occurred in Carden Bottoms. He made a few inquiries and determined that the fresh artifacts were coming from a clutch of Indian mounds in Le Flore County, southeastern Oklahoma, near a speck named Spiro. Locals called it Braden Bottoms. Armed with that information, he contacted his colleague, Forrest E. Clements, the chair of the Anthropology Department at the University of Oklahoma in Norman.[14]

Clements was cut from the same cloth as Harrington and Guthe. With his thin frame and dark hair, he looked equally at home in a pith helmet in the field as in a tweed jacket in front of the classroom. Still, he was a professional anthropologist with no use for pot hunters, and he firmly believed that only those with university training, people who understood archaeological techniques, should be allowed to excavate Indian sites.[15]

Clements reckoned he knew the mounds Guthe was talking about, so one day in spring 1934, he loaded up his car and left Norman for far eastern Oklahoma. These were the days before Interstate 40 cut directly across the state, so he had to take tiny State Highway 9. The 160-mile trip took most of the day. When he got to Le Flore County, it didn't take him long to find Braden Bottoms.

Clements was right—he had heard of this place. Just a cluster of Indian mounds and cotton fields a few hundred yards south of the Arkansas River. People in the area had long known of them. Around the turn of the twentieth century, they'd been known as the Mound Builder's Mounds. Later they were called the Fort Coffee Mounds because they sat about a mile away from the ruins of old Fort Coffee. By the 1930s they were being called the Spiro Mounds, and several of the larger mounds had their own names. A few houses sat far back from them, where the property owners lived. A nearby marshy depression marked the borrow pit, where the Indians so many hundreds of years before had dug up the dirt to make the mound the pot hunters were now digging on. The whole site sat maybe five miles north of the little crossroads named Spiro and about ten miles west of Fort Smith, Arkansas.[16]

It disturbed Clements to see the pot hunters, right at that moment, shoveling into the tail section of the long main mound, the one that came to be called Craig Mound. Later, it would earn the name Great Temple Mound. Craig Mound, named for the family who owned the property, was the largest of the twelve mounds on the site. It stood about 33 feet high, 120 feet wide, and over 180 feet long. At the time, it was covered with shrubs and trees, some three feet around.[17] Craig was actually four connected mounds, each one smaller than the previous, with the largest and tallest pointing northwest. From a distance, it looked like a giant caterpillar crawling across the landscape. About two hundred feet or so south of Craig Mound stood two smaller mounds, Ward Mound 1 and Ward Mound 2, also named for the property owners. Craig and Ward mounds seemed to sit off by themselves, isolated from the others on the site.[18]

About a quarter mile northwest of Craig Mound sat another grouping of mounds. Flat-topped Brown Mound was the largest of these at 200 feet long, 175 feet wide, and 15 to 18 feet tall. At one time it had been tilled over and cotton planted on top of it.[19] As Clements kicked around the site, he saw that pot hunters had already been scratching down into the top of Brown Mound. About 600 feet to the north of Brown sat squat Copple Mound, about 60 feet in diameter and only 6 feet high.[20] Just south and east of Brown and Copple mounds ran a semicircle of smaller "house" mounds, just bumps in the earth, really. The entire mound site, including both clusters, was only about eighty acres, and most of that was covered with oak, hickory, black gum, and honey locust. The mounds were all that was left of an ancient, long-abandoned Indian town and ceremonial center. Over the years, they had attracted pot hunters who'd picked over the surface and done a little shallow digging, but professional archaeologists also knew of them, and two of the mounds had already been excavated by university professionals.[21]

Between 1913 and 1917, Joseph B. Thoburn, an archaeologist at the University of Oklahoma, had dug into the two
Ward mounds. He found collapsed houses under both; each
structure was rectangular, about fifty by sixty feet, and held up
by four center poles. In Ward Mound 1 he found two sets of
burials. The four people buried in one set seemed to Thoburn
to have died suddenly, as if the house had collapsed on them
in the middle of the night. Later, the ruins had been burned
with the dead inside, and dirt had been piled over it until a
small mound resulted. Thirty-two additional skeletons had
been inserted into the mound sometime later. Along with the
skeletons, Thoburn found numerous artifacts, including T-shaped
pipes, spear points, bowls, and even copper ax heads.[22]

Thoburn had been struck by the large number of artifacts
and just how unusual they seemed. Both attributes made the
site important, begging to be studied. He'd planned on one day
doing a major excavation of the Spiro Mounds, but money and
the right circumstances never presented themselves. Meanwhile, he worried about pot hunters and wanted them kept out.
During the 1920s he wrote that "if an un-skilled amateur, who
is interested only in gathering 'relics' for a personal collection
or for sale, should disturb those interesting earth-works, he
may easily make it impossible for us to read the story that it
holds for the careful scientific investigator."[23]

Clements' own eyes showed him that Thoburn's fear had
come true. Virtually all the big mounds sported shovel marks.
Of course, the cluster of men right then digging on top of Craig
Mound also constituted pretty irrefutable evidence. Clements
wasn't really surprised to see the pot hunters at work. This
bend in the Arkansas River was just too well known for Indian
artifacts. If Clements knew about Spiro Mounds, everybody in
the area did too, as did the dealers over in Arkansas. And a
seemingly endless supply of artifacts was getting kicked up
around the mounds. Stone and clay ear spools, like finger-sized
pierced earrings, seemed to sprout from the ground. J. B. and
Thelma Brazeal from nearby Poteau, while just strolling around

the area, had found over fifteen hundred beads, arrowheads, and potsherds, as well as thirteen skeletons. Glen Newbern and his son had found scores of stone knives, beads, pipes, arrowheads, spear points, drills, and grinding stones.[24]

It could've been worse from Clements' point of view: the mounds could've been leveled. Fortunately, property lines crisscrossed the entire Spiro Mounds site, a few crossing directly over some of the largest mounds. While some landowners didn't mind the pot hunters, others refused to allow them on their property. Nevertheless, what the property holders wanted did not always deter pot hunters, especially because all the owners were African Americans, Choctaw Indians, or a mixture of both.[25]

At some point on that spring day, Clements walked over to the Craig Mound and introduced himself to the pot hunters, who'd been eyeing him ever since he'd driven up. There were six of them, or six, at least, who claimed they were the original investors in the Pocola Mining Company, as they were calling their relic-hunting consortium. They explained to Clements that they'd leased this part of the mound from the property owner and were digging for Indian relics to sell. It was all matter-of-fact and legal, the lease signed and money paid.

Still, the situation was more than Clements could take. The artifacts coming out of the mound were just too exotic and unusual to be left to pot hunters. He wanted to be the one to excavate and study the mounds, so Clements determined to put a halt to all pot hunting going on at Spiro. The Pocola Mining Company and its lease might be legal, but he was going to find a way around it. It was as good as a declaration of war.

2

The Founding

800–1100

Spiro sat on a commanding spot, a high, protected terrace overlooking a sweeping bend of the Arkansas River, right at the point where the river, barreling down from the Kansas plains, turned due east to thread its way through the Ozark bluffs. From this spot, heading back up the Arkansas a short way and following the Canadian River west, in a couple of hundred miles one would be off the prairies and into the buffalo grasslands of the Great Plains. A few hundred miles farther sat the growing Pueblo villages of what would become New Mexico. Along the downstream route east from Spiro, almost immediately the Arkansas began slicing through the Ozark Plateau, separating the Boston Mountains to the north from the Ouachitas to the south. From there, the river dropped out of the mountains and hit the Gulf Coastal Plain, where it crept through vast woodlands all the way to the Mississippi River and the Gulf of Mexico.[1]

So Spiro's inhabitants could reach out to the peoples living on the Great Plains and to those living among the great forests and rivers of the North American Southeast. And it was in the Southeast, about AD 800, where Indian people were just starting to scratch out a culture and civilization that would become truly spectacular. Along the Mississippi River and tributaries such as the Arkansas, hamlets were being planted, populations collecting, fresh ideas percolating. A new farming way of life was just beginning to emerge across the area drained by the Mississippi River, and Spiro would one day become a major part it.

So Spiro was a good place where an ambitious family might prosper. First off, it sat atop terraces well above the river, too high for the Arkansas' spring floods to reach. But it was those same floods, like those of Egypt's Nile, that covered and fertilized the lower terraces year after year. So here was plenty of well-watered land for gardening, as well as clays for pottery; cane for baskets and arrows; trees for bows; hickories, pecans, and walnuts for eating; cedars and junipers for rituals; herbs for healing; and a host of animals for food, clothes, and tools.[2]

Just as important, it was a strategic location. The Arkansas served as an east-west highway. Canoes back then were often just frames of sticks covered with buffalo hides, sometimes dugouts cut from huge logs, but there probably was not much canoe traffic on the upper Arkansas at 800. The river would become more important in later years.[3] River traffic was not uncommon, but most people in these parts, whether on the move to hunt, make war, or trade, often traveled afoot. Even then, they usually followed rivers and streams, which led them to other settlements. So this spot, situated directly at that great curve of the Arkansas, dominated the river for miles. Nearby Round Mountain, a tall, rocky outcrop two miles southeast of Spiro Mounds, was an excellent landmark. Situated on the margins between the southeastern woodlands and the southern Great Plains, Spiro had access to the resources of both and the potential to control all the river traffic between. It also sat at the head of what would eventually become a trail that meandered almost directly south to the Caddoan farming communities then springing up along the Red River.[4]

No one will ever know who the first family was that settled at Spiro. For millennia, Indian hunters wandered over the area. Spear points and campsites have been found nearby that date back eight thousand years.[5] During the 800s, small settlements, maybe just a house or two, began appearing along the Arkansas, Verdigris, Grand, and Illinois rivers of eastern Oklahoma, so it was about this time that a family settled on the bluff that would become Spiro.[6] The hunting, gathering, gardening, and trading proved fine, and over time the hamlet grew and attracted others to its prosperity.

Certainly these first Indian settlers recognized the spot's potential. Using slash-and-burn farming, the women cut out a few gardens along the terraces after men cleared areas by girdling trees. Using a stone ax, a man would scrape off a ring of bark about a foot wide, which would kill the tree in a matter of weeks. Later, the men burned the dead trees and underbrush, then mixed the ashes into the soil as fertilizer. The burnt trunks of particularly large trees might remain standing and the crops be planted among them. Once the land was cleared, the men helped turn the soil with hoes made of stones tied to wooden shafts. Sometimes they used buffalo shoulder blades.[7]

Then the women took over. Using digging sticks and hoes, they planted the seeds. Once these sprouted, the women and children watered them, weeded, scared off crows and other pests, and generally looked after the plants. Each family probably tended a four- to five-acre garden, and some might have worked communal gardens as well. While women gardened, men stalked the canebrakes and woods for deer, raccoons, and turkeys and sometimes prowled the riverbanks in search of fish, freshwater mussels, or waterfowl.[8]

As the gardens thrived, Spiroans built spacious rectangular houses with sturdy walls of wood and clay. To make the walls, they took log poles three to four inches in diameter and set them upright in the ground about six inches apart. They wove saplings between the poles, filled in the spaces with twisted grass, then covered it all with thick clay. Small fires were set next to the wall both inside and out to dry it. For the roof, inside the structure they set four large cedar logs upright into the ground as center posts. Crossbeam logs ran between them, while smaller cane rafters stretched from the crossbeams to the top of the walls. Grass was used to thatch the roof. Once dried and completed, the interiors became relatively cool in the summer and, with a small fire blazing, snug in winter. Beds were arranged around the walls, and containers made of hides or pottery might be suspended from the rafters to keep out mice. Small holes were dug in the floors, some to store food, others as trash bins for discarded animal bones and broken utensils. Extended families of five to fifteen people—often including parents, children, grandparents, even aunts, nieces, and nephews—lived in these houses. They were sturdy structures, but with so much dried grass around, the biggest danger came from a flying spark, a carelessly handled flame, or lightning.[9]

One of the great issues swirling about Spiro today is, Who were these people? If they can be associated with a later Indian nation, which one? Most, but not all, scholars believe that the people who settled at Spiro were Caddoans. "Caddoan" is the name of both a language family and a culture that spread along the prairies between the Great Plains and the eastern woodlands. By the 1700s, out of this Caddoan culture had come the Caddos and Hasinais of western Louisiana, East Texas, western Arkansas, and eastern Oklahoma; the Wichitas and Kichais of Texas, Oklahoma, and Kansas; the Pawnees of Nebraska; and the Arikaras on the Missouri River in South Dakota. Though all were different peoples, they were similar in that they all spoke a Caddoan dialect, all relied upon both gardening and hunting, all lived in grass houses, all made a similar style of pottery, and all had comparable political structures. The location of Spiro in eastern Oklahoma near the areas claimed by the Caddos, Hasinais, Wichitas, and Kichais leads many archaeologists to believe the Spiroans were Caddoan peoples.[10] Even this is not as simple as it seems, however, and the debate over who the Spiroans were or became still generates plenty of heat among academics and Indians.

Whoever those first people at Spiro were, at AD 800, they were at the end of a long, amazing history. Fourteen thousand years ago, small bands of Indian hunters had spread across North America, seeking out caves, rock overhangs, or other protected areas for camps. Some had even wandered over the general vicinity of Spiro. Using spears tipped with beautiful, but deadly, flint points, men formed hunting bands and tracked down such big game as mammoths, giant bison, camels, giant sloths, and giant armadillos. Women probably helped hunt smaller game but also foraged for what food they could and gathered firewood. However, the efficient hunting bands of fathers, sons, and brothers brought in the most food, so keeping the bands together was essential. Therefore, when a man married, usually courting a woman from a different group during summer gatherings, she went to live with him and his band, bringing new ideas and ways of doing things with her.[11]

However, twelve thousand years ago, the climate changed as the ice age came to an end. The temperature warmed, humidity decreased, and the glaciers melted and receded. Forests sprang up in some areas or gave way to prairies, plains, and deserts in others. Lakes shrank into ponds, while ponds became bogs or dried up altogether. Rivers and streams vanished, and soon so did entire species of animals. Between six thousand and twelve thousand years ago, hundreds, if not thousands, of animal species, including virtually all the big game these early Indians depended on, became extinct. By six thousand years ago, the mammoths, giant bison, horses, camels, saber-toothed tigers, and hundreds of species of birds and animals were gone.[12]

After the great extinctions, the only big animals left in North America were the buffalo, the bear, and animals of the deer family—antelope, deer, elk, and moose. To adjust, the Indian big-game hunters became true hunter-gatherers. Men now hunted smaller game, such as rabbits, deer, and fowl. Many took to fishing. Those people who lived on the margins of the Great Plains would venture out to hunt buffalo every now and again. Women's part in providing food jumped tremendously. Increasingly, families depended on women gathering seeds, roots, nuts, berries, and anything else they could. Rather than being constantly on the move, bands now cycled through distinct territories, going wherever the food was plentiful, then moving on once the season was over. Through this they acquired an intimate knowledge of a territory's plants, animals, and terrain.

They also created new tools to take advantage of it: fish hooks, bolos for catching birds, snares, smaller spear points, baskets, and the list goes on and on.

These Archaic Indians, as archaeologists call them, lived well, and a population increase is proof of it. Now many individuals began to specialize in making particular crafts, such as spear points, baskets, and other utensils. In some areas where food was always plentiful, Indian peoples built large communities and lived there just about year round. One such community was at Poverty Point in northeastern Louisiana, where by 1000 BC, the first major city in North America arose due to plentiful fishing on nearby Bayou Macon.[13]

For centuries to come, Indian peoples would provide food for their families by hunting, maybe fishing, and much gathering. However, something new was on the horizon, and by the time of Christ, it had hit the peoples of the American Southeast.[14] It began with a woman. After all, women were the gatherers of the band. She and her sisters had spent the day filling a few baskets with seeds and other wild grains. That evening, in preparing a meal for her family, she probably threw out a few handfuls of seed husks. They might have been from amaranth or sunflowers or the like, but among the husks were a few seeds. All this landed on a moist patch of ground, watered by a little runoff and sunlit much of the day. Over the weeks and months, the seeds sprouted and grew and ripened. One day she recognized the plants as those she and her sisters regularly gathered, and in that moment, she made a discovery that changed the universe for Indian America. She suddenly realized that rather than going out to the woods to search for the plant, she could bring the plant and its produce to her. So began the domestication of plants, a necessary prelude to farming.

This great discovery did not bring instantaneous change to these early American Indians. In fact, it was not agriculture or farming. It was barely gardening. Women might toss out a few seeds on a bare patch of ground, and the family would then set off on one of its hunting and gathering trips, leaving the seeds to fend for themselves. If all went well, ripe plants awaited them on their return months later. Over the next few centuries, women studied the plants, selecting the plumpest seeds from the most bountiful or hardiest plants. Some women began actually planting the seeds, rather than just scattering them on top of the ground, even watering them if the rains did not come on time. Soon, Indian women in the southern and eastern parts of America regularly scratched out small gardens of amaranth, sunflowers, little barley, bottle gourds, Jerusalem artichoke, squash, wild potato vine, goosefoot, and pigweed. Some of these plants, such as bottle gourds and squash, steadily gained in importance. Women turned gourds into dippers and spoons, as well as sturdy, lightweight, waterproof containers. Squash added a prolific and delicious food to their larders. This surer food supply increased populations even more, and by AD 300 in eastern Oklahoma, Indian peoples were using pottery and the bow and arrow.[15]

So while men still hunted, women began producing even more food from their gatherings and domesticated plants. This had important ramifications, because as families and bands became more dependent on their gardens, they were increasingly tied to one place. And as the population in any one area grew, it placed limits on the movements of a whole range of people. Now, traveling into other areas to hunt or gather often resulted in conflict and violence. Although trade and exchange might be welcomed, peoples took a dim view of strangers setting up camp on lands they claimed or taking resources they thought of as their own. Increasingly hemmed in, many bands found themselves limited to a certain territory and came to rely ever more on healthy gardens. When the first family settled at Spiro about AD 800, they were part of the gardening culture that was spreading along the rivers of the southern prairies. At that moment, the people at Spiro and throughout the American Southeast were poised for a great leap forward.

It came in the form of something new to garden, something that would change the world of Indian peoples—the entire world as well. Maize was one of its Indian names. Today most people know it as corn. It became as essential to some American Indians as rice was to Asians and wheat to Europeans. This was not corn's first appearance in America—from 200 BC to AD 400, Indian peoples in the eastern United States had grown a tropical flint corn—but after AD 400, as the weather cooled for the next few centuries, corn disappeared. Soon after, a new, hardier variety of corn, *maiz de ocho*, came out of Mexico. It reached Oklahoma about the ninth century and may have been in the people's hands when they first settled at Spiro. Following hard on corn's heels came beans. Both would become extremely important to Indians in the Southeast, though at first corn was just another domesticated weed. Not until about AD 1200 did corn and beans become really important to the people at Spiro, long after they were being grown extensively in other places in the Southeast.[16]

Spiro prospered, and by AD 1000, people around Spiro and across the American Southeast had come to depend on gardening. Large fields surrounded towns, and many crops, including corn, could be harvested twice a year. Now farming eclipsed hunting in the amount of food provided. This abundant food supply brought revolutionary changes not only to Spiro, but to all Indian societies along the Mississippi River and its many tributaries. Anthropologists call this time in eastern America between about AD 1050 and 1500 the Mississippian cultural tradition, or Mississippian period. It was a golden age for eastern Indian peoples, a time of amazing sophistication and complexity in politics, religion, art, and public monuments.[17]

During this time, Indian societies throughout the region drained by the Mississippi River were connected by and would interact through trade, warfare, kinship, diplomacy, and religion. Though they were different peoples possessing different cultures and languages, they shared the characteristics and traits that composed the Mississippian cultural tradition.[18] Now, a sure supply of food from farming touched off a population explosion among Mississippian Indian societies. Towns and villages surrounded by gardens and fields arose along the Mississippi,

Arkansas, Red, Tennessee, Cumberland, and Ohio rivers and their tributaries. Some of these towns, such as Cahokia on the Mississippi River across from present-day St. Louis, Moundville in western Alabama, Etowah and Okmulgee in Georgia, and Spiro on the Arkansas, would eventually become major cities or ceremonial centers dominating their regions.[19]

Farming changed the way Mississippian Indians saw themselves and thought about things, even whom they reckoned as kin. As long as hunting supplied the most food, the men's hunting bands of fathers, sons, and brothers remained essential to survival of the family and band. Since keeping the hunting band together was paramount, women left their families and married into their husbands' households. Children of these marriages traced their kin through their father's side. And because hunting was so important to the people's survival, religion revolved around ensuring a reliable supply of animals. Hunters prayed to animal deities for help. They appealed to cougar spirits or falcon spirits or other predators to impart their abilities. Some wanted speed; others strength or stamina; and still others wiliness, whatever would give them an edge to hunt down their prey.[20]

However, as people at Spiro and around the Southeast settled down, and crops eclipsed hunting in putting more food in their bellies, women's economic importance to the village skyrocketed. Since mothers, daughters, and sisters working in the fields now provided most of the village's food, it became essential to keep that farming team together. Men now married into women's families, leaving their own behind and taking up residence in their wives' houses, which women usually shared with their mothers and their sisters' families. Women controlled the land and the household, and children were born into their mother's clan. A person's clan membership never changed, and all members of a clan were considered kin. Since clan members were kin, husbands and wives had to be from different clans. And since children were born into their mothers' clan, fathers were in a different clan and not technically kin. Instead, the mothers' brothers, children's maternal uncles and members of the same clan, became their teachers and often the most important adult males in their lives. What few personal items or positions that might be inherited went through the mother to her children. And as leadership positions became more hereditary, the man who held one passed it on to his sister's children, not his own offspring.[21]

Some of the greatest changes brought about by farming are visible among the leaders of the Mississippian cities, towns, and villages. During the old hunting and gathering days, the best hunter or warrior might become the band leader, and this position was open to anyone good enough at hunting, warfare, or providing for his people to develop a following. Kinship ties to prestigious people or families also helped, as did showing wisdom and bravery. Still, a successful warrior and provider had a chance to go far. But as people settled into villages and increasingly relied on their fields to supply them with food, leadership often required developing different abilities. As in the old days, wisdom, success, and a warlike ability were still very much respected. The towns and their fields needed to be defended from wandering strangers, jealous neighbors, and rival towns. War parties needed to be raised and counterraids undertaken. So a great warrior, who was brave, generous, wise, and successful, earned high esteem.

As farming overshadowed hunting, however, ensuring successful harvests took on an importance all its own and required a different set of skills. Theoretically, in hunting, if animals were scarce, the band could move to where the animals were. Farmers, in contrast, could not just pick up their fields and move them. And as any farmer will tell you, it is not so much a person's skill that brings bountiful harvests as the cooperation of nature. Spiroan farmers understood that no matter how tenderly they cared for their crops, drought, floods, frosts, insects, and animals could destroy them all and leave their people starving. The Sun, Moon, Rain, River, Wind, Earth, even the Corn itself, all essential to bountiful harvests, had to be propitiated, manipulated, and enlisted for the people's survival. And those individuals who could do this—who could control the weather through prayer, magic, ritual, and ceremony—those people wielded tremendous power. Successful priests were people to be reckoned with.[22]

Good weather and bountiful crops meant these priests had the ear of the gods as well as knowledge of those arcane rites that kept everything in balance. Some of these rituals were public. For example, the green corn ceremony became the most common ceremony practiced across the Southeast and is observed by the descendants of these farming Indians to this very day. Held during the summer, it is a celebration of the harvest as well as a ceremony of renewal and regeneration. The ceremony, which takes days to complete, requires fasting, purification, and the forgiveness of debts and insults. At one great moment during the ceremony, all the fires throughout the nation are extinguished and relit with an ember from the one main sacred fire. Correctly done, the ceremony not only ensures a good harvest the following year but a harmonious and bountiful world for the people as well.[23]

Some rituals were semipublic family affairs, such as naming ceremonies, puberty rites, and death rituals. Still others were so sacred that they needed to be done in private by the priest, away from the prying eyes of citizens who might inadvertently disrupt the ceremony or contaminate the ritual.[24] At Spiro, as across the Southeast, citizens began building temples where priests presided over an eternally burning sacred fire, essentially a piece of the life-giving Sun here on earth. Built in the same manner as houses, temples tended to have a longer, foyer-type entryway. In these temples, priests communicated with various deities or the deities' representatives. The spirits of long-dead ancestors might also have been invoked. Because most deities and spirits possessed human traits, they often hungered for the same things humans wanted: honor, respect, even tangible goods. So priests performed rituals to divine the deities' desires and enlist their help. Any advice, instructions, or commandments were passed on to the people. A town with a successful priest possessed a powerful prize.

Although Spiro had been expanding during the past two hundred years, only during the eleventh century did these religious and political ideas as well as corn farming itself start to blossom at Spiro. By AD 1000, Spiro was a rapidly growing, decent-sized Mississippian town of square houses and temples scattered along a few acres of Arkansas River terrace gardens. It probably had a chief, a middle-aged man from a respected family who was related to many people in the town, someone who had over the years developed such virtues as bravery, generosity, and wisdom. He would have handled the town's day-to-day operations, such as welcoming visitors, ensuring the forests were cleared, commanding the building and rebuilding of houses, handing out food in emergencies, setting up festivals, and a host of other duties. His political authority, though, was tenuous. His kinship ties to the living and dead were important, but he led because people looked up to him, respected his wisdom, and benefited from his ability to provide for them. He had little coercive power, and most people could follow whatever course they wanted without risking too much. Worse, bad luck or wrong decisions could lose him followers and empower a rival.

Still, success bred success, and a successful chief drew admirers and followers to him. His success was Spiro's success, and this attracted more and more people to the Spiro area. Eventually, the people may have recognized the chief's family as being a leadership family, one that Spiroans expected to produce their leaders year after year. And this family, through well-arranged marriages, gift giving, and favors, cemented other families to it and so created a powerful political force.[25]

As Spiro grew during the eleventh and twelfth centuries, so did the number of leadership positions. For example, Spiro may also have had a war chief, a leading warrior who took the reins of power during periods of war or when the town was under threat. Only when peace returned did the war chief step down and the "peace" chief, the town's regular leader, take back his position of authority. Also, fearless warriors with several victories under their belts were highly respected, and their words were considered worth hearing. Commanding similar respect were older men, particularly older men who had once been successful warriors or medicine men. The chief often sought their advice. The town also had a priest, maybe several of them, who handled the religious duties of the population. These were the people who knew the correct rituals, who could command the weather, whose job it was to appeal to the gods for the preservation of the town by granting bountiful harvests, good hunts, and successful war.

All these primary positions needed a second tier of bureaucrats to make them work. As Spiro grew and the job of the chief became more complex, he needed functionaries to announce decisions and ensure they were carried out. Priests and medicine men needed helpers. All these secondary positions had a status in their own right. Of course, specialization was only getting more important, and skilled craftspeople might make their ideas known. As families, lineages, and clans became increasingly powerful and important, they might also have their own leaders and spokespeople. So at this time, not much precluded a smart, capable, ambitious person from the right family from rising to a top position. Leadership might go to a person from a certain family, but that did not guarantee he would become the next chief. Ability, particularly bravery, generosity, and wisdom were still highly prized characteristics that, theoretically, could take even a captive to the top ranks of power.

However, this changed after 1050 as Mississippian culture and ideology spread to Spiro and other southeastern towns and villages. Among farming societies, the demands of protecting their fields from invaders and of appeasing deities to ensure successful harvests brought about the rise of a ranked hierarchy of noble families and commoner families. The position of chief would now be hereditary, filled by the noble families, and the chief's political authority became greater. Religious authority went to a priest who performed the necessary ceremonies that ensured successful harvests and warfare. In some Mississippian towns, there was a political chief as well as a chief priest, each powerful in his own sphere. In other towns, a single person might embody both these powers as a priest-chief. Certainly, religion and political power went hand in hand in Mississippian America. At the top of this social pyramid were these political and religious leaders and their extended families, who made up the interconnected nobility. At the bottom were commoner families, those furthest down the social pyramid from the elite families, lineages, and clans.[26]

This rise in status of chiefly and priestly leaders and their families during the eleventh and twelfth centuries divided Spiro society. If the priest-chief possessed special knowledge that could deliver success and prosperity, that put him on a higher level than the other people of the town. Over the years and in some places, the prerogatives of the priest-chief evolved to amazing extremes. In some larger cities and towns, retainers carried the priest-chief on litters or placed mats in front of him when he strode about so his feet would never touch the ground. Priest-chiefs did not work in their own fields, but the people tilled and harvested them. Though some remarkable women might become priest-chiefs, men usually inherited the position from their mother's brother.[27]

Naturally, if priest-chiefs and elites lived differently than the commoners did, they certainly died differently, too. How to send off one's dead and ensure their entry into a comfortable afterlife occupied the thoughts of Indian people since earliest times. Exactly what that afterlife might be differed greatly from people to people. American Indian religion was and is complex and varied, making generalization dangerous. Still, many Indian peoples of the Mississippian culture believed it necessary to give the dead person a proper burial and send-off. Problems arose if the body had not been correctly cared for at death or if the living had not done the right rituals to help the soul enter the afterlife. If that happened, then the dead person might return as a ghost to cause problems for the living and throw life out of

balance. Therefore, every effort was made to ensure that one's
kinspeople received a proper burial.[28]

As early as ten thousand years ago, some North American
Indians covered their dead with red ochre and buried them
with stone spear points and bone and shell beads, and sometimes with bits of turtle shell, antlers, and bird claws.[29] Later,
Archaic peoples buried their dead in various ways: in the ground;
under the floors of rock shelters; under the floors or in wall niches
of caves; or under a carefully arranged pile of stones. Some were
cremated. Small cemeteries containing scores, even hundreds,
of Archaic burials have been found.[30]

Spiro residents during the 800s and 900s used similar methods
of handling their dead. Not many people lived in the area, and
the difference between the chief and his people was very small,
so everyone received much the same treatment. This normally
entailed the body being laid out in a burial in a common cemetery
on the edge of town. Maybe a few personal possessions and
some food went into the grave with them.[31] Death of a loved
one brought on a time of mourning, which may have included
cutting one's hair, crying for long periods, not washing one's
clothes, and often keeping away from public gatherings. After a
time, the mourning period was over, and the living went on
about their daily lives.[32]

The advent the Mississippian way of life changed the way
the people at Spiro handled their dead. Now the dead received
much more attention and honor—all the dead, both the nobility
and the commoners. So rather than immediately being deposited
in a grave, the corpse was taken to a temple, which doubled as
a charnel house, where the remains lay until the flesh rotted
from the bones. The skeleton was then collected, and the bones
jumbled together and interred elsewhere. In the first half of
the eleventh century, all adults at Spiro received this special
charnel house treatment. Children, however, still went to cemeteries intact. Charnel houses would become common across
the Southeast. Centuries later, in 1585, the first English explorers

at Roanoke on the North Carolina coast reported finding the Indians using charnel houses for their dead.[33]

Even though all the dead were honored, however, when priest-chiefs and nobles died, they received extra special treatment, far more elaborate than what a commoner got. Inside the charnel house, after the skeleton had decomposed, bone pickers stripped any remaining flesh from the bones of the nobility. After that, the noble skeletons might have their skulls removed and their remaining bones gathered and placed in a large earthen jar or cane box, which was then stored in the temple until ready for burial at a later time. Then again, cremation of some bodies began showing up in Spiro about this time. Exactly who got cremated and who got buried is unclear, but it is possible that cremation was reserved for those of the highest status or for people who died in battle.[34]

In other instances, bodies were buried under the floor of a temple. Ward Mound 1 in the southeastern section of the town seems to have been one of these temples. Several burials were placed in a grave beneath the temple's floor. Some of the skeletons appear to have been partially cremated. At some point, for unknown reasons, Spiroans collapsed the temple and covered it with earth. Over the next few hundred years, other graves were added as well as such grave goods as T-shaped pipes, clay jars, and arrow points. As layers of burials were added, an earthen burial mound arose.[35]

When Joseph Thoburn excavated Ward Mound 1 in 1913, he found it measured seventy-five feet in diameter and three-and-a-half feet high but had probably been taller when Spiro had been occupied. Not long after the first burials in Ward Mound 1, Spiroans created a sister mound next to it: Ward Mound 2. Smaller than Ward Mound 1, it was also a mound that began by collapsing a temple, then covering it over with dirt. Later excavations found three burials here but few artifacts.[36]

During the eleventh century, the ranked society brought major physical changes to Spiro. Along with the creation of burial mounds, the Spiro site now expanded toward the northwest. The area around the Ward mounds, the southeastern section of the city, became an area associated with dead elites. This had been the site where the earliest houses had been erected and the first fields planted more than two hundred years earlier. However, even after two centuries, Spiro itself was not all that large. A few houses squatted on the site, but many more connected farming hamlets and villages surrounded it. During the 1000s, Spiro moved from being just a small hamlet or village to being a major ceremonial center that would harness religious power for all the people in the region. The burials in the Ward mounds seemed to spark a demand for more elaborate interments for the nobility, particularly in the holy ground that was the original site of Spiro.[37]

In this area of the dead, Spiroans began doing something new: they began burying the bodies of their priest-chiefs and nobility in a conical earthen mound. Conversely, commoners still wound up in graveyards on the edge of town after their time in the charnel house. Sometime in the 1000s, maybe a hundred yards north of the Ward mounds, Spiroans built three relatively small burial mounds, each about twenty-five, thirty feet in diameter and only a few feet high. These would form the southeastern lobes of Craig Mound. In the smallest, southeastern-most mound, Spiroans took the bones of three skeletons from a charnel house and placed them in a grave along with several clay pots. The bones were placed around the center of a grave and then covered with sheets of red cedar bark sewn together with vines. Dirt was piled over the graves until a small mound arose. Immediately northwest of this small mound, almost attached to it, a second mound was created. It included several skeletons buried with a pipe. A crematory basin also appears to have been here. A few decades later, Spiroans would start a third lobe of Craig Mound. The area beneath this mound was initially an old cemetery containing many burials, but between 1050 and 1100, Spiroans deposited a few additional skeletons, laid them out in a circle, and then covered them with dirt.[38]

Burials were also becoming more elaborate. Some skeletons, one wearing a copper headdress, were put into woven river cane boxes and buried beneath the mounds. It seems that retainers, possibly war captives, were sacrificed and buried with these Spiro leaders. Certainly the increasing quantities of grave goods—incredible works of art in their own right—interred with these dead priest-chiefs and nobles indicated the dead's worth and importance to the community. The burials of the nobility would only become more elaborate over time, and additional graves would be added to Ward Mound 1 and Craig Mound. In fact, Craig Mound would grow considerably over the next hundred years.[39]

As the original town site became reserved for the dead, an area about a quarter mile northwest became the site where the major ceremonies would take place. Here between AD 1000 and 1100, Spiroans began building a great ceremonial center, which included a large central plaza surrounded by earthen mounds and temples that also served as charnel houses. The priest-chief ruled from this ceremonial center. Here he, his priests, and the nobility presided over the chiefdom's life-giving rituals. Commoners lived in small hamlets around the ceremonial center, where women farmed and men hunted and went on raiding parties. At other times, they worked on the plaza and mounds, and all participated in the religious rituals.[40]

As the southeastern area around the Craig and Ward mounds became the sacred graveyard of the Spiroan nobility, the central plaza and surrounding charnel houses became the active place of worship. Great flat-topped earthen mounds were soon being constructed around the plaza. Anchoring the plaza on the southeast is Brown Mound, one of the largest of all the mounds at Spiro. Initially, there was no mound here, only a temple. About 1080, Spiro men and women, basketful by basketful, piled a mixture of dirt and clay over the structure to create an earthen pyramid. Brown Mound was then about seven feet high with a flat top. The sides of the mound were steep, though there was a gentle slope to the north side, which allowed easy access to the top. At first, rather than a temple, huge sacred fires burned on top of it. Over the next few centuries, additional layers of dirt were added, and in the twelfth or thirteen centuries, three burials with a scant few grave goods were added to Brown Mound. By the early 1400s, flat-topped Brown Mound measured 200 feet long, 175 feet wide, and about 20 feet high.[41]

Just to say that these people built earthen mounds glosses over the devotion and organizational ability American Indian peoples displayed. These mounds were not built by slaves. Rather, they were labors of love, of religious devotion, done willingly by the people of Spiro who believed that what they were doing made their community stronger. Using only digging sticks, hoes made of stone or bone, and cane baskets, Spiroans hauled tons of earth to build Brown and the other mounds. No one really knows how Spiroans and other Mississippians organized their working parties, but men, women, and children worked for decades on some mounds. These became platforms for temples, places for priest-chiefs to conduct their rituals, or burial places for the honored dead.

About two hundred yards north of Brown Mound, Spiroans built Copple Mound, another flat-topped temple mound. Like Brown Mound, Copple did not start off as a mound, but started as a temple and charnel house. During the early part of the eleventh century, however, the structure was destroyed, accidentally or deliberately. The destruction may have been part of a renewal cycle in which the bodies in the temple were periodically removed and buried, the structure destroyed, ruins covered with a layer of dirt, and a new temple built on the same site. Maybe the death of a chief or some other calamity set off the renewal cycle. Or possibly the structure was destroyed by an accidental fire. Sometime in the late 1000s, this second temple was destroyed and the ruins covered with another layer of dirt about three feet thick. Copple Mound seemed to remain like this for about a century, and then in 1180, an additional five-foot layer of dirt was added. More dirt came in the thirteenth century until the mound reached a diameter of sixty feet and a height of six feet. No burials have been found in Copple Mound, only a few bits of pottery.[42]

With Brown and Copple mounds forming the east side of the plaza, a string of six structures curved around the west and south side of the plaza. Could these have been smaller temples or charnel houses belonging to specific clans or families? Like the process at Copple Mound, these structures were periodically dismantled or burned, covered with a fresh layer of dirt, and then another one was built over the ruins. Eventually, a small mound formed at each of these six locations. But where the Brown and Copple mounds eventually turned into large flat-topped mounds, these other "buried structure" mounds remained relatively small, merely humps on the ground. All together, Brown and Copple mounds and the six charnel houses circumscribed a huge grassy plaza of almost seven square acres, measuring roughly eight hundred feet by six hundred feet.[43]

The ring of temples and mounds around the great plaza were not placed haphazardly; the entire physical layout of Spiro was aligned to harness as much spiritual power as possible. One of the ways to do this was through correctly aligning the mounds to certain phenomena. Actually, three important alignments were at work in Spiro. First, the whole Spiro site seemed to align itself along a northwest-to-southeast axis. A look at map 1 shows the four lobes of Craig Mound, the two Ward mounds, and even the plaza and burial mound areas oriented toward the southeast. From Round Mountain, that outcropping of rock two miles southeast of Spiro, there is almost a straight alignment northwest through Brown Mound, Copple Mound, and finally to a small charnel house outside the ceremonial center that was itself later buried. Why the southeasterly orientation? The alignment seems to be generally oriented toward the winter solstice.[44]

That leads to the second major alignment at Spiro, which is the sun's track across the sky at the solstices and equinoxes. Here Brown Mound is the key. From atop Brown Mound on December 22, the winter solstice, the priest-chief would watch

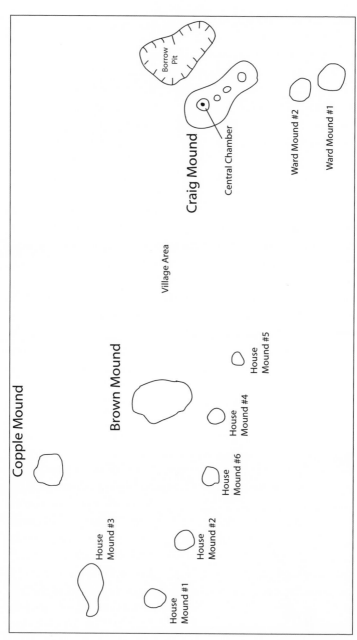

1. Spiro Ceremonial Center, 900–1420

the sun rise over Ward Mound 2 and then set over one of the temples on the other side of the plaza. On June 21, the summer solstice, the sun would set behind one of the other plaza temples. The same occurred for the vernal and autumnal equinoxes, March 20 and September 22, respectively: the sun would rise over where Cavanaugh Mound, near Fort Smith, would one day sit; pass directly over Brown Mound; go down behind one of the temples; and finally set over what would later become Skidgel Mound, a flat-topped temple mound about a mile to the west.[45] These four dates quartered the year and were probably the most holy days of the Spiro calendar, marked with processions, prayers, and rituals. It must have been awesome to see the priest-chief, dressed in his finery, complete with breastplate, mace, and copper headdress, stand atop Brown Mound and welcome the Sun to Spiro.[46]

The third alignment of the ceremonial center is related to the geometry of the site, the ratio of a certain distance between various mounds and structures. For this alignment, Copple Mound is the key, and the significant distance is 47.5 meters. Archaeologists call this the Toltec Module. Basically, 47.5 meters, or some multiplication of that distance, can be found in relation to all mounds and structures found around the great plaza. For example, from the center of Copple Mound to the center of Brown Mound is 191 meters, almost exactly 47.5 meters multiplied by four. Copple Mound west to the first charnel house is also 191 meters. From Copple Mound to the charnel house where the sun sets at the spring and fall equinoxes is 240 meters, or 47.5 multiplied by 5. Archaeologist James Brown, who has spent most of his career studying the Spiro Mounds, sees the mounds and charnel houses as forming a diamond shape. "It takes little imagination to visualize a symmetrical seven-mound configuration from these modular earthworks."[47] What is the significance of this? The layout of the ceremonial center, with its seven mounds and structures, almost looks like a mirror reflection of the Pleiades constellation, sometimes referred to as the Seven Sisters. Did the Spiroans have that in mind when they created the plaza? No one knows. These are just more of the many mysteries associated with Spiro Mounds. By the year 1100, Spiro seemed to be on the verge of something big. As a chiefdom and ceremonial center, it was quickly outpacing in size and complexity the other settlements in that region drained by the Arkansas River. No certain figure accounts for how many people lived there then. On the actual site, among the burial mounds and the ceremonial center, probably not more than a few score, maybe a little more, but just yards away and within sight of the mounds, scattered in hamlets and villages around the ceremonial center, probably lived several hundred to several thousand. Villages a few miles away also looked to Spiro for political and religious leadership. Certainly, there were enough people that could be put to work building mounds and burying the dead with elaborate ceremonies. But Spiro was poised for greatness, and over the next hundred and fifty years, it would become a powerful regional capital and one of the great ceremonial centers of Indian North America.

3

The Pocola Mining Company

1933–1934

No one could remember exactly whose idea it had been or how it all had gotten started. Had they known the commotion they'd cause, maybe they would have taken better notice. Guinn Cooper later said that it was his and Jim Vandagriff's idea, and it all had started with a gold-prospecting operation gone bad. Cooper outlived everyone and was the only one who ever talked about it at length, so his story is the one that takes.

It was the summer of 1933, and the heat and the Great Depression seemed to be making themselves right at home in these parts of Oklahoma and Arkansas. The new president, Franklin Delano Roosevelt, vowed to wage war on the Depression, but there were few jobs out here and not many ways to feed a family or even get by. Bad as it was, other things were weighing on Guinn Cooper that summer. He'd just watched his young wife die, and now he was looking for anything to keep his mind busy and off his grief. So he, Jim Vandagriff of Paola, Arkansas, and Kimball McKenzie of Pocola, Oklahoma, decided to try their hand at gold mining in the Kiamichi Mountains of southeastern Oklahoma. According to James Bruner, who interviewed Cooper not long before Coop died in 1992, the trio actually found gold. It was a concentrated ore they called "fines" and needed to have the gold extracted from it.[1]

The extraction process was far beyond what the three prospectors could do. Checking around, they heard of a fellow in Cripple Creek, Colorado, who could do it, so they took off for the Rockies with their fines. As Cooper told it to Bruner, they actually found the man, told him what they had, and negotiated a deal. They left their gold, and the extraction man promised to contact the miners when it was ready. Of course, the trio waited, and the call never came. When Cooper and the boys went back to Cripple Creek, they discovered the man had snookered them: taken off with their gold and leased their claim right out from under them. Whether they couldn't or wouldn't press the issue is not clear, but their gold had been permanently extracted from them. It was a sad lot of defeated prospectors who drove back to southeastern Oklahoma that summer of 1933.[2]

Needing something, anything, now more than ever, Jim Vandagriff first mentioned pot hunting. He'd been reared on stories about the Spiro Mounds and how with just a little effort, someone might scratch up some valuable Indian relics. They could team up with old John Hobbs, who lived down near the mounds. He was a pot hunter from way back and, by reputation, a good one. Hobbs, Vandagriff had heard, often dug in the Spiro Mounds and came away with some nifty pieces that he sold for a nice bit of change. That sounded good, didn't it? Mining for gold, mining for Indian relics, it was all the same thing. Problem is, Vandagriff warned, the mounds were on private property, and the owners weren't keen on letting people come dig in them. Anyway, odd things happened at Spiro, don't you know.[3]

And there were odd things about Spiro, like, what happened to the people who lived there? And why did they abandon it in the first place? Even stranger, when the inhabitants left the area in the fifteenth century, nobody replaced them. That part of the Arkansas Valley remained virtually deserted for the next four hundred years. Bands of Osages and villages of Caddos and Wichitas crisscrossed the area, but few, if any, made it home. In 1541, remnants of Hernando de Soto's ill-fated Spanish expedition across the American Southeast marched up the Arkansas River and got close to Spiro, but not quite, before retreating downriver. The eighteenth century saw French traders along the Arkansas, and by the early nineteenth century, a few American traders and explorers, such as naturalist Thomas Nuttall, were passing through. Although many wrote about the huge expanse of virtually impenetrable canebrakes along the river near Spiro, none mentioned the mounds.[4]

Not until the late 1820s and early 1830s did the first settlers come to the area, but they weren't American pioneers in covered wagons heading west; rather, they were Choctaw Indians being forcibly removed from Mississippi and Alabama over the "trail of tears." The Choctaws were one of the Five "Civilized" Tribes, the others being the Cherokees, Chickasaws, Creeks, and Seminoles. They got the "Civilized" nickname because by the early 1800s, many of their people, at least their leaders, spoke English, wore American-style clothes, went to school, attended church, and farmed the land. Some Choctaws even became cotton planters, and many owned black slaves.

Unfortunately for the Choctaws and the other of the Five Tribes, they happened to be living on some of the best cotton lands in America, and by the 1820s, cotton was the poor man's way to get rich. Wanting these lands for white settlers, the United States government decided on a policy of moving the Indians out of the East and placing them onto lands in the West. So began the ethnic cleansing of most Indians from the eastern United States.

By the early 1820s, that area west of Arkansas was dubbed Indian Country. Maps designated it as the Great American Desert, so many Americans thought it the perfect place to put Indians. Later officially named Indian Territory, it would eventually shrink down to what today is the state of Oklahoma. With the Indian removal policy in effect, during the 1820s and early 1830s, government negotiators met with the Choctaws. In a series of treaties, the Choctaws reluctantly agreed to a land swap by which they would exchange their land in the East for land in Indian Territory. Essentially, everything between the Red and the Arkansas and Canadian Rivers, from the Arkansas border to the 100th meridian, would now be their sovereign country. Beginning in 1831 and for the next few years, Choctaws were assembled into groups of about five hundred to fifteen hundred and moved west toward Indian Territory. The groups took different routes, most walking, though steamboats carried some up the Mississippi and the Arkansas. No matter which way they took, the journey was hard, with the Indians being hit by blizzards, hunger, and cholera. Of fifteen thousand Choctaws and one thousand black slaves who marched toward Indian Territory, over twenty-five hundred died along the way.[5]

Those Choctaws coming to Indian Territory by steamboat debarked on the south side of the Arkansas River at a large rock shelf only about a mile and a half upriver from the Spiro Mounds. Here the Choctaws built a town, which came to be called Skullyville, a derivative of *iskuli*, the Choctaw word for "money." It was an appropriate name because here the United States government built an Indian agency and disbursed the annuity payments promised to the Choctaws in the removal treaties. In 1834, the government constructed Fort Coffee to protect Skullyville and the surrounding Choctaw territory from the "wild" Wichita and Comanche Indians to the west.[6]

At Skullyville the Choctaws built their national council house. The Choctaws divided their new country into three districts, and Skullyville served as both the capital of the Choctaw Nation and the seat of government for the Moshulatubbe District. It somehow seems fitting that Skullyville became a capital city when just a mile and a half southeast of it sat the Spiro Mounds, itself once a great Indian capital. Skullyville quickly became a major center of trade in eastern Indian Territory, complete with a post office, docking facilities for steamboats, and several schools, including the New Hope Seminary for Choctaw girls. Old Military Road ran from Fort Smith through Skullyville, and in later years, the Butterfield Overland Stage made a stop there. The Choctaws even built a bridge near Spiro to make travel easier.[7]

Within just a few years, almost two hundred Choctaw citizens lived around Skullyville, many of them rather prosperous, their farms bursting with corn, cotton, and orchards. In 1834, when artist George Catlin passed through Skullyville, he painted a picture of well-to-do Choctaws playing stickball. Things were going so well that in 1847, the Choctaws at Skullyville raised money to assist the people of Ireland during their devastating potato famine. Two years later, when the California gold rush hit, Skullyville saw numerous forty-niners pass through on their way west.[8]

Still, all did not remain well for Skullyville. In the 1850s, the capital of the Choctaw Nation was moved to Doaksville. Between 1858 and 1862, the capital moved many times, spending time not only in Skullyville and Doaksville, but also at Nanih Waya, Fort Towson, and Boggy Depot.[9] When the Civil War began in 1861, federal troops abandoned Indian Territory and so abandoned the Choctaws to the Confederacy. During the war, Indian Territory suffered tremendous devastation as Union and Confederate forces battled across the region. In 1863, the Battle of Backbone Mountain took place near Spiro Mounds.[10] Though many Choctaw leaders actively backed the Confederacy, a host of other Choctaws remained loyal to the Union. As Union troops advanced south into Indian Territory, in 1864 these loyal Choctaws formed a separate Union government near the Spiro Mounds, but Union generals refused to recognize it as legitimate. When the war ended the next year, the Choctaws and other tribes reestablished their relationship with the federal government. As an indemnity, the Five Tribes were forced to give up all their lands in the western part of Indian Territory. They also had to free their black slaves and make them citizens of their respective nations.[11]

Not long after this, Skullyville began to fade. The capital of the Choctaw Nation had long ago moved away. Railroads came to Indian Territory, as did more and more non-Indians. Down in Le Flore County, large coal deposits had been found, perfect for driving locomotives. So in 1895 the Kansas City Southern Railroad (KCS)—sometimes known as the Old Split Log—built a line through Le Flore County on its way to Galveston, Texas.

The KCS bypassed Skullyville, however, and soon the citizens begin to abandon the town. As other railroads came through the county, they also bypassed Skullyville, essentially killing the steamboat traffic there.[12] So in 1895, just a few miles south of both Skullyville and the mounds, a new town on the railroad line sprang up—Spiro. The town was originally slated to be called Ainsworth, but the government rejected the name as too similar to the town of Alesworth. A citizen of the new community suggested Spiro after the name of his new son-in-law, Spiro Nicodemus. Somehow the name stuck. As the other railroads passed through the community, Spiro became a major agricultural center, with four working cotton gins and tons of corn and potatoes being shipped out. Spiro's prosperity was the end of Skullyville, as the last of Skullyville's citizens moved to the new community. Abandoned, Skullyville ceased to exist. Fort Coffee had long been closed, so Skullyville became a ghost town. Over the years, its buildings collapsed, and nothing remained. Skullyville became as lost as the mounds.[13]

The disappearance of Skullyville marked the political end of the Choctaw Nation, at least for a while. By the 1880s, Congress came to the idea that communal lands, such as reservations and the territories of the Five Tribes, were retarding the Indian assimilation process. Figuring that privately owned plots of land would force the Indians to become small farmers, in 1887 the government started breaking up the reservations and allotting each Indian head of family or single individual his or her own private tract of land. These tracts usually ranged somewhere between 80 and 160 acres. Though the Indians protested the allotment process, the government strong-armed it through. The Choctaws' turn came in 1896, when Congress forced them to sign an agreement that would divide their lands equally among their citizens. The former black slaves of the Choctaws would be included but get no more than forty acres apiece. Two years later, the Curtis Act abolished the Choctaw government as a political entity.

The actual survey and allotment of Choctaw lands began in 1903 and went on for the next few years. Any surplus land was to be sold off to white buyers. Although Choctaws had never mentioned mounds near Skullyville and Spiro, maybe the strange things reported about the place came into play, because the Choctaws allotted the Spiro Mounds to their former black slaves. Boundaries crossed over the mounds, and the entire Spiro Mounds site was divided between four, maybe five, landowners. The large Craig Mound became the property of "Aunt" Rachel Brown. The coup de grace for the Choctaws came in 1907, when Indian Territory was officially disbanded and Oklahoma became the forty-sixth state in the Union.[14]

Throughout their time in Indian Territory, the Choctaws ignored Spiro Mounds. They certainly knew about burial and temple mounds because their ancestors had been mound builders back in Mississippi and Alabama. In fact, their most sacred place, Nanih Waya, was a large earthen mound back in Mississippi. They also knew of the existence of Spiro Mounds as indicated by the Choctaw graves and Chickasaw pottery found nearby. But they never mentioned the mounds in writing, never held any festivals there, never recognized the place in any way. In fact, the first written mention of Spiro came in 1914, with Thoburn's excavation of the two Ward mounds.[15] So when it came to allot the land around the mound site, good river land except for the large canebrakes, no Indians kept any of it; rather, they assigned it all to their former slaves.[16]

Aunt Rachel Brown, the first owner of the tract that held Craig Mound developed a healthy wariness about the Spiro Mounds, as did the other African-Choctaw landowners of the site.[17] They knew the mounds held Indian burials, so they respected and revered them. This helped save the mounds. Although a few landowners planted cotton atop some of the mounds, most did not, and when Thoburn showed up in 1913, large trees were growing on Craig and the other mounds. Aunt Rachel and other landowners also refused to allow pot hunters to dig on the mounds. In fact, Clements claimed that "no Negro would approach the site after night-fall."[18]

Aunt Rachel's property line went directly across the middle of the long tail of Craig Mound. The largest lobe of Craig Mound, the one that would soon be labeled the Great Temple Mound, was on her land. She seemed particularly protective of it, maybe because she saw and heard things. From her cabin only a few hundred yards from Craig Mound, on dark nights, she reported blue flames shimmering around the mound and strange noises emanating from it. One night, a loud noise from the mound woke her. Looking out, she was frightened to see a team of ghost cats "harnessed tandem-fashion to a small wagon which they were pulling around and around the summit."[19]

Horses and mules, it was said, also sensed something strange about Craig Mound. Years before, a mule barn had been built at the base of Craig. In fact, one of the earliest photographs of the mound from about 1913 showed the dilapidated wooden barn at the mound's base. But the barn had to be abandoned because any mules housed there during the night came out terror stricken and couldn't be worked the next day. Locals admitted to Clements that "mules could only be urged to approach the earthwork with the greatest difficulty and with increasing expressions of panic."[20]

Of course, stories about lights, sounds, and wagon-pulling cats didn't deter everybody. Over the years, pot hunters had crept onto the mounds and dug out several nice pieces of pottery. The stories weren't about to stop Guinn Cooper, Jim Vandagriff, and Kimball McKenzie, but sneaking onto someone's property under the cover of darkness to dig out a few pipes or pieces of pottery wasn't what they had in mind. They hoped for something bigger, a full-scale mining operation into the mounds, all legal and aboveboard, complete with permission from the landowners. Though McKenzie was from the area, all three realized that for the project to work, they had to get John Hobbs on board.

Hobbs, a hard, wiry farmer with his trademark newsboy cap always perched atop his head, was older than the others, and by

1933 was probably in his forties but looked younger. He'd lived around Spiro since before Indian Territory had become a state back in 1907. He'd even married a Choctaw woman. Their home was only about a mile and half northeast of the mounds.[21] As early as 1915, Hobbs had developed an interest in the Spiro Mounds and what they contained. As he later told the *Kansas City Star*, back then he dug into the Craig Mound and found an odd-shaped clay bottle and a foot-long copper "chisel," which was so hard it could cut nickels. He'd often picked up ear spools on his walks around the mounds. His finds had interested others. As Hobbs told it, a wealthy oil man had come down to the mounds and spent about two thousand dollars trying to open one of the mounds, but he didn't find anything.[22] Nevertheless, Hobbs had, over the years, found enough relics to put him into contact with Pilquist, Balloun, and Daniel, the artifact dealers in Dardanelle, Arkansas.

So in the summer of 1933, still smarting over their gold fiasco, Guinn Cooper, Jim Vandagriff, and Kimball McKenzie went down to Le Flore County, Oklahoma, and met with John Hobbs. The big problem, as always, was leasing the mounds from the property owner, but things on this front seemed to be looking up. Aunt Rachel Brown, the original owner of the property, who had been so adamant about pot hunters not disturbing the mound, had since died. The property passed to William Craig, for whom the Craig Mound came to be named. Craig was also black and somewhat well-to-do in the local African American community. Like Aunt Rachel, he protected the mound and refused to allow pot hunters on it. But he'd died about 1930, and the property was divided among his two grandchildren, Helen and James Craig. Both Helen and James were about twelve or thirteen years old in 1933. Their maternal grandfather, George Evans, was named as their guardian. Evans didn't have the same reverence for the mound that Aunt Rachel and William Craig had had, so he was open to the idea of leasing it. One thing that spurred his decision was that young James Craig had been stricken with tuberculosis and needed money for doctor's bills. Adding to Evans's willingness to lease the mound was the toll the Great Depression was taking on rural African Americans.[23]

Still, though Evans was open to leasing, Cooper, McKenzie, Vandagriff, and Hobbs knew he wouldn't rent it out for a pittance. The four began to discuss the project among themselves and eventually brought in Kimball McKenzie's father, W. M. "Bill" McKenzie, a respected store proprietor in nearby Pocola, Oklahoma. Understanding that the negotiations with Evans might be touchy, the five approached Reverend R. W. Wall, a black preacher in the area. They offered to make him a full partner in the project if he could get Evans to lease Craig Mound for a decent price. They also made a pact in which whatever they found in the Spiro Mounds would be divided equally among all six. So in the summer of 1933, the Pocola Mining Company was formed with Guinn Cooper, John Hobbs, Bill McKenzie, Kimball McKenzie, Jim Vandagriff, and R. W. Wall as partners. Now all they needed was the lease to Craig Mound.[24]

The formation of the Pocola Mining Company came just in time, because at that very moment, another party was trying to lease the mounds. Before the company could negotiate its lease with George Evans, Joe Balloun, one of the artifact dealers out of Dardanelle, Arkansas, contacted Percy Brewer, who owned the tract of land next to Evans's. In fact, Brewer's property line went directly over about a quarter of Craig Mound, giving him ownership of the smallest southeasternmost lobe of the mound. Joe Balloun, along with Van Balloun, Roy McKelvey, Charlie Banks, and Ike Dowell made some kind of deal with Brewer, the details of which are not clear. Nevertheless, in the summer of 1933, Balloun and his associates began digging into the southeastern tail of Craig Mound, but for whatever reason, they soon gave up their lease. Possibly, since they were relegated to the fourth and smallest lobe of the mound, they didn't find much. Or maybe Balloun had heard that the Pocola Mining Company was forming, and since he was really a relic dealer more than a digger, he might have reasoned that giving up his claim would put him first in line to buy any items the Pocola men might find.[25]

With Balloun out of the way, Preacher Wall went to work on George Evans. In November 1933, they finally hammered out a deal. Evans would lease his part of Craig Mound and any other mounds on his property for a flat fee of three hundred dollars. The six members of the Pocola Mining Company would put up fifty dollars each. The lease would run for two years, ending on November 27, 1935. During that time, the men could excavate the mounds and sell whatever they found. Aside from the three hundred dollar lease payment, Evans was also supposed to get a small percentage of whatever the miners found and sold.[26]

Fifty dollars apiece and three hundred dollars for George Evans wasn't small change back then. And it was going to cost even more to clear the land and dig the mounds. Still, nobody puts up money expecting to lose it, so for the men of the Pocola Mining Company, this was a serious investment, and they firmly believed valuable things were to be found in the mounds. It was not to be archaeology either. There would be no study of the artifacts or leaving them in place to see what they could tell about the people who made them. These were hard times, and the men wanted to recoup their investment and then some. As the company name proved, this was to be a full-blown, slash-and-burn mining operation. They were going to be tomb raiders, grave robbers—burrow into the mound, dig out any Indian artifacts they could find, then sell whatever turned up. Although professional archaeologists would call it looting, they were doing what John Hobbs and the farmers in Carden Bottoms, Arkansas, had been doing for years. They were just stepping it up a notch.

With the ink on their lease barely dry, the men of the Pocola Mining Company set up a tent camp next to Craig Mound. Now came the hard part. Craig Mound and all the other mounds on the property were covered with trees that had to be cut down before digging could start. And that led to another problem. Wall had delivered on his part, so he wasn't going to dig. Bill

McKenzie wasn't, either. He was older than the others and had his store in Pocola to tend. Anyway, he was seen as something like the money man behind the mining company. So Guinn Cooper was designated site manager, living on the property and guarding whatever they found. He, along with John Hobbs, Jim Vandagriff, and Kimball McKenzie, would chop brush and dig. Even then, they needed more hands, so Will Vandagriff, Jim's brother, came down to work. Soon they'd need even more help.[27]

Making it all the more difficult was that everything had to be done by hand. Whether they couldn't afford a bulldozer or couldn't get one back there, the excavators used only picks and shovels. For that reason, they concentrated on the two smaller lobes of Craig Mound just west of Percy Brewer's property. These mounds were less than fifteen feet high, so the men felt it would be easier to hit pay dirt. Even then, as Hobbs pointed out, the three smaller lobes had been so picked over and pitted by pot hunters over the years that they didn't even look like separate mounds anymore.[28]

Still, almost immediately, the men uncovered artifacts. About seven feet down, they hit a burial containing numerous skeletons and relics. As Hobbs later told it, they found "hundreds of these skeletons, lying in pockets sometimes three and four deep."[29] The bones, he said, were blackened. Among the skeletons, they found some T-shaped pipes ranging in length from five to thirty-one inches. There were also a few copper needles and ear spools, several heavy stone maces, some burned pieces of baskets and cloth, and thousands of beads and arrowheads.[30] This was a good beginning because the pipes, copper items, and maces were rare.

Finding these artifacts was one thing; marketing them was something else. About this time, late 1933, the Arkansas relic dealers showed up: Joe Balloun, Goodrich E. Pilquist, and H. T. Daniel. Dardanelle, Arkansas, was a small town on the Arkansas River, maybe 150 miles downstream from Spiro, so John Hobbs was probably familiar with them from his many years as a part-time relic hunter. Similarly, Joe Balloun certainly knew most of the diggers and had probably been tracking the excavations since the Pocola men had started their project. It had been Balloun who had tried to lease part of the mound in the summer of 1933 but had given it up when the Pocola Mining Company got their lease on the Craig side of the mound. As for H. T. Daniel, not much is known of him.

The most professional of the three relic dealers was Pilquist. Born in Georgia in 1879, his family had moved to Dardanelle in the early 1900s. By 1933, he was fifty-four years old, married to a woman ten years his senior, and known around Dardanelle as a rather odd man who distrusted modern things like gas stoves and automobiles. Never having a steady job, Pilquist supported his family by trapping, hunting, and relic dealing.[31] And it was relic dealing that really captured his fancy. He'd been involved in the Carden Bottoms relic rush in 1924 and had been the one to call in Harrington of the Heye Museum of the American Indian in New York to see the artifacts.[32] From the Carden Bottoms rush, he knew that relics got people's money fever going. "I have seen as many as 100 people digging on one acre at one time. It was just like a gold rush. Everyone was trying to see who could find the most pots, beads or whatever they could find. There would be a wagon load of pottery dug every day."[33]

Pilquist became so adept at finding and buying artifacts that he printed up letterhead billing himself as the "Largest Dealer in Arkansas Pottery," with "Flint and Stone Relics from Every State. Thirty Years in the Business."[34] Besides Arkansas, he often traveled through Oklahoma, Texas, and New Mexico in search of exotic artifacts.[35] Eventually, his collection numbered over thirty-seven thousand items.[36] In *Hobbies* magazine, he listed over twenty thousand arrowheads for sale, ranging from $1.75 to $3 per hundred. He also advertised vases, bottles, and even "one perfect skull" for $8.[37] Every now and again he wrote short articles on relic collecting for *Hobbies*.[38] When he died on December 29, 1962, at eighty-four, his occupation was listed as "retired relic dealer."[39]

So now, as the Pocola men dug into the top of Craig Mound and found exotic artifacts, they had ready buyers waiting for anything they hauled out.[40] Balloun, Pilquist, or Daniel might swing by every now and again, offer some low prices on what the diggers had found, buy the artifacts, then advertise them for sale in *Hobbies*. If something was really exotic or outstanding, they hit up their usual customers, those collectors who specialized in Indian artifacts. What kind of money the Pocola Mining Company got for these first relics is not known. It probably wasn't all that much, because the dealers low-balled them. Still, it was enough to keep the Pocola men digging. In fact, they expanded their operations. They began to hire relatives, out-of-work neighbors, even unemployed Le Flore County coal miners to help dig.[41]

By December 1933, these early finds from Craig Mound hit the curio markets, where they caused quite a stir. They were so extraordinary and so fine that many collectors thought they were fakes. Academics also sat up and took notice. The director of the Illinois State Museum at Springfield, Thorne Duel, came down to Spiro in late 1933 to see what was happening.[42] And it was these artifacts that caught the attention of Carl Guthe, who contacted Forrest Clements at the University of Oklahoma.[43]

So in the spring of 1934, prodded by Guthe's phone call, Clements made his first visit to Spiro only to find the Pocola boys digging into the top of Craig Mound. Spiro Mounds had been on Clements' list of possible university excavation projects, but that was to be in the future. Money was always an issue, as were the property owners. Others before Clements had run into the same problem. In 1928, Joseph Thoburn, who had excavated the Ward Mounds between 1913 and 1917, had tried to negotiate a lease in order to conduct a real archaeological excavation on Craig Mound. However, "some one told the negro owner that I had plenty of money, so he receded from his previous agreement and refused to permit me to do any work there unless I would first pay off the mortgage on his 40-acre farm, which I was not in a position to do."[44] Now, Clements realized the pot hunters had managed to do what Thoburn could not.

While he was there on his initial reconnaissance, however, Clements figured he might throw his weight around and see if it worked. He met with the men of the Pocola Mining Company and tried to convince them to give up their lease and allow trained archaeologists to do the excavating. He probably cajoled and threatened, but nothing came of it. These were hard, raw-boned men, overalls men who distrusted suits and ties.

Anyway, for the Pocola men, this was an investment. They'd each put up fifty dollars, and there was no way they were going to give up their claim and lease. Besides, as they saw it, all was right and tidy. George Evans was the legal guardian of the Craig children, so he could lease their land for them. The Pocola men had explained to George what they'd planned and he'd agreed. In their minds, considering the hard times and all, it was a good deal for Evans and the children. Anyway, their lease ran until November 1935, so whatever they found in the mounds was theirs, and they could do with it whatever they wanted. And they had the papers to prove it.

Clements went back to his university office in Norman disappointed and distressed at the diggings going on at the mounds. He was determined to put an end to it somehow. He didn't have any law to stand on, but that wasn't going to stop him from trying. So for the next year and a half, a low-level war began between the men of the Pocola Mining Company and Forrest Clements, chair of the Department of Anthropology at the University of Oklahoma.

On one side, the Pocola men continued potting around the mounds, unearthing skeletons and a few artifacts. These were quickly sold to the Arkansas dealers who put them on the curio market. On the other side, Clements hoped to end the excavations. He tried to persuade George Evans to cancel the lease, but Evans had already spent the money. Clements, with money put up by the Oklahoma Historical Society, offered to buy out the diggers. The Pocola men thought hard about it; after all, they weren't finding as many artifacts as they'd hoped. But in the end they could never agree on a price. Clements seemed to think that he almost had the Pocola men convinced on selling out, but their backbone got a little stiffening from outside interests. If that's true, then it was probably the Dardanelle relic dealers who convinced them to hold out.[45]

Nevertheless, while Clements was distressed at the destruction of the mounds, he soothed himself with the thought that time was on his side. Using shovels to pot around on the tops of the mounds was hard, time-consuming work. It wasn't systematic either, so shoveling might prevent them from hitting a really large cache of artifacts. Also, Clements knew that only intact relics would bring the big money, and that required unhurried, cautious digging. If he could just keep the diggers working slowly and carefully until their lease ran out, then he could jump in and get a crack at it. So Clements, giving his professional but not unbiased opinion, suggested the miners confine themselves to the smaller mounds and dig them very carefully.[46]

But Clements was worried. He didn't know what was under there. Maybe something big. And he was afraid that if left to their diggings long enough, the miners might just find it. While he waited for the lease to run out, he tried to ensure his success by taking his grudge with the pot hunters to the Oklahoma legislature. Throughout the rest of 1934 and into the spring of 1935, Clements, using his position as a respected anthropologist and department chair at the University of Oklahoma, lobbied the state legislature to pass an antiquities act. This would prevent nonprofessional pot hunters from digging into Indian mounds by mandating that only academically trained archaeologists had a right to excavate and study them.

It didn't take long for the Pocola boys to get wind of Clements' legislative machinations. It seems they had every reason to be suspicious of Clements, but in their minds, they had law and right on their side. And they weren't about to back down.

4

Ceremonial Center

1100–1250

At the beginning of the twelfth century, Spiro was just one of many towns growing up along the rivers and streams of the American Southeast. It possessed the foundations of an impressive ceremonial center, but so did other towns, some even in the general vicinity of Spiro, such as the Harlan site many miles to the north. However, the next 150 years would propel Spiro to fantastic heights, dominating eastern Oklahoma, western Arkansas, southwestern Missouri, and heavily influencing the entire region east to the Mississippi River and beyond. Four things, all connected and intertwined, brought Spiro to greatness. These included internal stability, success in war, control of trade, and religious power.

One of Spiro's greatest assets during this time was its economic, social, political, and religious stability. Every community, no matter how large or small, wants things to happen according to plan, or at least in predictable ways. For a growing chiefdom such as Spiro, stability meant a population expanding through natural increase and immigration. This was a good time for Spiro because even Nature seemed to be working in her people's favor. The weather was pleasant and constant. Great soaking rains came on time, and every spring the Arkansas deposited rich silt along the lower terraces. The growing season lasted from April through October, and women farmers took advantage of it, expanding their gardens and increasing their yields. Little

barley and other plants still made up the lion's share of culti-
vated foods, but corn was becoming increasingly common.
Men continued hunting, bringing home deer, turkeys, squirrels,
gophers, rabbits, and other meats, which women turned into
delicious soups and stews.[1]

For most Spiroans, both commoners and nobles, there was a
predictable sameness to their years. The seasons themselves
determined it. In the warm season, April through October,
farming governed everything, and every family participated.
Without any draft animals to help, men cleared the land and
turned the soil, but after that, the women took over. It fell on
the household's mother, daughters, and sisters to plant the
seeds, weed the gardens, scare away the birds and raccoons,
and then, when the time was right, harvest their crop.

Of course, a woman's world meant much more. She birthed
the children, doted on them, and while they were infants, carried
them on her back in a cradleboard while she went about her
chores. She comforted her husband, cooked the meals, and
made most of the baskets, pottery, ropes, blankets, clothing,
and utensils every household needed. In the warm season,
almost everything happened outside. Women cooked under
brush arbors, and on hot nights, the entire family might sleep
under them. For men, the warm season was a time for war and
some hunting. If not at war or beating the woods for small
game, they remained at their village, fixing their equipment,
gambling, gossiping, and dancing.[2]

During the cold season, November through March, the
hunt took precedence. Although a little hunting was always
going on around the area, come winter, some Spiro families
ventured out on long hunting and gathering expeditions that
might cover several hundred miles and many weeks. Some
went a hundred miles or more to the west to hunt buffalo on
the southern plains. There they butchered the animals they
killed, taking and tanning their great hides, but also cutting off
long strips of meat to dry into jerky. When the hunting season
was over, they carried these hides, jerky, and any other buffalo

items they needed back to Spiro. Without horses, this was done either overland by foot or by canoe when possible.[3] Deer and smaller game also provided substantial amounts of meat. Hunters often returned with large quantities of this meat, as well as with hides, bones, and sinews that could be turned into tools. Along with this, households lived off food that had been stored after the harvest.[4]

During the cold season, Spiroans not on the hunt moved back inside their snug square houses. A smoky fire burned constantly, and in this gloom women passed the cold days weaving cloth of buffalo or rabbit fur; tanning deer hides; making clothing, shoes, rope, pots, baskets, and a host of other utensils. A woman might tell stories to teach and entertain her children, or the boys and girls, bundled up against the cold, might scurry to the lodge of their mother's brother to learn what it meant to be Spiroan. It was also a good time for men and women with certain skills, specialists, to work on their crafts. Cold winter days were just right for the medicine woman or midwife to dry her herbs; the flintknapper to make his arrowheads; the potter to throw and bake her jars and bottles; the pipe maker to work on his stems and bowls. Many of these products would later be used in the everyday lives of the people of the towns and hamlets. Many would be shared with kinspeople or given away through gift exchange. Some were so special, so beautiful, that they were slated for use by the priest-chief and his principal men and eventually wound up buried with them.[5]

Nevertheless, no matter what specialty they practiced, Spiroans lives were shaped by farming. It certainly affected their health. The same farming lifestyle that brought population growth also proved hard on their bodies. Spiroans tended to be of average height—five feet, five inches, to six feet for men, six inches shorter for women. If Spiroans looked anything like the realistic human figurines made at Cahokia, they looked very "Indian," with almond eyes and full lips.[6] However, studies show that the bones of Indian farmers of this time at the great ceremonial centers of Spiro, Moundville, and Etowah had more arthritis, more wear, and higher infection rates than the nonfarming hunter-gatherers of the day. Many people also seemed stricken by a disease that caused bone lesions.[7] Parasites, such as hookworms and flatworms, probably bedeviled them, as well as parasitic ailments, such as Rocky Mountain spotted fever. Skin ailments such as ringworm may have been common. Besides illnesses, Spiroans, like all active people, suffered fractures, sprains, twists, cuts, scrapes, ruptures, and tears. Sometimes these became so severe that a person might lose the use of an arm, a leg, or an eye.[8]

The social division played into the health of Spiroans. The nobles seem to have been healthier and to have lived longer than commoners.[9] Toothache also separated the classes. As any corn eater knows, bits of kernels tend to get stuck between one's teeth. As corn became an increasing part of the Spiroan diet, tooth problems resulted. Commoners seemed to have more wear to their teeth, more cavities, and more teeth lost than did the nobles. This may indicate that corn was considered a food for the commoners, while the older, more traditional foods, such as little barley, sunflower seeds, squash, and such were reserved for the nobility. That is not unlike Mexico today, where corn tortillas are associated with the lower class and flour tortillas with the upper. For Spiroan commoners, the process of grinding corn with stones often meant that grit got mixed in with the meal. Over time, sandy meal wore down teeth and caused gum inflammation. This brought on painful abscesses and tooth loss. Even then, Spiroan commoners seemed to have fewer cavities overall than did their counterparts at Cahokia, Moundville, and Etowah. This may have resulted from the buffalo meat Spiroans added to their diet.[10]

Still, when compared to Indians peoples living centuries later or even to Europeans living at that same time, Spiroans were downright pictures of health. None of the terrible diseases that had swept across Europe, Africa, and Asia over the past few thousand years had reached the Americas. Smallpox, typhus, plague, malaria, measles, and diphtheria were all unheard of at Spiro. On the downside, Europeans and Africans had long contact with epidemics and had developed some immunity to them, but American Indians had none. Any immunities had been washed out of their blood in earlier times when the population was small and scattered. Also, Indian peoples lacked domesticated animals, the herds of cattle, horses, pigs, and sheep that served as breeding grounds for disease. This lack of immunity would prove disastrous for American Indians after the fifteenth century, when Europeans and Africans began arriving in the Americas. But until then, Spiroans did not have to worry about these killers.[11]

So the stability of a ranked society was there. Priest-chiefs ruled. Nobles occupied the important political, military, and religious positions. Commoners did most of the work. Spiro elites not only were healthier than the commoners, they also dressed differently. Noblemen might wear large snake-like necklaces and cloaks made of feathers. Their earlobes were pierced, actually slit with a knife, and large round ear spools were inserted into the slits. These heavy ear spools of clay or stone, many later decorated with the cross-in-circle or forked-eye motifs, stretched their earlobes like taffy.[12] In fact, these ear spools seemed to have been one of the markers that identified and separated the nobility from the commoners.

A nobleman also wore his hair in a prickly roach on the top of his head, sometimes with ponytails, or bound at the back into a bun with long braids hanging down on either side of his face. He might wear a hide breechcloth or a skirt made of grass or buffalo- or rabbit-fur yarn. If the effigy pipes are any indication, some rituals called for a man to be naked except for his feather cloak and necklaces. A warrior would wear a large beaded shell on a front piece of hair, which hung down over his forehead. In battle, men wore wooden armor, light skirts, and moccasins that wrapped up to their knees.[13]

Commoners, in warm weather, wore simple breechcloths or skirts made of hides or woven cloth made from animal fur. In colder weather, everyone, commoner and elite alike, bundled

up and wore longer, warmer clothing. Still, commoners rarely
wore jewelry because that was a privilege usually reserved for
the nobility. Both classes practiced body and face painting,
especially in war. Tattooing, which was widespread among
Caddoan peoples, was also probably done by both nobility and
commoners to identify them as Spiro residents and to mark
their position in society, their accomplishments, and possibly
even their clan membership.[14]

Spiroans, both the commoners and the elites, often deformed
their skull in particular ways. Various aspects of cranial deformation became common throughout the Southeast, though
many peoples chose not to do it all. As late as the early 1700s,
French explorers saw it among the Caddos along Red River,
and the English saw it among the Waxhaws of the Carolina
Piedmont. Cranial deformation seems to have been associated
with Mississippian peoples. What led some people at Spiro to
deform their skulls one way, some another, and others not at all
is unknown. The most common form of skull molding practiced
throughout Mississippian America was "flat heading." A mother
strapped her baby into a cradleboard and then bound another
board across the child's forehead until the forehead was flattened, the sides swelled outward, and the eyes developed a
bulging look to them. Although this practice died out in the
early 1700s, some Indians believed flat heading gave them
better vision. This type of forehead flattening was common
among Mississippian peoples of the Caddoan area and across
the American Southeast.[15]

A second type of cranial deformation was a circular type.
Mothers tightly wrapped strips of animal hides around the top
of a child's head until the skull was elongated into a cone
shape. Most other peoples in the region used the flat head look,
but the elongated skull seemed particular to Spiro and may
have been used by Spiroans to separate themselves from their
neighbors in appearance. Archaeologist Frank Schambach,
looking at what he sees as Spiroan traders buried in mounds at
a Red River trading center, believes that their elongated skulls

instantly identified them as Spiroan and, in this case, important traders. There would be no mistaking them, because their conehead would identify them even if they were naked. There may be something to this because some very realistic statues and masks found at Spiro seem to show this elongated, cone type of skull molding.[16]

Whether they had shaped their heads or not, commoners at Spiro lived their lives as they seemingly always had. They farmed, hunted, worked, played, courted, joked, laughed, cried, and loved. They cooked, ate, gossiped, gambled, refurbished the temples, and continued hauling earth to build up the Brown and Copple mounds. Were they oppressed by the priest-chief and nobles? They probably did not think they were. How rigid the line was between commoner and noble is unknown, but it was probably much less than it was in Europe at that time. In fact, it might be better to think in terms of important families rather than important individuals. However, if Caddo societies in the late seventeenth and early eighteenth centuries are any indication, leaders could administer a switching to people who showed up late for labor details. Some punishments could have been even more drastic. Slavery existed, but slaves were captives taken during war and might eventually be adopted into a Spiroan family. Nevertheless, for the commoners, the nobility and the priest-chief were essential for their town's harmony and prosperity. The priest-chief's rituals ensured the sun went along the correct path, the rains came regularly, the corn grew, and their warriors triumphed. And it all seemed to be working for Spiro during the twelfth and thirteenth centuries. The power and prestige of the Spiroan priest-chiefs awed all.[17]

During these years, when priest-chiefs died, their bodies went into the charnel houses, accompanied by many pieces of artwork and symbols of their status. Once the body had fully decayed, a procession of Spiroan nobles carried the dead chief's bones on a cedar pole litter to his final resting place. It must have been one of the most solemn occasions in the life of any Spiroan. With huge sacred fires burning atop Brown and Copple mounds, long lines of chanting priests, mourning Spiroans, and awe-struck allies followed the litter to its final resting place in one of the burial mounds. The new priest-chief presided over the interment of his predecessor, and when the ceremonies were over, men selected for the duty buried the bones, litter and all, amid grave goods of pipes, pottery, and copper. The really fantastic grave goods, such as the huge effigy pipes, would come later, after 1250.

Stability cannot be overestimated, but it does not explain everything that fueled Spiro's rise to greatness. At 1100, many towns in that part of the country were in about the same shape as Spiro. The Harlan site on the Neosho River in northeastern Oklahoma was a serious rival. Like Spiro, its people were building mounds and interring their dead elites in them.[18] Similar sized towns and smaller villages, hamlets, and farmsteads clustered around Spiro and throughout the region. But by 1250, Spiro would dominate them or at least seriously influence them.[19]

Another way that Spiro may have ensured its rise to power was through the successful waging of war. Warfare was common throughout the Mississippian area. Evidence of this is that most major cities of this time fortified their main plaza and temple area with log palisades. A good example is Cahokia, across the river from modern-day St. Louis. During the 1100s, it was the largest town in North America, boasting a population of more than fifteen thousand in the city alone, and thousands more in the general vicinity.[20] Even smaller towns built palisades. Hernando de Soto had to overcome the palisades of Mabila when he attacked that Alabama city in October 1540. English explorers on the North Carolina coast in 1584 reported log-enclosed villages. As late as 1758, the Caddoan Wichitas and their allies had built a log-walled fort on the Red River and from it successfully repelled a furious Spanish attack.[21]

Strangely, no palisade has ever been found at Spiro, and not because archaeologists have not looked.[22] Could it be that Spiroans did not need to protect their temple area with a palisade because serious warfare never threatened the city? Internal stability certainly helped, but so did good borders. Outwardly, the Great Plains to the west served as a formidable defensive barrier. The plains were sparsely populated at this time, maybe a few scattered camps along some of the river valleys. And there were no horses then to make Plains people the fearsome mounted warriors they would become. Similarly, the Arkansas River as well as the surrounding mountains and hills protected the city.[23] So did the many settlements and villages radiating out from Spiro, serving as pickets. A raiding party would have been spotted and disposed of long before it got to the sacred Spiro ceremonial center. Another possibility was that Spiro did not need a palisade because none dared attack this holy place. Maybe the priest-chief's connection to the natural elements made the other towns view it as important, even essential, to the health of the entire region. Or maybe they feared the wrath of a Spiro counterattack.

Despite the lack of a wooden palisade around the city's ceremonial areas, warfare seems to have been very important to Spiroans. Over the next few centuries, nobles were buried with large quantities of military items or items that had military images carved onto them. For example, in the Southeast, the most common weapon was the war club. Though bows and arrows were also used, the thick underbrush of the Southeastern forests necessitated hand-to-hand combat. And the best weapon for this was the war club. So common was it that a red-painted war club became the symbol of war among Southeastern Indians.[24] Surely it is more than coincidence that after 1100, we find Spiroans increasingly burying their elite with scepters, maces, and celts, all essentially ceremonial war clubs and the very emblems of nobility at Spiro. Other military items buried with the nobility were various spear and arrow points, ax heads, clubs, and the like. Additional grave goods show a similar tilt toward war. One of the most common animal images scratched onto conch shell cups was that of the falcon. Spiroans honored the falcon for its aggressiveness, and as one archaeologist theorized, the bird was "a symbol of appropriate military behavior in successful war."[25] A Spiro grave also produced one horrific depiction of the war club's use in the form of a giant ceremonial effigy pipe. Originally made at Cahokia from Missouri flint clay in the early twelfth century, it arrived in Spiro during the mid-thirteenth century. The pipe stands almost a foot tall and shows a warrior bending over a downed enemy, grabbing him by the hair and hitting him on the side of the face with a war club.[26]

This heavy emphasis on warfare and death seems almost unique to Spiro. For example, flint clay figurines recovered at Cahokia emphasized "aspects of the Underworld, regeneration, fertility, green corn ceremonialism, and world renewal." But the people at Spiro marched down a different road. The artwork and figurines at Spiro exalted ancestors and the nobility and the rituals associated with them, but they especially emphasized warfare, such as oversized spear points, stone maces, ax heads, the effigy pipes, and the death motifs engraved on the conch shells and pottery. Priest-chiefs and nobles deliberately chose to acquire these symbols of war. It seems war and death permeated Spiroan society.[27]

Were Spiroan warriors marching out across the region, attacking enemies and subduing towns? Possibly, but a few more questions need answering. How was war waged, and what would make Spiroans go to war? Back in the twelfth, thirteenth, and fourteenth centuries, waging war was rather simple because combatants were limited to weapons made of stone, wood, and bone. A heavy wooden war club or a stone ax, either of which could break bones or smash skulls, served well. Most warriors could swing these and do some damage on a crowded battlefield. Requiring more skill were wooden bows and stone-tipped arrows. The best wood for bows was bois d'arc wood, also known today as Osage orange. A bois d'arc bow was about sixty-five inches long with backward-curving tips and a leather hand grip. It had a seventy-pound draw weight, making it more than adequate to kill a man, a deer, or even buffalo. Bows made of bois d'arc were highly prized weapons across the American South. However, most bois d'arc grew south of the Red River, in North

Texas. Arrows might be made of cane or any straight stick, though Indians used special tools to straighten crooked ones. Arrow points were usually made from flint, though obsidian, bone, or even large fish scales might be used in some parts of the continent.[28]

So armed, how did Spiro deploy its troops? First off, in Indian societies, all men could be considered warriors. If attacked, virtually every man, and some women as well, rallied to fight the invaders. The Spiro nobility, however, steadily applied themselves to warfare, so being a warrior was equated with being a noble. It is in the graves of the nobility where so many of these military-style items are found.[29] Some commoners also proved particularly good in battle and became warriors, even war leaders with high prestige, possibly even being admitted to the nobility. On the other hand, most Spiro commoners probably fought only when needed and felt no special desire or need to become full-fledged warriors. These men applied their time to developing other skills, such as hunting, medicine, various arts and crafts, or just being good husbands, fathers, and citizens. So the nobles served as the trained warrior class, while commoners served as the rank-and-file soldiers, called up when needed.

If warfare was becoming a noble's occupation, then the positions of priest-chief and war chief might have merged during these years to become a holy warrior king, something like what Moctezuma of the Aztecs would become in early sixteenth-century Mexico. If so, did the priest-chief actually participate in battle, like Alexander the Great did, or did he remain back at Spiro and allow his war chiefs take control of the fighting? We will never know for sure, but probably the latter, although it does seem that the priest-chief was honored not only for his knowledge of the rituals that ensured prosperity and his generosity and wisdom in governing his people, but also for his ability to win wars.

What would make Spiroans go to war? At the top of the list would be revenge. In this, warfare could be punitive, an effort to punish another town or people. Spiroans, like most Indian peoples, believed in a cosmic harmony and that bad things happened when life got out of balance. One of the surest ways to let things go out of kilter was to allow insults, attacks, and deaths to go unavenged. The law of blood said that vengeance must be taken to put the dead's soul to rest and to restore harmony to society. If a Spiroan hunting party was ambushed on the trails and some members killed or taken captive, then Spiro had to retaliate. In this case, it might come in the form of a small war party made up of the dead people's relatives. They in turn would ambush a party from the offender's town and either kill or capture the party members. Those taken captive would be returned to Spiro, where they would be tortured to death, enslaved, or adopted by the dead man's family. Only then would the dead be avenged, their souls put at peace, the tears of the mourners dried, and harmony restored. If the insult or attack was big enough, the entire town might become involved.[30]

Then again, the Spiro priest-chief might have political or economic reasons to go to war. Subduing a nearby village or town, dominating its leadership, and pulling it into the Spiro political orbit might prevent the rise of a dangerous rival or provide access to important resources. What resources? Food was apparently not a reason for war, but exotic resources or items the priest-chief deemed essential for various rituals might have been. The need or desire for a certain type of stone might entail conquering a city that had sure access to such a commodity. These commodities would then be funneled back to Spiro through tribute, by regulating the production of resources, or by controlling a trade route. This last might have been the most likely.[31]

Once a major war had been decided on, various protocols would go into effect. The priest-chief would meet with a council of wise elders, war leaders, and principal men to discuss the war and its prosecution. Spiro's warrior nobles and commoner soldiers would be called up, diplomats fanned out to rally allies, and ambassadors sent to the enemy town to announce war and make demands for surrender. A red war club would be ceremonially hung at the outskirts of town, announcing to all visitors that this was a nation at war. Prior to their leaving, warriors would spend several days in secluded purification while the priests performed rituals to ensure a successful battle.[32]

If the attack was merely punitive, the strike force might have been pared down to a band of warriors who would set up an ambush, make a quick hit-and-run strike, or if the gods were on their side, they might manage to sack and burn the enemy's temple. A major campaign to subdue a town and control a nearby trade route, however, required a large party of warriors and auxiliaries to march to the enemy nation, always on the lookout for ambushes. As Spiroans arrived on the foreign city's doorstep, the enemy would bring out its warriors, and the two armies would meet in lines on an open plain. There the warriors might yell insults, dart in for a quick slash with a war club, fire off an arrow when opportunity afforded, or maneuver into position for taking a captive.

Sometimes these turned into brawling melees, with some killed and many captives taken. Other times, it was almost a show battle. In either instance, Indian warfare produced few fatalities because too many would show that the issue was not favored. Too many deaths threw things even more out of balance. At some point, one side or the other would yield.[33] In reality, big battles were rare, and most warfare was low-level feuding, with small hit-and-run parties from one village trying to burn the temple of or take a captive from another. The sheer size and importance of the Spiro ceremonial center seemed to protect it from this.

Still, it is uncertain whether Spiro had to use military power to become the most important chiefdom in the region. Certainly by 1200, Spiro was extending its influence. It was the main ceremonial center between the plains and the Mississippi River. Here were flat-topped Brown and Copple temple mounds, the great plaza, the steadily rising cone-shaped Craig and Ward burial mounds. Spiro was where the great priest-chief lived and the important political and religious ceremonies took place. Essentially, Spiro had become an expansionist chiefdom that either ruled or dominated rivals throughout its region. The mounds and plaza sat surrounded by allied settlements, each with maybe fifteen or twenty houses spread over only twenty acres, compared with Spiro's eighty acres. A settlement might be governed by a political leader, possibly connected to a Spiro noble family, who made the day-to-day decisions but was bound to the Spiro priest-chief. Around settlements came villages, with only about five or six houses, governed by a principal man whose lineage may also have been connected to the Spiro nobility. Hamlets of two or three houses, hived off villages, and a farmstead of one house were usually the farthest from Spiro.[34]

By the thirteenth century, probably ten thousand people more or less within a ten-mile radius of the city considered themselves Spiroans. They lived scattered among fifteen to twenty villages and thirty to forty hamlets. The number of farmsteads was probably even higher. For all these people, Spiro was their home, their provider of political and religious leadership. And as citizens, they provided grain, meat, information, any special commodity that might be found in their area, labor for mound building, and conscripts for warfare.[35]

Even then, Spiro's power reached much farther. By the mid-thirteenth century, Spiro had become the largest, most significant chiefdom in this part of country and one of the largest on the continent. It dominated every city, town, and village in eastern Oklahoma, western Arkansas, southwestern Missouri, and southern Kansas. It wielded significant influence on people in northwest Louisiana, northeast Texas, and far onto the Great Plains as well. On ceremonial days, "the residents of the smaller communities would gather . . . at the local ceremonial center. When death struck, at least the important individuals in the small communities were buried at the nuclear center rather than in a local cemetery. Perhaps for the great ceremonies of the year, Indians for many miles would gather at the primary center located at Spiro."[36] At its height during the thirteenth century, Spiro might have had two hundred to three hundred towns and villages scattered across present-day Oklahoma, Arkansas, Louisiana, and Texas, with a population of maybe 250,000 people who looked to it for leadership.[37] And the city's influence reached beyond the Mississippi River. Archaeologist Don Wyckoff noted that Spiro "maintained ties with other key political, religious centers in the Mississippi Valley, such places as Cahokia in East St. Louis, Angel Mounds in Indiana, Etowah in Georgia and a number of political religious centers in various parts of the United States" (see map 2).[38]

Rather than war, two things that probably did more to attract immigrants and allies to the Spiro chiefdom was the religious power it possessed. That and the massive amount of exchange and trade its people were involved in. These two go hand in hand because Spiro's religious power brought in trade items, particularly those special prestige goods needed for offerings to the gods or used in the ceremonial rituals or for burial with the nobility. In turn, possession of these items by the priest-chiefs and nobility only enhanced their prestige and power. Like European kings' crowns, scepters, and royal seals, possession of these prestige goods meant the bearer was a very important person. The very success of the city played to its advantage. Spiro was politically and economically stable, militarily potent, and religiously powerful, so it made sense for nearby towns, settlements, and minor chiefdoms to put themselves in the hands of Spiro's obviously successful priest-chief. And it made just as much sense for other major ceremonial centers across the Southeast to trade with Spiro.

Trade goods could be broken down into two categories: status goods and commodities. Status goods are those items that increase the prestige of the person who possesses them. Commodities were items most people had access to and were often the necessities of life. Grain, meat, hides, chunks of flint to make arrowheads, bois d'arc wood for bows—all are commodities, though some could at times be considered status goods. One might envision buyers waving currency and negotiating prices, or a straight trade or barter, but commodities were more often

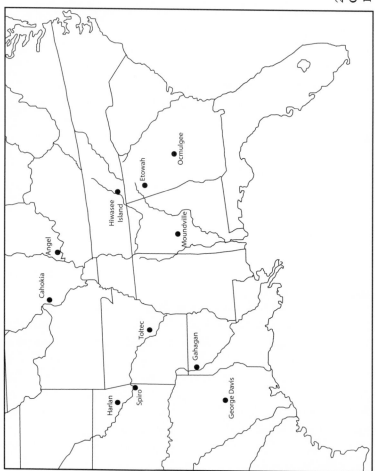

2. Mississippian Ceremonial Centers, 1050–1450

exchanged than traded. Sometimes they were given as gifts, which would bring back gifts of other needed goods, corn in return for bison hides or the like. But straight trade was not unheard of, and Spiroans may at times have exchanged so many deer hides for so many shanks of dried buffalo meat, or so many bois d'arc staves for so many conch shells.[39]

Spiro's location on the river between the plains and forests made it an excellent bottleneck for commodities and status goods passing through the area. As Wyckoff observed, "If anyone wanted to control the flow of raw materials, finished goods, and ideas between Plains villagers and Puebloans and populous Southeastern chiefdoms, the people who founded Spiro picked the right place."[40] Naturally, Spiro drew in the surplus commodities from the settlements and villages within its orbit. However, Spiroans were also very active in long-distance trade with other regions and chiefdoms. Spiro officials would welcome any trading band trudging in from a distant city, while roving Spiroan traders followed certain trade routes and sent back whatever they found.

Spiro had consistent needs for certain goods, particularly status goods, and these needs only got stronger after 1250. Status goods were offered to Spiro's guardian spirits to help control the weather keep the crops growing and the harvest bountiful, and assure the success of Spiro in war. These goods also bolstered the power of the priest-chief and nobility because possession of these items was seen as communion with these spirits and therefore proof of the possessor's leadership. These status goods were so important to the priest-chief and nobility that when the person died, these items usually got buried with him or her.[41] To ensure a steady of supply of these needed status goods, Spiroans sent trading bands to distant regions where they would live on an almost permanent basis. There these traders would acquire the needed merchandise and periodically ship it back to Spiro. Sometimes carriers hauled large packs of items on their backs, their skeletons showing the damage these heavy burdens and long trips had on their joints and bones.

Other times, whenever possible, they paddled dugout canoes from place to place.[42]

Spiroan traders headed up the Arkansas and Canadian rivers to the Great Plains, where they set up small trading camps. The Nagle site, 170 miles west of Spiro on the Canadian, is a good example. There Spiro traders met with hunting-gathering peoples of the plains and exchanged pipes, pottery, ear spools, and bois d'arc bows for buffalo hides, shoulder bones that could be used as hoes, and dried meat.[43] The city also had a similar bois d'arc trade to the south with peoples along the Red River. Archaeologist Frank Schambach sees Spiro aggressively dominating a far-off trade route by creating a village of Spiroan traders on a bluff overlooking Bois d'Arc Creek near the Red River in North Texas. The Sanders site, located at the north end of a giant bois d'arc forest in the territory of the Red River Caddos, was a 150-mile southward trek from Spiro.[44]

At Sanders, Spiroan traders exchanged engraved conch shells and shell breastplates to Caddo traders for bois d'arc wood slated to be turned into bows. Once the deal was done, the Spiroan trading crew hauled the thirty-pound bundles of bois d'arc staves back to Spiro. It was a long, hard trek that took weeks. Spiro craftspeople turned the staves into some of the best bows ever made by Indians. Spiroan warriors and hunters kept some of the bows, while traders took others to the Nagle site to exchange for buffalo products. Other Spiro traders went to the great cities of the Southeast, where they exchanged buffalo hides from Nagle and bois d'arc bows from Sanders for conch shells, embossed copper sheets and ax heads, and after 1250, huge effigy pipes. And Sanders and Nagle may well have been only two of many Spiro connections; Schambach believes other Spiroan trading camps were located across the plains of central Oklahoma and east toward the great Mississippian ceremonial centers as well.[45]

Trade and exchange meant more than merely items changing hands. There were also aspects of diplomacy to it. Many trading bands lived almost full-time at their posts, where the chief traders also served as Spiroan diplomats, representing the city in their dealings with their host peoples. These chief traders were Spiroan elites serving on both trade and diplomatic missions, and they wielded engraved conch shell cups or greenstone maces as proof of their status and connection to Spiro's power. These diplomat traders carried much weight in these foreign territories, bolstered as they were by their symbol of office, which linked them to the great Spiro priest-chief. They might even be brought in for consultation when that chiefdom's elders had to decide on certain courses of action and wanted to know what the great chief of Spiro thought.

Carrying a stone mace or wearing an engraved shell breastplate would certainly have signified a person as one of the Spiroan nobility, but the Spiroan practice of elongating their skulls through circular deformation provided an immediate means of identification. Should a war party think about ambushing a caravan of traders, a quick glance at their cone-shaped heads revealed they were from Spiro and any attack would bring a terrible retaliation. Should a city not want to welcome strangers showing up at their gates, the elongated skull of a Spiroan diplomat trader showed immediately who they were dealing with and made them think twice about refusing. Spiroan diplomat's conch shell cups, stone maces, and even their appearance announced to all that they were Spiroan nobility and therefore worthy of all respect and honor.[46]

These status goods, emblems of the nobility and proof of their connection with the Sun and other deities, became very important at Spiro. In many ways, the possession of these goods was one of the biggest differences between the Spiroan nobility and commoners.[47] And when cargoes of these status goods showed up at Spiro, the priest-chief or his principal men acting in his stead took control of them. In turn, the Spiro priest-chief redistributed these status goods. He parsed out some to diplomat traders, some to political leaders in allied cities and villages, others to his own officers and nobility, and of course, some to himself.[48]

Naturally, what passed for a status good might change over time and from city to city, people to people. At Spiro, where almost everyone had access to commodities, status goods were those rare and exotic items that were appropriated and controlled by the elites who used them to bolster their power and position. During the twelfth and thirteenth centuries, an incredible quantity and variety of status goods from all across America began showing up at Spiro: flints from Illinois, Tennessee, Oklahoma, and Arkansas; mica from North Carolina; galena, hematite, and limonite from the Missouri Ozarks; turquoise from New Mexico; copper from the Great Lakes.[49]

Besides these raw materials, vast quantities of finished goods, items that had already been engraved or turned into scepters and such, began turning up in Spiro. Today, these are considered some of the finest pre-Columbian artwork ever made. The Spiroan nobility now acquired oversize spear points made of Smoky Hill jasper from Kansas; pottery, as well as various stone points, that originated in the Ouachita Mountains; and painted bottles from the Tennessee River Valley. The Appalachians contributed the greenstone that was turned into ceremonial ax heads. Giant conch shells from the Florida Gulf Coast made their way to inland cities, where they were turned into engraved cups, amulets, and breastplates or drilled into pendants and beads. Eventually, these too made their way to Spiro, as did bushel baskets of freshwater pearls. Similarly, somewhere in the Southeast, people hammered out great thin sheets of copper, pressed amazing images onto them, and then sent these along to Spiro. Beautiful Caddoan pottery from the cities along the Red River also began arriving in the city. After 1250, the huge figurines from Cahokia began showing up in Spiro, where they were turned into smoking pipes.[50]

The extraordinary number and variety of these exotic items is what makes Spiro so special, as archaeologist James Brown explains: "In terms of wealth items and prestige goods, the sheer number of marine shell beads, shell cups, and repoussé copper plates is so much greater than any other single site that site-wise measures cannot help but place Spiro at the top of any index of wealth."[51] Probably the most exotic of all things were the many items made of shell, particularly the engraved giant conch shells. These conch shells were huge, often weighing several pounds and measuring almost eighteen inches in length, much larger than what we think of as conch shells today.

At Spiro, most conch shells show up as cups, the center coiling taken out and the outer shell engraved with a variety of figures and designs: warriors, rattlesnakes, spiders, crosses, falcons, and such. These shell cups were probably used during the black drink ceremony. The black drink was a tea made of toasted yaupon holly leaves. Just about all Southeast Indians used the black drink, though some called it by other names. It was a purification drink commonly used in councils and rituals.[52] These engraved shell cups, when buried with the bodies of priest-chiefs and other nobles, were usually filled with pearls or beads or balls of galena. Hundreds of conch shells or items made of conch shells wound up at Spiro. Other shell items used by the Spiro nobility included engraved breastplates, pendants, cameos, and beads.[53] In fact, twelve hundred pounds of shell beads were found at Spiro, and some archaeologists believe they may have served as an early form of currency.[54]

While the conch shells are evidence of Spiro's participation in a cross-country trade network, the engravings cause the most excitement. Most have a warfare theme, though many have obscure motifs that still leave scholars scratching their heads. These symbols include the eye in hand; forked eye; cross in circle; the sun circle; the bilobed arrow; and various death motifs, such as skulls or leg bones. Some engravings are of human warriors or priests, making them the only realistic images we have of Indian peoples before the coming of Columbus. Other images are of animals, such as eagles, woodpeckers, turkeys, panthers, and rattlesnakes.[55] Others are a blend of human and animal beings, sometimes snakes or spiders. The falcon man, with his forked-eye symbol of bravery, was common at Spiro and across the entire Southeast.[56] Significantly, the human engravings are usually of men, and they are often dressed in ceremonial regalia. Conversely, Cahokia artwork shows many more women.[57] As for the engravings, archaeologist Jeffrey Brain saw a strange terribleness in them. "There are weapons, often broken ones, corpses and severed heads. Most of the animals depicted, whether in whole or in part, are predatory creatures—raptorial birds, rattlesnakes and felines. Some of the activities suggested are obscure in meaning, but they too, like so much of the decoration, seem somehow sinister. It is clearly a man's world; there is no intimation of procreation or of domestic pursuits. The designs seem strange and frightening, perhaps because we do not understand their significance or function."[58]

Spiroan priest-chiefs and nobility also had an affinity for copper. Large quantities of Great Lakes copper came to Spiro in the form of copper sheets, axes, breastplates, headdresses, hairpins, beads, and coverings for wooden items. Indian peoples of that day did not have a smelting process, so all copper had to be cold-hammered and then carefully cut with stone tools. Even then, Indians still found ways to rivet large pieces together. On the large sheets, rather than engraving, artisans embossed images in relief. This is called *repoussé,* and like the conch shells, the embossed copper sheets are examples of exquisite Indian artwork.[59]

Besides being a political powerhouse, Spiro by the midthirteenth century was also an important religious center. Major rituals were periodically conducted at the city, and a host of minor ones was done almost daily: the greeting of the sun at dawn, the welcoming of official visitors, the sending off of war parties, and such. No business, no ritual, could be fully completed without the smoking of a pipe. Pipe smoking was everywhere in Indian society. Men and women smoked for pleasure, but they also had ritual pipes in their houses. The nobility and the priest-chief used large symbolic and stylized pipes when leading the city's rituals. And like the engraved conch shells and embossed copper, these beautiful and important pipes wound up buried with their owners. Some are T-shaped pipes, meaning they look like an upside down T, with a single bowl in the middle and two long stems on the sides. Some have double bowls. These most certainly were used in ceremonies, possibly cementing diplomatic relations because two people would smoke from the same bowl.[60] The huge effigy pipes, pipes in the form of a figurine, are the ones that catch the eye. Made of red flint clay quarried near present-day St. Louis and created by Cahokian artisans, some of these pipes weigh as much as ten pounds. Most are in the shape of humans, though some are of eagles, owls, and frogs. The pipes were originally made as figurines, but the Spiroans drilled holes in them to change them into smoking pipes.[61]

These great ceremonial effigy pipes used at Spiro, which began showing up there about 1250, represent some of the most amazing, most fantastic artwork ever made in Indian America. And we can only guess at what ceremony the priest-chief used the Big Boy pipe, also known as the Resting Warrior pipe. At ten pounds almost eleven inches high, the pipe is in the form of a man, a priest or leader, seemingly lost in prayer, sitting crosslegged, hands on his knees. He is naked, genitalia exposed, except for a thick necklace, large ear spools, and a feather cloak on his back. An oval headdress angles back across his sloped, elongated forehead. Part of the headdress hangs down the left side of his face. His hair is gathered in a bun at the back of his head, while a long braid hangs down the right side of his face. Two large holes perpendicular to each other have been drilled into the figure's back, making it a pipe, one hole for a smoking bowl, the other for the wooden stem.[62]

Another effigy pipe, almost ten inches high, depicts an armored warrior, his pointed skull peeking above a wide headband, bending over the face-down body of an enemy. The warrior grasps the downed enemy's hair with his left hand while he smashes his enemy's face with a war club. This pipe also has a bowl in the back for tobacco and another for the stem. Could this huge pipe have been used by the priest-chief to declare war or to send off war parties?[63] And there were others. One, known as the WPA

Rattler, looks almost like an open-mouthed, gap-toothed demon holding a ceremonial rattler. Some of the few women images at Spiro come from the pipes, such as a fourteen-pound effigy of a woman and an eagle; another of about the same weight has a woman kneeling before an altar with a cradleboard on her back, and another is of a woman holding her child in her arms. And these are just a few of the great effigy pipes at Spiro.[64]

Archaeologists, using modern detection techniques, believe these pipes were created by Cahokian artisans between 1100 and 1150. But by the early thirteenth century, the great city of Cahokia was past its prime and beginning its slide into obscurity. Whatever power these figurines once possessed at Cahokia was gone by then, no longer respected or needed by the Cahokian elites, so the items were traded away. Spiro, which was hitting its ceremonial peak around 1250, saw value in these amazing status goods. After 1250, Spiroan elites began acquiring as many of these figurines as they could. The conversion of these figurines into pipes seemed to happen only at Spiro and other Caddoan areas. As some archaeologists have pointed out, this shows that a major change in Mississippian religious ideas took place between 1150 and 1250. It also highlights the difference between how Spiroans and Cahokians viewed their deities. "There is a vast difference between bowing to an ancestral being and smoking one."[65]

As if the conch shell engravings, repoussé copper, and huge effigy pipes were not enough, an extraordinary amount of other exotic goods cemented Spiro's place as one of the most powerful and richest chiefdoms of the Mississippian period. Spiroan priest-chiefs and nobles displayed numerous flint maces and just as many stone and copper axes. There were also oversize spear points of jasper and rare flint, along with hundreds, if not thousands, of beautiful but unused arrowheads. And that is the point. None of the items could be used for utilitarian purposes. The maces were too weak to be used as weapons; the stone and copper axes too fragile for chopping; the pipes too large for casual smoking; and thousands of arrowheads deliberately never used. All just for show; power goods that were used for manipulating spirits and as symbols of the nobility.

The indication that these pieces of art worked to bolster the position of the nobles was that most of these exotic items went to the grave with them. When the priest-chief or an important noble died, the shell cups, embossed copper plates, effigy pipes, large carved wooden statues representing ancestors, expertly woven baskets of cane, large flower-shaped clay pots painted red or white and inscribed with intricate designs, scores of ear spools, and blankets made from buffalo and rabbit fur; as well as thousands of pounds of beads, all wound up in the charnel houses to be buried later with the Spiro nobles. In fact, some of these goods were made *only* to be placed in the graves of the nobility. And Spiro charnel houses and graves became choked with these exotic items. Eighty percent of all these types of artifacts that have ever been found have come out of Spiro, much more than from any other Mississippian city of the day. For example, few conch shells show up anywhere else and certainly not in the quantity found at Spiro. And Spiro was not one of the largest ceremonial centers of the day, nowhere near the size of Cahokia in Illinois or Moundville in Alabama.[66]

These status goods at Spiro raise important questions. First, were these finished goods, such as the engraved shells or embossed copper or the effigy pipes, created at Spiro or were they made somewhere else and transported to Spiro? Scientific methods have proved that the great effigy pipes found at Spiro were actually made at Cahokia during the early twelfth century, so what of the shells, copper, and such? Respected and knowledgeable archaeologists have come down on both sides. Some believe that Spiro imported the raw materials, and then the nobility, calling upon obligations of reciprocity, prevailed upon Spiro artisans to transform the shells, copper, and pottery into works of art.[67] Certainly some of the stonework, pottery, baskets, cloth, and smaller pipes were made by Spiro craftspeople.[68]

Archaeologist Jeffrey Brain, who has done much work on the Mississippian Southeast, believes the items were created among the many settlements and villages connected to Spiro, if not at Spiro itself. He sees the style of engravings found on the shells, copper, pottery, and some of the pipes as being distinctly Spiroan and not typical of other ceremonial centers.[69] There may even have been an exceptional class of artists who specialized in these engravings. However, Brain believes that about seven hundred different artists engraved the Spiro shells, and the same artist can be detected only in two cups. So Brain believes that if these were engraved at or around Spiro, "a considerable part of the male population was engaged in this activity."[70]

However, the biggest problem facing those who think the status goods were finished at Spiro or thereabouts is that no workshops, craftspeople's houses, or even piles of debris have been uncovered at Spiro or any other nearby site. That does not necessarily mean they do not exist, only that they have not been found.[71] Still, the lack of any workshops, which have been found at places like Cahokia, leads some archaeologists to accept the idea that these finished goods were imported into Spiro. They believe that, as shown by the effigy pipes, the most exotic items—the shells, embossed copper, stone maces, and oversize points—were actually created or engraved somewhere else, then transported to Spiro. Even the artwork on these items seems to point to another Mississippian city.[72]

And that city seems to be Cahokia. Spiro, it seems, was an emulator, a copier, of Cahokia. It wanted the status goods that Cahokia produced and the power that came with them. Archaeologist James Brown believes the giant metropolis at Cahokia sent Spiro "notched points of crescent flint, ceremonial ax heads and crown-shaped bifaces (maces) of Kaolin and Mill Creek cherts, red pipestone effigy pipes, and a few vessels (Powell Plain). The Braden style artwork in marine shell, copper repoussé work, and carved stone probably came from the Cahokia area."[73]

All this raises another question. What brought this amazing artwork to Spiro? Why would a Florida Gulf Coast conch shell, plain or engraved, wind up thousands of miles away at Spiro?

How did Great Lakes copper get to Spiro? What brought these incredible Cahokian effigy pipes and the heavy stone maces and ax heads to this city? Why are these items here? And why did they stay here? What did Spiro have to offer in return?

The decline of Cahokia during the hundred years between 1150 and 1250 seems to be the answer. As the chiefdom at Cahokia collapsed and its people abandoned that great city, it released all those amazing status goods. No longer needed, the goods were put into the trade networks, where the Spiroan nobles went out of their way to acquire them. But why did so many wind up at Spiro and so few at other emerging ceremonial centers in the Southeast, such as Moundville or Etowah? Because Spiro could offer something the other centers could not: bois d'arc bows and buffalo products. Cahokia's splintering brought about an increase in feuding, raiding, and warfare across the Southeast, which helps explain the rise of fortified plazas and villages. Combatants now sought the best weapons. Embattled Cahokians and other Mississippians were more than happy to exchange their now seemingly useless conch shells and clay figurines for very useful bois d'arc bows.

Buffalo products also proved attractive to more easterly Mississippians. Buffalo shoulder blades made excellent hoes, much better than digging sticks. Dried buffalo meat was another source of valuable protein. Hides, much larger than those of deer, as well as cloth made of buffalo fur, a Spiroan specialty, were always in demand. For the descendants of Cahokia, a sure supply of bois d'arc bows, buffalo hides, hoes, and meat, combined with their own resources of corn and deer, could easily ensure their people's survival and prosperity. And in return, the Spiroan nobility was more than happy to acquire the figurines, shells, coppers, maces, masks, beads, and points. After all, Spiroans probably saw themselves as the next Cahokians. Possession of these power goods simply proved it. And by 1250, it seemed that the Spiro chiefdom might just be on its way to becoming the next great Mississippian metropolis.

5

The Great Temple Mound

1934–1935

Getting the Pocola Mining Company thrown off the Spiro Mounds and having a state antiquities act passed was not as easy digging as Clements had hoped. First off, not everyone agreed with him. In the 1930s, archaeology was still in the process of becoming professionalized, and it suffered a sort of identity crisis. Until about the end of the nineteenth century, most people who called themselves archaeologists were really just glorified pot hunters. Ever since 1802, when Lord Elgin returned from Greece with the famed Parthenon marbles for the British Museum, archaeology was pretty much a search for exotic treasure. Sensation was everything, and the more exotic the artifact, the better. Heinrich Schliemann had the same idea when in 1870 he went searching for Troy. And Howard Carter certainly created a sensation in 1922 when he found King Tut's tomb and all its golden grave goods.

The same mentality took hold in America in connection with the Indian mound builders. From the earliest days of colonization, Europeans, and later Americans, were both repelled and fascinated by American Indians. On one hand, Indians were everything the Europeans were not. Indians were rude and rustic, swarthy too. They stressed kinship and community over the rights of the individual. Their religion differed from Christianity. By European standards, Indians appeared wholly barbaric. The earliest Spanish explorers in the Americas even wondered if they were human beings or if they possessed a soul. The Pope had to step in and declare Indians both human and soul worthy. And if being different wasn't bad enough, even worse from the European and American point of view, Indians sat on valuable lands and tended to fight being driven from them.

On the other hand, Indians were everything Europeans and Americans admired. As Europeans saw it, Indians were brave people who lived free. They went where they wanted, lived in a state of nature, and though their technology was no match for that of an industrial nation, they seemed to have a spiritual connection to the earth. Europeans, it seemed, had knowledge, but Indians had wisdom. In fact, to Europeans, it was this free way of life that was most dangerous. It seduced Europeans into "going native." So, as the American government determined early on, this "Indianness" had to be eradicated. This was to be done not so much by killing Indians, but by destroying their tribal cultures, replacing Indian methods of learning with vocational training and American education. Essentially, the goal was to transform Indians into American farmers. By 1930, that seemed to have been just about accomplished.

So whether white people back then saw Indians as red devils or noble savages, most were still fascinated with them. This fascination only intensified as Indians were put on reservations, where missionaries and government officials tried to rub out all aspects of their Indian way of life. During the mid-nineteenth century, many scientists concentrated on Indian skeletons, particularly skulls, to explain why Indian technology lagged so far behind that of Europeans and Americans and why Indian culture seemed so different. Reservation doctors, government scientists, even famed anthropologists, such as Franz Boas, dug up Indian graves, cut the skulls off skeletons, and sent them back east to museums and universities. There they were measured against those of Europeans and, in academic eyes, found wanting. The demand for Indian skeletons for study became so great that in some instances, Indians would bury their dead in the afternoon and that night archaeologists would steal in and dig them up. Over the years, thousands upon thousands of Indian skulls and skeletons wound up in museums around the country.[1]

Although controversial, the study of Indian skeletons was a step in the professional growth of archaeology and anthropology. By the early twentieth century, university-trained archaeologists were making their mark. These academics still supported the excavation of skeletons and artifacts, but now they stressed the benefits, such as preservation of the items as well as studies that would shed light on ancient America. Unlike the pot hunters, they weren't planning to sell artifacts on the open market for profit.

However, the demand for great and exotic artifacts still dominated. As Buffalo Bill's Wild West Show and the early silent movies could attest, there was already a powerful wave of nostalgia for the "old" America. With the early twentieth-century Indians mired in poverty on reservations or in rural enclaves, a far cry from their storied past, white Americans became more and more interested in Indians prior to the coming of Columbus. And the place to look for pre-Columbian artifacts was in the thousands of earthen mounds in the eastern part of the United States. As American settlers moved west, it didn't take them long to discover these humanmade mounds. Some were huge, such as those at Moundville, near Tuscaloosa, Alabama, and Okmulgee in Georgia, north of Atlanta. The largest were at Cahokia, just across the Mississippi River from St. Louis.

These were only the most spectacular. Most mounds were small, maybe only a few feet high. And it didn't take long for curious people to discover that there were several types of Indian mounds. Effigy mounds were in the shape of an animal. Though none of these exist at Spiro, the most famous is Serpent Mound, near Locust Grove, Ohio, in the form of a winding snake. Flat-topped, pyramid-shaped temple mounds were associated with the Mississippian culture and were used as platforms for temples or sacred fires. Monks Mound at Cahokia was a pyramid mound, as were many of the mounds at Moundville.

Spiro's own Brown and Copple mounds fell into this category. Another type was a burial mound. These tended to be cone-shaped and usually filled with skeletons and grave goods. Spiro's Craig Mound was a classic burial mound. Sometimes temple mounds and burial mounds had structures buried in them. A temple or charnel house, usually burned or collapsed, would be covered with dirt and a mound built over it. Craig Mound, the Brown and Copple mounds, and the Ward mounds all had buried structures in them. The smaller house mounds at Spiro were also buried structure mounds. Though just small humps of dirt, a structure had been burned, deliberately or accidentally, and earth piled on top of it until a small mound formed. Sometimes there might be several burned structures on top of each other.

These mounds across the eastern United States had fasci-nated Europeans and Americans from the very first. Travelers commented on them, and even President Thomas Jefferson dug in them.[2] It didn't take long to discover that amazing artifacts could be found inside the burial mounds, and so they began to be cracked open with a vengeance. By the nineteenth century, the beautiful pottery and beads coming out of the mounds began an argument over who had built them. For some, there was no mystery. The mounds had been created by Indian peoples, the ancestors of those living today.[3] As early as 1779, Athanase De Mézières, the Spanish commandant at Natchitoches, Louisiana, commented on a small mound near the Neches River in Texas. It was situated near the main village of the Caddoan Nabedaches Indians, "which their ancestors erected in order to build . . . a temple, which commanded the nearby village, and in which they worshipped their gods."[4] Even Thomas Jefferson conceded that the mounds had been made by Indians.[5]

Others weren't so sure. Many, taking their cue from skull-measuring anthropologists, believed Indians were genetically inferior to white people. Others saw the poverty of Indians and doubted that the ancestors of these peoples could create such majestic mounds and beautiful artwork. So in many minds, some peoples other than Indians must have built them. But who? There were plenty of suspects: Aztecs, Mayans, lost tribes of Israel, the Knights Templar, Irish priests, Vikings, and the list went on and on. Anybody would do except Indians.[6] But in the end, it really didn't matter to most people who made the artwork; only the artwork itself mattered. Amateur pot hunters broke into mounds, tossed aside skeletons, and tore up tombs to get at anything of value, and in doing so, they destroyed much.

Forrest Clements was in that group of archaeologists who were trying to change the nature and reputation of archaeology. By the early twentieth century, as archaeology and its parent discipline anthropology matured and became professions that were taught at universities, there was a move away from tomb raiding and skull measurements, though these remained important aspects of the "sciences." More and more academically trained archaeologists insisted that mounds be excavated carefully, systematically. The intent was not so much to acquire fantastic grave goods, though that was nice too, but to learn about the culture that had made them.[7]

So in 1934 and 1935, as Clements and the men of the Pocola Mining Company faced off over the Spiro Mounds, each represented different ideas and philosophies. Clements carried the torch of the new, professional archaeology. To him, Spiro and every other archaeological site in the country should be protected from pot hunters. These legacies of the past should be studied only by accredited, university-trained archaeologists, slowly and carefully, under strict methodological rules and supervision. Records would be meticulously kept, photographs taken, site maps sketched, reports drawn up, articles written, books published, and academic careers made. As Clements saw it, "If the at present almost wholly unknown prehistory of Oklahoma is to become a matter of scientific record, the archaeological work must be done by formally trained persons and published in the orthodox scientific journals before the relatively few sites have been irretrievably ruined. Scratching around can never be useful and is always damaging."[8]

Of course, while the systematic excavation was going on, any valuable artifacts found would be sent back to university museums to dazzle the alumni and potential donors. Here they would also be stored in vaults, protected and preserved for future study. Clements certainly saw himself as different from the Pocola men, who weren't archaeologists and had no claim to such a title. For him, the pot hunters were looters, destroyers of knowledge for the sake of a quick buck, and they should be prevented from taking what he felt rightly belonged to him and members of his profession.

The partners of the Pocola Mining Company, in no uncertain terms, saw it differently. They were hard-working, honest folks representing good old-fashioned American free enterprise. These artifacts belonged just as much to them as to Clements. Even more so because they had acted on it and gotten a legally signed lease. The way they saw it was that until now, few academics had been interested in Oklahoma archaeology, but now that they'd found the treasure, everyone wanted it. And they probably saw Clements as just as much a looter as he termed them. They wanted the artifacts, Clements wanted the artifacts, so this was just sour grapes on his part. And if Clements wanted relics, then he could buy them on the curio market, same as anyone else. At least their way, everybody would profit a little: the diggers, the dealers, and the collectors. It was all the same. Whether they or Clements got the goods, the artifacts would still wind up in collections somewhere. But Clements was trying to cut them out of the deal. Just like their gold venture, someone was trying to swindle them out of their find.[9] One writer described the miners as "united in their deeper suspicion of outsiders, which really amounted to a distrust of city slickers and professional museum men. They belonged to a distinctly unprosperous rural world in which the downtrodden were heroes."[10]

Throughout 1934 and into the spring of 1935, the miners dug around the tops of Craig Mound and maybe a few others. They continued to turn up nice artifacts, which they immediately sold to Joe Balloun, Goodrich Pilquist or H. T. Daniel from Arkansas. And if the diggers were suspicious of Clements before, by mid-1935, they'd come to downright hate him. Support for his antiquities bill was growing across the state. For years, professionals such as Clements and Thoburn had protested the pot hunting of archaeological sites. Any disturbance ruined the chance of getting reliable information about the site's previous occupants or what Oklahoma was like before the coming of the white man. A popular groundswell against pot hunting was also on the rise. As word of the exotic artifacts coming out of Spiro spread, wealthy philanthropists and members of historical societies became worried about the loss of Oklahoma's historical heritage. So with Clements leading the charge, in the early summer of 1935, the Oklahoma legislature passed the state's first antiquities act.[11]

The law said that anybody wanting to do archaeological excavations of any kind within the state must first apply to the chair of the Department of Anthropology at the University of Oklahoma for a license. Without approval from the Anthropology Department, pot hunting would be an arrestable offense. Of course, it just so happened that Clements was then the chair of the Anthropology Department at the University of Oklahoma, and there was no way in hell he'd ever issue an approval for the Pocola Mining Company or any other pot hunter to dig anywhere in Oklahoma.[12] As Clements had pointed out, licenses would be issued only to those who had "the necessary scientific and professional qualifications. This worked no hardship whatever on reputable scientific institutions or persons, but did serve to make commercial looting illegal."[13]

With his antiquity act passed, Clements immediately sent word to the mounds to cease all excavations. The Pocola men ignored him. So in July 1935, Clements sent the law down. He filed a complaint with the Le Flore County district attorney and sheriff's office, who sent a deputy out to clear the diggers off the site. The deputy explained that continued digging was against the new law and that they had to move on. And, as

Clements later wrote, "amid loud recriminations and threats of mayhem the lessees gathered up their tools and departed."[14]

Though Clements may have run off the miners, Spiro wasn't his yet. The Pocola Mining Company still had a lease that ran for four more months. He would not be able to touch the place until November 1935, and that was only if he could work something out with George Evans. According to Clements, he made one last attempt to buy out the Pocola Mining Company. Financially backed by the Oklahoma Historical Society, Clements claimed he offered the six Pocola investors a buyout with a 300 percent profit for them. The men, he said, turned him down.[15]

Even if he couldn't get his hands on the mounds for a few more months, it was a solid victory for Clements, both professionally and personally. He'd saved the mounds from looters and gotten powerful and influential people interested in them. Once the pot hunters' lease ran out in November, he'd approach George Evans and negotiate another lease, but one much more realistic, in keeping with the shallow pockets of a state university. Then he'd lead a team of graduate students to conduct a major professional excavation. If he was right, these mounds might reshape the history of pre-Columbian Indians of the American South. Smug, satisfied, and certain that everything was running smoothly, Clements headed out to California to teach summer school and wait for November, when the Pocola lease would run out. It was a move he would regret for the rest of his life.[16]

Pocola Mining Company investor Guinn Cooper was outraged at Clements and his high-handed tactics. Some suit was cheating them out of their claim, a hostile takeover to screw them out of their hard-earned money. Every one of the Pocola men felt the same way. They all knew that Clements got the antiquities act passed just to spite them. Hell, they could work harder than any men alive, but what could you do when an ivory-tower professor had the law in his back pocket? It was hard times in this country. People were starving, and relic digging was how they put food on their tables, how food was put on a lot tables in Le Flore County. It just wasn't right. And then word came down to them that Clements was gone. Wouldn't be back until later in the year. What a bastard! Stops them from working, then heads out to California to make more money for himself. It just wasn't right.[17]

Once again, no one was really sure who came up with the idea, but somewhere along the way, a "cat's away" mentality took hold of the Pocola Mining Company. They knew the law was against them, but this was a law they didn't believe was fair. With Clements out of town, they had four months to wrap up their dig, but potting around with shovels on the tops of the mounds wasn't the best use of this narrow window of opportunity. They'd been doing it that way for a year and a half, and though they'd turned up some relics, they hadn't found enough to make it worth their while. Instead, they needed a new, speedier approach. So rather than digging around the mound tops, now they planned to tunnel straight into the heart of Craig Mound. Then they'd see what was there. The coal miners they'd hired a while back had suggested this, and now the Pocola men believed tunneling was the last best hope.[18] Get in, get the relics, get out, and leave what's left to Clements.

So in August 1935, with Clements off in California, the Pocola Mining Company crept back to Spiro and began digging a tunnel into the northeast side of Craig Mound. The shaft was large, big enough for a man to push a wheelbarrow through it, which they loaded with dirt and debris and hauled away. A few of the investors might have helped dig, but the unemployed coal miners and other hired hands probably did most of the tunneling.[19] As the tunnel lengthened, the men used miner's lamps to see what they were doing. But that was about the only safety precaution. In such a rush to hit pay dirt, they refused to shore up the tunnel with timber supports.[20]

At about twenty-six feet into Craig Mound, they hit piles of conch shell fragments, pieces of some of the large engraved shell cups. There were so many piles of these broken shells that the diggers claimed they had hit a low wall of them. Since the shells were broken and the pieces believed to be worthless, the men merely shoveled these fragments, engraved with Mississippian faces and symbols, into the wheelbarrow and dumped them outside the entrance.[21] No one paid them any more attention, while workers and visitors tramped through the piles, crushing the pieces underfoot. There were so many, one later visitor thought the broken shell fragments looked like "new-fallen snow."[22]

Just beyond the shell piles, the men hit harder earth, much more compact than the loose fill they'd been digging through. In fact, they seemed to have hit a hard mud wall supported by cedar posts. Cedar posts six inches in diameter and nearly eighteen feet tall had been stuck into the ground to form a large circle. The posts were spaced about six feet apart and angled inward toward the top, with the mud seemingly packed around them.[23] This would be one of numerous controversies and arguments about Spiro: Did the men actually hit a sort of mud wall surrounding a hollow central chamber that had been deliberately prepared by the Spiro inhabitants so many years ago? It certainly seemed that way. The wall earth was harder than the other earth and had a heavy lime content.[24]

For the men of the Pocola Mining Company, the wall seemed manmade, but what was important was what lay beyond it. This was big, and any actual Pocola investors on site had probably taken over the digging. John Hobbs was there for certain. So were Kimball McKenzie and Guinn Cooper.[25] Exactly how many people were in the tunnel right then, nobody could remember. Still, the excitement must've been electric as the men pressed toward the back of the tunnel, their miner's lamps flickering in the gloom as they ran their hands over the hard earthen wall.

Eventually, someone, probably John Hobbs, grabbed a pick and ordered everyone to give him room. He swung away, the pick digging deep into the wall. The hard earth was about a foot and, a half thick, so he probably had to hit it several times. Then the pick blade broke through into empty space. Immediately there was a hissing noise, as humid Oklahoma summer air rushed into the hollow chamber beyond.[26] "As the wall was cut through, and the dead air rushed forth, the stench from the inside was almost unbearable."[27] A low rumble came from the room beyond as outside air rushed in, and the sudden change in pressure caused a minor cave-in inside the chamber.[28]

Not wasting any time, and not giving a damn about a cave-in, Hobbs cleared out the wall and stuck his head into the cavity beyond. His miner's lamp threw only a little glow into a room that hadn't seen light in over five hundred years. As his eyes adjusted, he could tell he'd broken into a large burial chamber, formed by the cedar poles and dirt, about sixteen feet in diameter and eighteen feet high. The actual floor of the chamber was about five feet below where the tunnel came in. The interior of this vault was "draped with colored cloth woven of fur, hair and feathers."[29] The central chamber, as it came to be called, very much resembled a dirt-walled tepee.[30]

The dim light of their miner's lamps revealed an amazing tomb. Cedar poles lay strewn about the floor. These came from a litter burial in which the honored dead was carried like a king to his grave. On top of the poles lay hair blankets and robes piled to a thickness of about a foot. Beneath the blankets they would find cane mats as well. Around the edges of the chamber, at the four cardinal points, small earthen altars had been built. On each altar was a blanket and a pottery urn filled with about one hundred pounds of shell beads. Small statues sat on the altars as well. Around the room and interspersed between the four altars sat scores of large engraved conch shells.[31]

On top of the blankets rested more conch shell cups, filled with freshwater pearls, beads, and balls of red, yellow, black, green, and gray mineral pigments, such as galena. There was even a copper-covered basket full of blue and white kernels of Indian corn.[32] A closer look showed a skeleton grinning back at the diggers, surrounded by "copper breastplates, engraved conch shells, beads and carved stone ear spools. Pottery vessels decorated with incised designs and sculptured stone effigy pipes were found on the floor near the tapestried walls."[33] The men could see at least two skeletons atop the piles of blankets.

One lay on its back, cloth and human hair still clinging to the skull, with thirty-two flint blades across its breast. The blades ranged from twenty to twenty-seven inches in length. Alongside the skeleton lay another fifteen flint knives, nine pottery bowls, and sixteen pounds of galena.[34] The diggers would later find many more skeletons.

The tremendous quantity of beads and pearls astonished the men. Hobbs reported that he found thousands of shell beads carved in all sorts of shapes, each with a string hole drilled through it. There were thousands (at least eight quarts) of freshwater pearls as well. Unfortunately for the diggers, the pearls were "dead," meaning they'd lost their luster. Some powdered into dust as soon as the men touched them.[35]

Guinn Cooper was equally amazed at what they'd dug into. He reported seeing numerous skeletons lying among the piles of blankets. "There were thousands of artifacts of all descriptions. . . . One of the most prized finds was a copper box with what appeared to be surgical instruments inside. These were stolen from the tent one night and we never found out what happened to them."[36]

While thousands upon thousands of artifacts came out of the central chamber and other parts of Craig Mound, several items proved incredibly fantastic and valuable. These included the many large effigy pipes and figurines; the cloth and cane matting; the items made of embossed copper; and the long stone maces. The conch shells were extraordinary. The Pocola boys said they'd found eighty-six engraved shells, nine shells done in bas relief, twenty-seven engraved breastplates and pendants, four cameos, ninety-four engraved shell fragments, five hundred conch core pendants, and twelve hundred pounds of shell beads.[37]

The copper was equally amazing. The diggers uncovered seventy pieces of embossed copper sheets, sixty-two cedar objects covered with copper, one hundred fifty copper hairpins, eighteen copper-covered baskets, a quart of copper beads, and a quart of cedar beads covered in copper. There were scores of wooden masks, some covered in copper, others with shell inlays. Some

masks even had carved deer antlers attached to them. Woven
and feather cloth seemed equally astounding. Maybe the most
spectacular were the twenty-three effigy pipes, including the huge
one of the naked sitting Indian, the conquering warrior pipe, the
one of a woman holding an ear of corn, and many others. The
long flint maces and scepters excited all who saw them.[38]

According to the Pocola men, the central burial chamber,
and Craig Mound as a whole, yielded twenty-three effigy pipes;
fifteen long double-stemmed plain T-shaped pipes; six double-
bowled T-shaped pipes; eighty other pipes; four stone effigies;
seven effigies made of cedar; three effigy stone bowls; sixteen
pottery vessels; fifteen chipped stone maces; thirty-five large
stone blades; nineteen "spuds," similar to a ball-headed club;
fifty hoes and diggers; twenty celts; thirty copper-headed axes;
four stone axes; forty stone ax heads; eighteen plummets; six
banner stones, small grooved weights for atlatls; five stone
pendants; five hundred pounds of worked galena balls; one
thousand pounds of unworked galena; five thousand projectile
points; sixteen stone disks in various sizes; twenty boatstones,
stone bowls shaped like little boats; two baskets in the shape of
trays; twenty-eight fragments of cane matting and basketry;
nine large pieces of animal hair cloth; one hundred forty small
pieces of animal hair cloth; two gallons of pearl beads; twelve
hundred pounds of shell beads; a gallon of stone beads; a quart
of cedar beads covered with copper; a quart of copper beads;
one hundred fifty copper needles; seventy pieces of embossed
sheet copper; sixty-two bladelike cedar objects covered in copper;
eighteen baskets covered with copper; four hundred stone ear
spools; twenty cedar ear spools; eighteen bone artifacts; five
hundred pendants made from the core of conch shells; twelve
shell fishhooks; twenty-seven engraved shell breastplates and
pendants; four engraved shell cameos; eighty-six engraved shells;
ninety-four engraved shell pieces; and nine whole shells carved in
bas relief.[39] And this was just what was noted. There must have
been scores of artifacts destroyed, thrown away, lost, or stolen,
like Guinn Cooper's copper box of "surgical instruments."

None of the men there that day ever fully recorded what he was thinking as he gazed into the central chamber. Astonishment? Probably. Ecstasy over hitting the mother lode? Certainly. As Glen Groves, head of the North American Indian Relic Collectors Association, reported, "One great find followed another, satisfying the most fantastic dream of any collector. Ear spools, large spears, larger spears, stone effigy dishes, copper implements with wooden handles attached, monolithic axes, scepters, effigy pipes of unbelievable size, double bowl peace pipes and effigies in galena lead."[40]

It was one of the most amazing archaeological finds in American history. The men of the Pocola Mining Company didn't know it, but they had discovered the single largest trove of pre-Columbian Indian artifacts north of Mexico. And the Spiro record holds to this day. There has been nothing else like this in all of North America. Spiro was not the biggest mound site in North America. Cahokia, Moundville, Etowah, and Okmulgee all had larger mounds and covered a larger stretch of ground, but Spiro produced the largest quantity of the most exotic grave goods.

One of the great controversies surrounding Spiro was whether the diggers actually hit a true hollowed-out central burial cavity created by the upright cedar poles. The Pocola diggers insisted they'd dug into a great tomb, a hollow chamber. Later archaeologists did not think so. Many believed that the central chamber was just a natural anomaly. Clements thought it was the work of the coal miners. In later years, archaeologist Don Wyckoff felt that the natural settling and decay of the blankets and such caused a small space to develop.[41] Phil Newkumet, however, a later excavator at Spiro, certainly believed there was a central chamber.[42] So it seems that the people who were actually on the scene at Spiro believe in the chamber; most archaeologists who came later believe otherwise.

For the men of the Pocola Mining Company, whether the chamber was real or not was beside the point. What it held was more important; after all, it was what they'd been working for.

But there was no time to stand around gawking; Clements was sure to come back from California any time. Now a sort of frenzy took hold of the Pocola men. They dug air vents and other tunnels into the mound for easier access, though they shored up none with timbers. They trundled wheelbarrows into the heart of Craig Mound and immediately began stripping the burial chamber of its goods.[43]

Unfortunately, the men were not careful. In fact, they seemed deliberately careless. Handfuls of beads, pearls, and arrowheads were carried out of the chamber and spilled across the work site. Later visitors reported "the ground around the mound was strewn with thousands of them."[44] The cedars poles, both from the litter burials and the wall supports, seemed to have no value to the diggers, so they hauled them outside and burned them as firewood.[45] Many of the engraved conch shell cups were roughly handled and broken, their fragments scattered about the mouth of the tunnel and then trampled underfoot.[46] And there would not be any eternal rest for the skeletons. The human remains were carried outside and dumped somewhere at the rear of the camp. Sam Dellinger of the University of Arkansas visited the dig and retrieved a skull, but most of the ancient skeletons lay out in the open air, a curiosity for visitors, until the bones crumbled away to dust.[47] The destruction of so many artifacts along with the knowledge they could have imparted enrages and saddens professional archaeologists to this day.

Once the Pocola men cleaned out the central burial chamber, they began digging into the interior sides of the mound, where they found additional artifacts. That only spurred them on. They turned their attention to other parts of the mound and once again hit the smaller lobes on George Evans's property. They found fifteen to twenty burials there, but destroyed the mound in the process. Percy Brewer, who owned the smallest and most southeasterly of the Craig Mound lobes, jealous of what the Pocola men had found, leveled his small mound with a mule team and scraper. He managed to smash what few artifacts were in the small lobe, their pieces mixed and strewn about the tailings.[48] As Clements pointed out, "the result was a demolished mound, ripped up burials, and scattered artifacts."[49] Percy Brewer, through his carelessness, received nothing for his effort. One observer later commented that the destruction of Craig Mound rivaled the Spanish priests' burning of the Aztec codices. What knowledge was lost through the carelessness of the diggers, no one can say.[50]

Now no mound was safe. Looking for another burial chamber, the company dug into Brown Mound, about a quarter mile west of Craig Mound. Brown Mound sat on property owned by Bill and Mamie Brown, black farmers. How the mining company got permission from the Browns is unknown; the men probably did not put up any money, but just made deals in which the Browns would get a percentage of anything found. So while the partners continued digging into Craig Mound, Jim Vandagriff took a team and, using a mule-drawn scraper, dug straight down into the top of Brown Mound. Their experience at Craig told the diggers that burial chambers sat deep inside the mounds, and this was a direct attempt to get into the heart of the mound. Eventually, they removed the entire center of Brown Mound. With the sides left standing and only the northern side taken out as an exit, one observer said it was like looking down a well. Although a lot of work went into the Brown Mound excavation, it was disappointing. They didn't find much, only a single long, chipped blade and the remains of a long-buried wooden structure.[51]

If Brown Mound had been a bust, then Craig Mound more than made up for it. In fact, the Pocola Mining Company found itself with an embarrassment of riches. Like vultures, the Dardanelle dealers, Balloun, Pilquist, and Daniel, showed up, but there were so many artifacts that the glut drove down prices. The three dealers began snapping up fantastic relics at bargain-basement prices.

No matter how much the dealers would have liked to have kept it a secret, something as big as the Craig Mound discovery quickly leaked out. Almost immediately, the area newspapers told of the finds. In late August 1935, the *New York Times* reported the discovery of the Indian relics, which they dated at six hundred to two thousand years old. Not only were the dates incorrect, the *Times* was dead wrong in stating that "each item taken from the mound is catalogued and photographed and careful records are being kept." In reality, the men kept no records nor took any notice of anything perishable. However, the *Times* was correct in reporting the large quantities of "human bones, beads of wood and stone, pearls, and large conch shell" found.[52] It was truly an amazing find, ranking up there with some of the great archaeological discoveries of all times. Newspapers, recalling Howard Carter's 1922 discoveries in Egypt, began referring to Spiro as an American Tutankhamen's tomb.[53] They were not exactly wrong. Soon Craig Mound was being called the Great Temple Mound.

The publicity brought visitors to the excavation site, which in turn brought trouble among the Pocola partners.[54] Several professional archaeologists showed up to see what was going on. Dellinger, director of the museum at the University of Arkansas at Fayetteville, came by while the digging was going on and managed to purchase a few artifacts, including a cane burial box.[55] Robert E. Bell, who later became an archaeology professor at the University of Oklahoma, also stopped by Craig Mound.[56] Both were shocked by the destruction. Warren K. Moorehead, director of archaeology at Phillips Academy in Massachusetts, called it "an archaeological crime."[57]

By far, most visitors were curious locals and artifact collectors who came to make deals on the spot.[58] In August, the *Daily Oklahoman* ran a story about the Spiro dig, which only sent more visitors to see what was going on.[59] Archaeologist Jeffrey Brain wrote that "some entrepreneurs set up shop outside the tunnel with cash boxes and fistfuls of dollars, selecting from among the artifacts as they were brought out. Whole engraved shells sold for two dollars apiece—good enough money for the depressed 1930s, but a pitiful undervaluing of objects which, today, move through the antiquities market at prices upward of $10,000."[60] And Brain was writing in 1988.

Kenneth McWade and a friend from Kansas City heard rumors about things coming out of Craig Mound and wanted to see them for themselves, so they loaded up their Ford Model A and headed down to Spiro, where they witnessed the diggers hauling artifacts out of the central chamber. They also saw the destruction that went with it. McWade reported, "many ear spools covered with copper and long copper needles which were just discarded as not valuable enough to bother with."[61]

With interest in Spiro getting hotter, and with money being flashed around, the members of the Pocola Mining Company became suspicious of their visitors and of each other. They refused to permit visitors to enter the tunnels, much less go into the central chamber.[62] Since other collectors were showing up wanting to make their own deals, the partners became concerned with what each other was doing. All relics were supposed to be placed into a common pool and later divvied up fairly among them. Instead, they suspected each other of pocketing valuable artifacts and withholding "them from the common pool."[63] And there was good reason for their suspicions. Some of their hired diggers did pocket small artifacts and sold them on the side.[64]

Nevertheless, over the next few months, the Pocola Mining Company cleared out most of the Great Temple Mound, its smaller lobes, and Brown Mound as well. They had to work fast because their lease was scheduled to run out on November 27, 1935. Even more worrisome, they knew Clements would eventually hear about the excavation and come storming back from California to put an end to everything.

John Hobbs, left, was one of the leaders of the Pocola Mining Company who found the central chamber and its huge cache of Indian relics. The other men are unidentified pot hunters. Photo courtesy of Sam Noble Oklahoma Museum of Natural History, University of Oklahoma.

In their search for artifacts, members of the Pocola Mining Company dig on one of the smaller lobes of Craig Mound. Photo courtesy of Sam Noble Oklahoma Museum of Natural History, University of Oklahoma.

View from the interior of Craig Mound's central chamber, where most of the artifacts were found, and back into the tunnel dug by the Pocola men in August 1935 to reach the chamber. Photo courtesy of Sam Noble Oklahoma Museum of Natural History, University of Oklahoma.

A cache of pristine arrowheads made to be buried with the Indian nobles interred in Craig Mound. Photo courtesy of Sam Noble Oklahoma Museum of Natural History, University of Oklahoma.

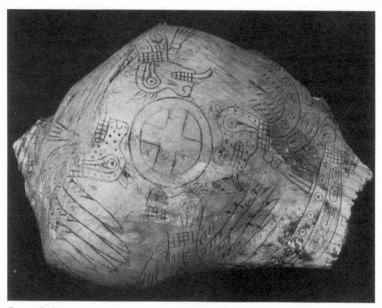

One of the many engraved conch shells found interred with the dead in Craig Mound's central chamber. Photo courtesy of University of Arkansas Collections.

Some of the thousands of pearl beads found in the central chamber at Spiro. Photo courtesy of University of Arkansas Collections.

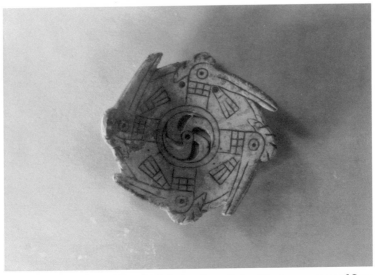

A conch shell gorget with a bird design from Spiro. Photo courtesy of Sam Noble Oklahoma Museum of Natural History, University of Oklahoma.

The Big Boy effigy pipe, made of Missouri flint clay, weighs more than ten pounds and is over a foot tall. Photo courtesy of University of Arkansas Collections.

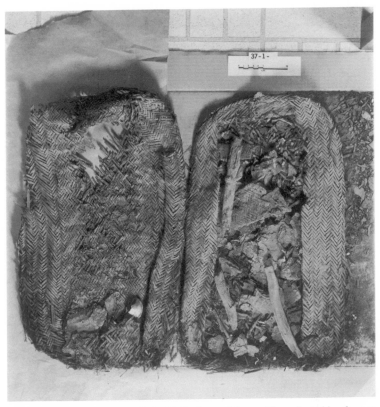

One of the cane baskets buried with Indian nobles and later found by the pot hunters in Craig Mound's central chamber. Photo courtesy of University of Arkansas Collections.

A reproduction of one of the many repoussé copper plates found buried with the dead in the central chamber. Photo courtesy of University of Arkansas Collections.

Harry Trowbridge, right, an amateur archaeologist from Kansas City, Kansas, bought many Spiro artifacts from the relic dealers. Photo courtesy of Wyandotte County Museum, Bonner Springs, Kansas.

The severely wounded Craig Mound after the Pocola Mining Company finished its pot hunting excavations in 1935. Photo courtesy of Sam Noble Oklahoma Museum of Natural History, University of Oklahoma.

The December 15, 1935, edition of the *Kansas City Star*, which announced the discovery of the Spiro Mound central chamber. It sparked an artifact rush on Spiro by hopeful artifact dealers.

Kenneth Orr, a WPA supervisor, examines Spiro artifacts. Note the car of one of the many relic dealers who hoped to buy up the artifacts before museums could acquire them. Photo courtesy of Sam Noble Oklahoma Museum of Natural History, University of Oklahoma.

WPA excavation of Craig Mound, led by Forrest Clements of the University of Oklahoma. Clements and his crew began excavating the ravaged Craig Mound after the pot hunters had finished their looting. Photo courtesy of Sam Noble Oklahoma Museum of Natural History, University of Oklahoma.

Present-day reconstruction of Craig Mound at Spiro Mounds Archaeological Park. Photo by the author.

A re-creation of one of the Spiro houses, Spiro Mounds Archaeological Park. Photo by the author.

6

City of the Dead

1250–1450

By the middle of the thirteenth century, the Spiro chiefdom was reaching its peak. The ceremonial center with its mounds and plaza stretched along eighty acres of Arkansas River terraces and served an immediate surrounding population of several thousand people and thousands more across the region. The flat-topped Brown and Copple mounds were about as high as they were going to get and were in full ceremonial use by the priests and priest-chief. The charnel houses on the west and south sides of the great plaza had been emptied out several times over the years, the bones buried, and the structures burned, covered with dirt, and then rebuilt. The houses now sat on small humps of earth.

Spiro was the most influential chiefdom between the Mississippi River and the Pueblo towns of the American Southwest. It dominated all the smaller settlements and villages in the area and was active in the long-distance trade networks spanning the continent. Spiro's rise to power occurred about the same time as other major ceremonial centers and chiefdoms around the Southeast, such as Moundville and Etowah, to name two of the largest. The emergence of Spiro and these other regional centers can be attributed to the decline of Cahokia.

For two hundred years, from about AD 1000 to 1200, Cahokia was the only real city in North America. And what a city it was! At its height, it boasted fifteen thousand people living amid a jumble of houses, craft shops, temples, charnel houses, wood-henges, and mounds, making it one of the largest cities in the world. Led by a priest-chief within a ranked society of nobles and commoners, Cahokians constructed 120 huge earthen mounds. As at Spiro, some were temple mounds, such as the enormous Monks Mound at more than one hundred feet high. Until twentieth century skyscrapers, it was the largest humanmade object in North America. Others were burial mounds filled with bodies, bones, and beautiful grave goods.[1]

Cahokia strongly influenced the entire eastern two-thirds of what would become the United States. The city sucked in raw materials from across the continent, such as conch shells, flint clay, copper, exotic stones, and minerals. Its craftspeople then turned these into art: engraved shell cups, human figurines, pipes, ear spools, breastplates, scepters and maces, embossed copper sheets, and spear points. These were power goods, items used in religious ceremonies and rituals that dealt with fertility, regeneration and renewal, the underworld, as well as warfare, glorification of the nobility, and death.[2] As Cahokian traders fanned out across the eastern United States, they took news of their city's politics, culture, and religion with them.

Then, after 1150, Cahokia went on the decline. Population dwindled as people migrated away from the city. Cahokia's huge size worked against it. It became unwieldy, and anything might make its people look for a fresh start elsewhere. A drought, a fire, an earthquake, an attack on the temple, overuse of wood, a rising water table, each could have put too much stress on the city. Whatever it was would have to snap those bonds that had held the people of Cahokia together for so long—and what had bound Cahokians together were their religious beliefs, espe-cially those that connected the authority of the priest-chief and nobility to the gods' favor and the city's prosperity. And the power goods and religious ceremonies were part of that authority. Something shook the people's faith in that authority and so broke the bond between the Cahokian people and their leaders. Possibly it was the burning of the city's temple or the earthquake that undermined a corner of Monks Mound. Factional disputes among powerful families seemed to flare up and cause a sort of secession movement. By 1200, Cahokia had slid far, its traditional religious rituals and ceremonies discredited. By 1275, the once great city was abandoned.[3]

Cahokia's downfall was Spiro's gain. As Cahokia shed its power, the Spiro nobility and those of other emerging regional centers across the Southeast hoped to grab a share of it. And one of the best ways to acquire this power was to acquire the visible symbols of it. As Cahokians underwent their political revolution, artwork that had been powerful fifty to a hundred years earlier now had no power. At least among the Cahokians. So during the late twelfth and early thirteenth centuries, Cahokians began putting this once sacred and powerful art into the trade networks, and in the case of Spiro, exchanging them for bois d'arc bows and buffalo products.[4]

From the amazing quantity of goods at Spiro, we can track this evolution of Mississippian power goods and cultural beliefs. When Spiro was first founded around the ninth century, stone beads were popular, but after 1100, shell beads became common. At the year 1000, large ceremonial double-edged spear points were made of Smoky Hill jasper. By 1250, these large points had become more elliptical and were made from flint. From about 950 to 1350, large T-shaped pipes were common at Spiro, but after 1350, L-shaped pipes made inroads. The same kinds of changes occurred with ear spools. At 1000, there were many, many different styles of ear spools, but a hundred years later, there were fewer styles, but they were more highly decorated. Then by the late 1300s, the use of ear spools tapered off altogether.[5]

After 1200, as Cahokia disgorged its artwork, it created a new way of thinking at Spiro and other regional centers. The spread of Cahokian ideology and artwork around 1200 created what archaeologists have called the southeastern ceremonial complex, or Southern Cult. There were many local variations on the Southern Cult. At Spiro, the cult was seen in the rise of divine rulers, specialized priesthoods, elaborate death rituals, and power goods that stressed warfare, weapons, and death. The Southern Cult brought incredible veneration, a divinity, to Spiroan priests and nobility. But Spiro, though certainly influenced by Cahokian culture and religion, was not a mere copy of that once great city. For example, Spiroans concentrated on acquiring certain types and styles of Cahokian artwork. Cahokians seemed to honor women, especially their role in fertility and regeneration, and created many female figurines and etchings; however, Spiroans seemed to ignore these trade items, as only a few female figurines and such wound up at Spiro. Rather, Spiroans focused on "male" items, concentrating on acquiring power goods that symbolized warfare and death, such as maces, oversized weapons, points, and figurines showing downed enemies.[6]

Along with this warfare belief, Spiroan priest-chiefs now saw themselves as little brothers to the Sun. They became akin to pharaohs, and their governments became theocracies through which they wielded tremendous power.[7] But that power and its legitimacy rested on the priest-chief's ability to bring about the desired results. So when the priest-chief presided over the sacred fire of the green corn ceremony, or when he stood on Brown Mound at the solstice and celebrated the arrival of the Sun, his acts were more than just rituals of crop renewal, they were also proof of his kinship with the Sun. Fortunately, the gods seemed to find favor with their little brothers; the late twelfth and early thirteenth centuries saw regular rains and floods, plenty of food, and apparent success in war.

As befitting their newfound status, the priest-chief and his family became linked with the steadily arriving Cahokian power goods. Just as the crown, scepter, and throne became associated with the European monarchy, over time stone maces and giant spear points, shell breastplates and beads, copper headdresses and axes, pottery figurines and statues, engraved conch shells, and huge ceremonial pipes became associated with the priest-chief, as did warfare symbols carved onto wooden masks or engraved onto shells, pottery, and sheets of copper. These symbols included the cross, sun circle, arrows, forked eye, eye in hand, rattlesnakes, birds of prey, human warriors, and some that were outright bizarre, such as snakes with seven deer heads or humans with snakes coming out of their backs.[8] All together, these items and symbols became part of the rituals and ceremonies the priest-chiefs used to control the elements, keep the crops growing, ensure successful warfare, and maintain the prosperity of the area.[9]

Now, during the second half of the thirteenth century, Spiro became incredibly wealthy, its nobility possessing a trove of some of the most spectacular status goods and artwork ever found in North America. Hundreds of engraved conch shells made their way to Spiro, as well as exquisite copper work, from thin riveted sheets embossed with figures to copper axes, ear spools, and hairpins. Scores of pipes were in use, from single and double bowl T-shaped pipes to the huge ceremonial effigy pipes in human shape. Flint maces and ax heads; stone scepters; giant oversize spear points and pristine arrowheads; expertly worked and elaborately decorated pottery bottles and jars; woven cloth of rabbit and bison fur as well as feather headdresses; and maybe over a hundred thousand beads of all different types and shapes were in use at Spiro. Spiro had it all, and in quantities greater than at just about any other place in America.[10]

It all provided visible proof of the nobility's deification to even the most rustic bumpkin or sophisticated town dweller. But as noble families appropriated this status and the prestige goods, much more was expected from them. The engraved images told as much. The falcon man and rattlesnake images engraved on so many shells held the nobility to a high standard of bravery and aggression. Arrowhead images did the same, while crosses and sun circles denoted the priest-chief's kinship with the life-giving Sun. Eye-in-hand images may have invoked a sort of overseeing, omnipresent authority. Turning Cahokian figurines into huge effigy pipes allowed priests to interact with ancestors or deities.[11]

The engraved images could also tell a story that explained these sacred concepts.[12] For example, a common image engraved on Spiro shells is that of a spider. Some southeastern Indian stories say it was the spider who brought fire to animals and humans. And fire was very sacred to Mississippians because it was a visible piece of the Sun on earth. As the story goes, Thunder struck a sycamore tree with a bolt of lightning, and the tree began to smolder. The animals craved fire and saw this as a chance to get it, but the sycamore sat on an island, difficult to get to. All the animals got together to devise a way of retrieving a piece of fire. The Raven flew over and perched near the flame but got burnt permanently black for his trouble. The Owl went, but as he looked down the hollow tree, the hot smoke and ash blew in his eyes and forever more owls would have wide eyes with white rings around them. Several snakes tried, the black racer and the great blacksnake, but they just got burned, and that is why they are black today. Finally, the water spider, the one with downy hair and red stripes, wove a small pocket of silk, a *tutsi* bowl, as Cherokees called it. She swam over to the island, placed a hot coal in her silken bowl, swam back, and delivered fire to the world. The Spiroan noble who quaffed black drink from a shell cup engraved with a spider image might be one of the all-important fire keepers, charged with ensuring the sacred fire never went out.[13] Burying the shell cup upon that noble's death, essentially sacrificing it, might be a testament to the fire keeper's powers and an attempt to keep the spider spirit or the fire spirit appeased and working in Spiro's favor.

At first, Spiro may have acquired the shells or copper by happenstance. Some happened to show up by trade or exchange and were promptly appropriated by the nobility, who realized their potential. Or maybe an ancestor or a deity told a priest what they wanted, what they needed to make them happy, and the priest tried to acquire it. Nevertheless, priests and noble families throughout the Spiro chiefdom went out of their way to get their hands on these power goods. These were not personal property; rather, they became community objects or associated with certain families, sacred items, used during ritual or special occasions, and often buried along with an important family member. Come the solstice celebrations of the late 1200s, and the Spiro priest-chief was truly a sight to behold, wielding a stone mace, drinking from a shell cup, wearing a copper breastplate, and smoking from a giant effigy pipe.

As the city expanded and the nobility grew in size and power, the nobles needed more of these goods. In return for in-demand bois d'arc bows and buffalo hides, the Spiroan nobility dominated the market for the old Cahokian power goods. When cargoes arrived from other towns and villages, the local chief took control of them. Powerful noble families tried to get their hands on some. Naturally, the priest-chief, if at all possible, took control of any that showed up near him, and he might have demanded that regional families send some of their power goods to him. Later, the Spiroan priest-chief would redistribute them to his priests, nobles, allies, and diplomat traders. As Spiro traders fanned out to various regions and cities, they carried with them shell cups or flint maces or special pipes as symbols that they were Spiroan noblemen from high-ranking families as well as diplomats representing this great and powerful chiefdom.[14]

As Spiroan diplomat traders traveled across the region, they carried with them these emblems of nobility. Like the Cahokians before them, they passed on the good news of these divine beliefs that the images and items told. So the death of Cahokia united Spiroans and other Mississippians in their Southern Cult religious beliefs, just as the demise of Rome united western Europe under Catholic Christianity. As archaeologist David Hurst Thomas explained, "There was a high degree of social interaction at work. The conch shell gorgets and cups, the copper plates, the ceremonial axes and batons, the effigy pipes and flint knives found at Spiro and elsewhere contain a distinctive set of Southern Cult symbols. The Forked Eye, the Cross, the Sun Circle, the Hand and Eye, the Bi-Lobed Arrow, among others, suggest a shared symbol system that extended beyond the limits of any single Mississippian empire."[15] In some instances, the Spiroan priest-chief might have sent a carved shell, an embossed piece of copper, a special pipe, or a flint mace to his counterpart at Moundville or some other Mississippian town as evidence of the kinship between the two.

By 1300, the Spiro ceremonial center was truly extraordinary. Incredibly wealthy with beautiful artwork and status goods, it was the largest, holiest, and most powerful chiefdom west of the Mississippi River. The other ceremonial centers in the Southeast certainly knew of and respected Spiro. The smaller towns and villages around Spiro revered it. Years later in the late 1700s, the Cadodachos, a city-state of the Caddo Indians of western Louisiana and eastern Texas, who claim descent from Spiro, believed themselves to be the founding lineage of the entire Caddo people as well as the fathers of most Indians in that part of the country. As one early nineteenth-century observer wrote, the Cadodachos "are looked upon somewhat like the Knights of Malta, or some distinguished military order."[16] If the same held true for Spiro, then an engraved shell breastplate, stone mace, or effigy pipe sent by its priest-chief was very valuable. It enhanced, if not deified, those who possessed it.[17]

So the Spiro nobility continually traded for the shells, copper, and statues. Some items were for use in rituals, some for redistribution to make and maintain alliances, and others were for what represented the biggest difference between Spiroan nobles and commoners—their burials. One can imagine the pageantry of a Spiroan priest-chief's funeral. Although we have no written records detailing the life and death of Spiroan leaders and nobles, in 1725, an official in French Louisiana witnessed the funeral ceremony of Tattooed Serpent, brother of the Great Sun of the Natchez Indians. By 1725, the Natchez were the last remnant of the great Mississippian chiefdoms. As such, their politics, society, and funeral ceremonies are the closest to what Spiro must have had. At the top of the Natchez chiefdom sat the Great Sun. Seen as divine, his people "obey him in everything he may command them."[18] Natchez society was divided into two classes: the noble class, called the Suns, and the lower class, called the Stinkards. Though Tattooed Serpent died four hundred years after Spiro, his funeral might shed some light on what took place at Spiro upon the death of a priest-chief.[19]

Because Tattooed Serpent was a Sun, one of the highest nobles in all of the Natchez chiefdom, several citizens were selected to die with him, including his two wives, a sister, his head servant and the servant's wife, his first warrior, his nurse, a maker of war clubs, an infant, and several older women.[20]

The body of Tattooed Serpent lay in state for three days, dressed in his finest clothes and a feathered headdress, his face painted vermillion. Food was brought to the corpse as if it were alive. During this time, emissaries from allied villages arrived for the funeral. After the three days, the body was placed on a litter of cedar poles and cane mats. Six temple guardians carried the litter, while behind them others carried chests of Tattooed Serpent's belongings to the temple, where his body was to be buried. Two older women had already been strangled, and the infant had been strangled by its parents, who threw the body in front of Tattooed Servant's funeral procession.[21]

The procession slowly meandered its way around the town. There was an order to it. First came an old priest, the master of ceremonies. Behind him came the oldest war chief. In one hand, the chief carried a pole festooned with forty-six cane hoops, each hoop signifying a person Tattooed Serpent had killed in battle; in the other, a large ceremonial pipe, "a mark of the dignity of the deceased."[22] After the war chief "came the body, after which marched the procession of those who were going to die at his burial. Together they circled the house from which they had come out three times. At the third turn they took the road to the temple." Pulling up the rear were the relatives of those who were to die. And at every turn of the procession, the parents of the sacrificed infant threw its little body down in front of the marchers so it could be trampled.[23]

For those who were to die with Tattooed Serpent, red pigment had been rubbed into their hair, as if symbolizing blood and impending death. Each of these was attended by eight of his or her closest male kin, all dressed in their finest. These were the executioners. Once Tattooed Serpent's body reached the temple, where his body would remain until the flesh decayed, mats were laid down for those who were to be sacrificed. The wives had their mats placed on either side of the temple door, then "afterwards according to their rank, 6 or 7 feet apart on the two sides of the road."[24]

Once the doomed were sitting on their mats, their eight relatives gave the death cry, and those to be sacrificed swallowed a few pills of ground tobacco. This heavy dose of nicotine dazed and calmed them. Then the death cry was given again. At that signal, the relatives threw a deer hide over the heads of the condemned. Others held them down as a knotted cord was slipped around their necks and pulled tight. They strangled to death within minutes.[25]

Tattooed Serpent, along with his two wives and his possessions, was buried in a trench inside the temple on the right. His sister was buried in front of the temple to the right, while his chief servant and his wife were buried to the left. The other dead were carried back to their own villages for burial there. "After this ceremony the cabin of the deceased was burned, according to custom."[26] A few months later, the bodies of Tattooed Serpent and his main retainers were dug up and the bones cleaned of decaying flesh, then placed in a basket and deposited in the temple.[27]

As among the Natchez four hundred years later, the death of the great chief of Spiro initiated a time of national mourning. Immediately, the priests would begin performing all the necessary rituals to get the priest-chief's soul to the afterlife. Succession would most likely pass to the priest-chief's sister's son, not his own. After all, royal blood could only be guaranteed through one's mother. A man could only hope the child by his wife was his and not some other man's. But if a man's mother is of royal blood, then it is assured that he, his sister, and his sister's children are all of the same blood.[28]

As with the funeral of Tattooed Serpent of the Natchez, in short order and with all the pomp and circumstance befitting his position, the Spiroan priest-chief's body would be borne on a litter to the temple, which also served as a charnel house. Around him would be stacked the shells, copper sheets, pipes, and other status goods associated with him and his office. There the body would lie for a time, the flesh rotting from the bones. Only later, once all the nobles and emissaries could gather, would the bones be taken from the temple and buried with honor in one of the mounds.

Similar things took place for lesser chiefs, members of the Spiroan nobility, and the diplomat traders, but on a smaller scale. After the right amount of time in the charnel house, they would be interred in one of the burial mounds. If the bodies could not be brought back to Spiro, then, as happened at the Sanders trading village in Texas, they would be buried where they'd died, with full honors and the emblems of their nobility. Numerous Spiroan status goods have been found at Sanders site burials, including six conch shell cups, twenty-one conch shell breastplates, six shell pendants, six shell discs, about five thousand conch shell beads, a celt, two stone elbow pipes, some copper-stained ear spools, and some pottery.[29]

Still, these engraved shells, embossed copper, effigy pipes, and such were powerful items, and some were just too powerful to be permanently buried. If a successful priest-chief had used them, then his exploits only added to their power. When the priest-chief or some other important person died, many of these goods went into the charnel houses with them. In fact, the temple charnel houses became important storehouses for these items. When it came time for the body to be buried, some items would go into the grave with the dead, while others would remain stored in the charnel house. Each noble family or lineage probably had its own charnel house for its dead, and each house would become a place of family power, a place where not only the bones of the lineage's honored dead remained while awaiting burial, but also where these spiritually powerful status goods were stored. Sometimes items would later be taken out and reused. Ancestors were particularly admired, even worshipped at Spiro, so imagine the prestige a later priest-chief would have if he conducted black drink rituals using the same cup that had been used by one of Spiro's most gloried leaders. Or if a now dead chief had been a great warrior, then taking his ancient mace from his family charnel house and having Spiroan warriors carry it into battle would give them great spiritual power, maybe certain victory.[30]

Besides being a storehouse for power goods, a charnel house was a place where the bodies of both nobles and commoners were stripped of their flesh and prepared for burial. Charnel houses were associated with families or lineages and were scattered throughout Spiro, though during the thirteenth century, the most important one was located near the base of Craig Mound.[31] Here in death are visible the differences between commoner families and noble families. The bodies of commoners were piled into large mortuaries where they might remain for some time, their bones often jumbling together. After months, maybe years, once the commoner charnel was full, it would be cleaned out and the bones and skeletons buried in cemeteries at the edge of mounds, or even at the edge of town, and often in mass graves. Few grave goods of any kind wound up with them.[32]

However, for the nobility, burials, especially after 1250, could be very elaborate. In the charnel houses, the bones of the nobles received far more attention than those of commoners. After a time, bone pickers removed any remaining flesh, and the skeleton would essentially be disassembled and the bones gathered into a pile. The more a skeleton's bones had been disjoined, the higher the status of that elite. The burial came next, but even these changed over time at Spiro. Between 950 and 1100, the bones of most nobles were disjointed, placed in a jar or a box woven from river cane, then buried. Some were cremated. From 1100 to 1250, the disjointed skeletons of nobles were often buried in a cedar pole litter in the smaller lobes of Craig Mound. Grave goods of the time were buried with them.[33]

Cremation became more common between 1100 and 1250. In fact, a sixteen-foot-diameter crematory basin was built over a cache of burials directly next to what would become the northwesterly lobe of Craig Mound. A great crematory basin, complete with drain holes for human grease and rainwater and a rim about a foot and half high, sat at about ground level. To the immediate west of the crematory basin, and actually connected to it, was a small platform mound and altar. Incredibly hot fires burned in this basin, and later excavations found several years' worth of ash, matting, and bits of human bones encrusted in it.[34]

About 1250, after the arrival of the Southern Cult at Spiro, elite burials changed again. Litter burials and cremation fell out of favor. In fact, the great crematory basin in Craig Mound was covered with dirt and became part of the mound itself. Next to it, Spiroans expanded Craig Mound's base in order to construct the fourth and largest lobe. A temple, which also served as a charnel house, was placed on top of it. Burials began to take place in the floor of the structure. Outside, Spiroans surrounded the structure with an earthen berm, and burials were inserted into it.[35] At that time, lesser nobles were being buried in the other three lobes of Craig Mound.[36] One of the biggest changes seen after 1250 was a move away from disjointing all parts of the skeletons of nobles. Now the bodies of some nobles were laid out extended, with most of their bones connected. Any disassembling of the skeleton usually entailed putting the skull and arm bones on the chest. Sometimes hands and feet might be missing. Of course, the great artwork and power goods would still be placed in the burials as grave goods. All of these practices seem reminiscent of Cahokia.[37]

If anything, elite burials after 1250 showed the widening gap between elites and commoners. Besides Craig Mound, some elites now demanded interment in Brown Mound, which as a flat-topped temple mound had not been used for burials up to this time. In these burials, some commoner bones were laid down on the floor of the grave and elite bones placed over them.[38] Could the commoners have been retainers, or possibly war captives, sacrificed to accompany their lords into the afterlife? This had been common at Cahokia, and would be the same at the funeral of Tattooed Serpent of the Natchez in 1725.[39] It is also after 1250 that Ward Mound 1 received additional burials and a cap of dirt finally placed on top of it.[40]

Significantly, after 1250, there seems to have been fewer newly made grave goods being put with the bodies. The grave items are there, but now it seems that the only new goods were locally made pottery. There do not seem to be any more arrow points, *newly* engraved conch shells, or embossed copper sheets coming into Spiro. This can be attributed to the demise of Cahokia. When these goods went into a burial after 1250, they were already old and well used. Most had been made at Cahokia a hundred years earlier and had arrived at Spiro during the late twelfth and thirteenth centuries.[41]

As the Spiroan nobles adopted aspects of the Cahokian Southern Cult, they brought about a major physical change at the ceremonial center, creating one of the great mysteries of the Mississippian period. Right about 1250, the population of the Spiro ceremonial center, the scores of people who actually lived and worked among the mounds, abandoned the place. They took up residence in the smaller towns and villages surrounding it. Food doesn't appear to have been scarce, because it was during the thirteenth century that corn became ever more important to Spiroans. Rather, the abandonment seems to have been a religious issue. The priest-chief, a Southern Cult demigod, must have ordered all the residents to leave their homes and gardens and move beyond the town limits. With the arrival of the Southern Cult, the Spiroan ceremonial center and burial ground was now just too holy for anyone but the priest-chief and his helpers, the town's guardian spirits and honored ancestors. It became a city of the dead.[42]

This meant a shift in the power structure of the Spiro chiefdom. Now the priest-chief was too holy to participate in mundane political affairs. As a demigod, he concerned himself only with major religious affairs. He continued performing the necessary rituals during the solstices and equinoxes atop Brown Mound. He still officiated over the various farming ceremonies. He also presided over the dead, and after 1250, besides the priest-chief, only the dead came to reside at Spiro proper.[43]

The Spiro ceremonial center, except on ceremonial days, became a ghost town: a living, breathing, vibrant town suddenly abandoned by its people. The Spiroan political seat of government apparently moved about a mile due west, across the Arkansas River, where Spiroans built another town, but much smaller than the one they had left. There they began constructing another pyramid temple mound, and by 1350, they had built Skidgel Mound. It, too, was aligned at the equinoxes with Brown Mound. Skidgel, along with its own burial mounds, temples, and charnel houses, sat on a bluff overlooking the Arkansas and was itself surrounded by several decent-sized villages.[44]

However, Skidgel was just one of several villages in a few-mile radius from Spiro that soaked up the town's former population.[45] Today, these Spiro suburbs include such nearby archaeological sites as Littlefield, about two and half miles southeast of Spiro; Choates site, just north of Spiro; Gertrude Bowman site, near the former Fort Coffee; Hall, two miles south of Skidgel Mound; Louis Jones village site, northeast of Spiro near Skidgel; the Moore site, southeast of Spiro, with eighty burials of its own; and the Hamilton and Tucker 1 and Tucker 2 sites, west of Spiro on the Arkansas. Some Spiroans moved even farther, constructing larger sites, such as Cavanaugh Mound near Fort Smith, Arkansas, which was also aligned with Brown Mound; Parris Mound in Sequoyah County, Oklahoma; and Eufaula in McIntosh County on the north bank of the Canadian River. And there could have been many more.[46] In these surrounding villages and towns, peoples re-created their lives as they had been in Spiro, often building mounds and temples and following their usual religious ceremonies.[47]

Although people left the limits of Spiro proper, they did not necessarily leave its orbit. Spiro, or at least Spiro religious leadership, continued to dominate the area and influence the Southeast for another hundred years. Nevertheless, this move physically isolated the priest-chief from his people and meant he probably gave up actually running the chiefdom's day-to-day affairs, handing them over to other nobles. He essentially went from being a priest-chief to a high priest. Now Skidgel Mound conducted the more routine political and religious ceremonies. When a lesser noble living at these outlying villages died, he or she might be buried in a mound at that site. But for the really important ceremonies, particularly at the solstices and equinoxes, people from miles around went to Spiro and its mounds, where the high priest presided over the ceremonies.[48]

A look at the Hasinai Caddos of East Texas four hundred years later might show what happened at Spiro. During the late seventeenth and early eighteenth centuries, the overarching Hasinai chiefdom consisted of ten smaller town chiefdoms. A *caddi* served as the local leader of one of the smaller chiefdoms and handled the town's political and bureaucratic affairs. However, there was only one Hasinai *xinesi*, a priest-chief who did nothing but conduct the major spiritual affairs of the ten Hasinai towns.[49] In a way, this dispersal of the nobility only extended and solidified Spiroan influence. As the Spiroan nobles spread out and took up residence in the surrounding settlements and villages, they took over the secular leadership, and bound these villages ever more to the Spiroan high priest and the ideas of the Southern Cult.[50]

If the high priest believed he and a few lesser priests were the only ones holy enough to live among the dead at Spiro, that is one thing. But to actually give up political power to elites in other villages is a major step. Why would a priest-chief do this? After 1250, the priest-chief possibly found himself more concerned with weather rituals, and these may have taken up all his time and power. After 1250, Nature quit being so good to Spiro. Droughts began to hit the southern plains. Some got so bad that much of the oak forest around Spiro died out. This had a significant effect on the animals men could hunt. Things only got worse after 1300 when the coming of the little ice age dropped the average temperature by four degrees. It lasted for the next five hundred years. For Spiroans and other Mississippians, droughts followed by weeks of drenching rain followed by early frosts and mild summers played havoc with the crops.[51]

One attempt to get around the drop in crop yields was through trade. After 1250, Spiroan peoples actually increased their trade and influence, particularly toward the west. The vagaries of weather could hurt one area but help another, and after 1250, the buffalo herds on the southern plains began to increase in size.[52] This surer source of food brought a population increase to the river valleys cutting across the plains. Some of this was a natural increase by the peoples who had long lived there. Some of it was Puebloan peoples from the West moving onto the plains. Some of this increase might have come from Spiroans who felt they might prosper better toward the West. As they moved and prospered, Spiroans opened up additional trade routes to the peoples of the plains and the pueblo Southwest. Besides more buffalo hides and such, other Plains Indian–style implements, such as diamond-shaped knives, scrapers, and L-shaped pipes, began showing up at Spiroan towns. Even a scraper made from Mexican obsidian arrived at Spiro from the west. At the same time, Spiro goods such as shells, pipes, and pottery, as well as Pueblo obsidian and turquoise, began appearing in more Plains Indian encampments.[53]

To take advantage of these Plains goods, Spiroans blazed additional trails west. One, established between 1250 and 1300, was a northern route, up the Arkansas River to some small Plains villages in central Kansas, and then overland to the Pueblo city of Pecos. During the 1540s, the Spanish conquistador Francisco Vázquez de Coronado and his army would travel this same northern route to reach Quivira, a sprawling Wichita village along the Arkansas River in Kansas. About 1350, Spiroans extended their southerly Caddo bois d'arc route along the Red River to Plains peoples farther west and then on to the Pueblos in New Mexico. This trade route became so used that Plains peoples began to copy

Spiroan artwork on their own pottery.[54] It would not be surprising if Spiroans and Pueblos had exchanged ambassadors or developed some type of cross-plains trade because Spiroan-type pottery has shown up in the Pueblos, and turquoise and cotton cloth from the Southwest has turned up in Oklahoma.[55]

While Spiroan trade increased with the Plains peoples after 1250, it became more sporadic with the great Mississippian chiefdoms in the East. Cahokia was abandoned by this time, though its culture and artwork were making tremendous impacts on Spiro and the other southeastern ceremonial centers. Certainly, Spiro knew of Moundville and Etowah and other major sites and vice versa. But after 1300, the little ice age was forcing these other regional centers to face their own environmental crises.[56] Conversely, Spiroan trade increased with the Caddoan peoples in the Ouachita Mountains and Red River area to the south. These areas now provided much of the pottery and clay pipes bound for Spiro. In fact, between 1250 and 1400, the most diverse types of pottery were being deposited in the burials of Spiroan elites.[57] Still, after 1350, Spiroan trade to the east was in steep decline, although for another fifty years, Spiro would continue to wield some influence both east and west.

Nevertheless, Spiro and its high priest were living on borrowed time. So were all the great Mississippian chiefdoms. The unpredictable weather patterns affected Spiro in many ways. Something as mundane as house structures began changing, from four center posts holding up the roof to only two.[58]

More important, after 1350, the uncertain weather began to take its toll on the high priest. Since the 1000s, the priest-chief's power and prestige had rested on his ability to control the weather through his knowledge of ritual and ceremony. But now, nothing seemed to work. It was as if the gods had turned their back on Spiro. Drought burned seedlings, then drenching rains, which lasted for weeks, turned gardens into bogs. The flooding of the Arkansas did not always materialize, or if it did, it came at the wrong time, washing away fields of ripening corn and grain. As had happened at Cahokia two hundred years earlier, Spiroan people's faith in their high priest was shaken, and many soon turned their backs on him. With the priest unable to deliver a proper climate, farming faltered, and the social contract between the commoners and their hereditary leaders snapped. By 1350, no one paid attention to the Spiro high priest. In fact, the position may well have ceased to exist at Spiro. Brown Mound was no longer used to celebrate the arrival of the sun at the solstices and equinoxes.[59] Now newly built Skidgel Mound, just west of Spiro, itself aligned to the equinoxes, became the main temple mound for ceremonies. But Skidgel was a shadow of the size and glory Spiro had been in its heyday. And its priest had no better luck in controlling the weather than did Spiro's last great high priests.[60] The days of the demigod nobility were over.

By 1400, the center was not holding at Spiro. The abandonment of Spiro by its general population in 1250 initiated a dispersal of people and settlements that the unpredictable weather only exacerbated. As the climate disrupted Spiroan society, it forced some villages and hamlets to move further afield in their search for better farming. Their search often led them beyond the range of the fading Spiroan nobility. Rather than looking toward a priest-chief or nobility for leadership, these people took up a more egalitarian lifestyle. They did what they could to deal with the weather, and leadership shifted again to the wisest, bravest, and most generous, and not so much to the person who thought he knew what ritual could influence an increasingly uncontrollable climate.[61]

Then about 1415, the remaining people around Spiro decided to make one last major effort to get the climate under control. There was to be one final try to halt the splintering of their chiefdom. Since 1350, with the solstice and equinox rituals not being conducted at Brown Mound anymore, at Spiro only Craig Mound remained in use as a burial place for the elite dead.[62] Now what remained of the Spiro nobility, those who had seen their power drained by an uncooperative climate, decided to try to shock the weather deities into compliance. They would turn Craig Mound into one of the largest repositories of spiritual power in the history of Indian North America.

It was a solution on a truly grand scale. These last Spiroans planned to gather all the skeletons, bones, and prestige goods of every Spiro priest-chief, every high priest, and every important noble who had ever lived and rebury them all in a great mortuary inside Craig Mound. If all went according to plan, this great concentration of power goods and powerful ancestors would correct the weather, restore harmony, and bring the world back to the way it used to be. It was Spiro's last-ditch attempt to save itself. And if this sacrifice of all that was holy at Spiro did not appease the spirits, then nothing would.

They began with the great mortuary, disassembling the charnel house then atop the fourth and most northwesterly lobe of Craig Mound. This area, about eighteen feet in diameter, was covered with dirt, and then a layer of bones from more than one hundred commoners was taken out of nearby cemeteries and laid down.[63] Placed there to serve their noble masters? To show how all the people of Spiro were begging the weather deities for help? Whatever the reason, the bones of these commoners were covered with another few inches of dirt as well as cane matting, and then Spiroans began reinterring their elites. They cleaned out every elite charnel house and even dug up long-dead chiefs and arranged their bodies and status goods on the floor of the great mortuary. Some of these bones and goods were over four hundred years old. Old-style jar burials, which had not been seen since the late 900s, were placed in the great mortuary. There were eighteen woven cane burial boxes, which had gone out of style in the 1000s, as well as fourteen cedar-pole litter burials, which had been popular in the early 1200s. There were so many cedar poles that they almost covered the floor. In went the giant Big Boy effigy pipe of the sitting chief and other effigy pipes, which had originally come to Spiro around 1250. A true mish-mash of artifact styles that ranged throughout Spiro's six hundred year history was now dumped there.[64]

All the ancient bodies and burials were placed together on the floor. There were even a few bits of cremated bone inside a conch shell cup, and cremations had not been done at Spiro since before 1250. Many of these remains were waterlogged or blackened with minerals from having been in the ground so long. However, there were also about ten extended burials, in which the skeletons were laid out whole, and these ten were the only dead contemporary to the building of the great mortuary. Were these members of the last great Spiro chiefly family who had sparked the renewal effort? Or were they retainers or captives sacrificed for this great spiritual undertaking? In all, there were forty-two elite burials, but only a scant few were children. Over a hundred commoner skeletons were placed there, most reburied from the distant past. The interesting thing is that of all the bones, only a few intact skulls were found. Still, virtually everything, bones and artifacts, were all old things. The only items contemporary with the great mortuary itself, besides the ten extended skeleton burials, were a large stone celt and a circular breastplate.[65]

One of the greatest troves of Mississippian period artwork went into the great mortuary. Shells, copper sheets, pipes, maces, pottery, balls of galena, all of which had been big before 1300, were dug up from burials or taken from charnel houses and placed among the bodies.[66] But this effort was to be something bigger. The whole great circle was to be a temple, a ritual in itself, harnessing all the power of the dead Spiroan priest-chiefs and their status goods to influence the spirits, change the weather, and bring back the happy times. Raised altars were set at the four cardinal points, and on each were placed blankets and about a hundred pounds of shell beads. In the eastern part of the mortuary stood several cedar effigies of Spiroan ancestors. At the north were human effigy pipes made of Missouri flint clay. Across the floor were piles of human bones; cups, figurines, and breastplates made of shell; copper-covered baskets, some with blue and white kernels of Indian corn in them; pristine projectile points; numerous ear plugs and ear spools, some of stone, others of wood covered with copper; and a tremendous variety and number of pottery vessels, many hundreds of years old. There were seven maces, thirty-two small wooden human head effigies covered with copper, copper hairpins, one in the form of a snake, as well as numerous copper sheets.[67]

Spiroans placed over 950 different conch shell cups and breastplates in the great mortuary, but many shells had been ritually broken, "killed," to ensure all their power would be released because they would never be used again. Great stone blades had been deliberately broken in half. Pottery jars deliberately smashed. Some copper plates were intentionally crumpled. Even some beads had been burned. Piles of blankets made from woven animal hair were scattered throughout the chamber, with beads piled on top of them. An exquisitely carved quartz locust without wings went into the chamber. There were even Archaic Indian items, such as atlatl banner stones, which were already thousands of years old by the time Spiro came about. Among it all were shell cups, many filled with beads or balls of glittering galena, as well as red, yellow, black, gray, and green mineral pigments, over five hundred pounds of them. There were baskets containing copper-headed axes, beads, smashed copper sheets, and other artifacts. And the number and variety of beads were astronomical: over twenty-one thousand in one pile, fifteen thousand in another, as well as thousands of pearls and pearl beads.[68]

Then, as if to channel the power, Spiroans ringed the great mortuary with conch shells and built a cedar pole frame over it.[69] The frame, a cone of poles leaning inward, reached maybe eighteen feet high. This would be a conduit to funnel the power of the dead priest-chiefs and their goods upward to the top of Craig Mound, where weather-changing rituals would be conducted. Earth was packed over the poles to create a hollow vault, a central chamber, over most but not all the graves and power goods. All this had taken place inside the original berm, and now Spiroans placed a few additional bodies here and piled dirt over the entire great mortuary, central chamber, and berm. Just before the ends of the vault's cedar poles were covered, another conical frame of cedar poles was put in place over the first one, and it too was covered with dirt, finishing the largest and most significant lobe of the Craig Mound.[70]

Despite its great riches; despite it holding more Mississippian artifacts than any one place in the United States; despite being both a shrine and a mausoleum for the bones of Spiro's glorious priest-chiefs, the Great Temple Mound, or Craig Mound, was an act of desperation. Once the Spiroans decided this was what they had to do to get things back on track, it all happened very fast. The charnel houses and ancient graves were cleaned out so rapidly that stray deer bones got mixed in with the human bones. Pieces of mussel shell, confused for conch shell, were also mistakenly mixed in. Hurrying workers left buffalo-bone digging tools behind. They also forgot some goods in the graves they had dug up, because several ear spools did not have mates. In their rush, the Indian workers accidentally broke many relics.[71]

Even then, though the central chamber was covered and Craig Mound capped, last-minute burials were added to its sides. Although these were elites, they received few grave goods because most had already gone into the great mortuary below them.[72] Now Craig Mound was the most holy of all Spiro holy places, reserved as the resting place for the Spiroan past elites— and the one hundred commoner skeletons interred with them.[73]

But all the work was for nothing. By the time Craig Mound was finished in 1420, with all four lobes now connected, it sat over thirty-three feet high and almost two hundred feet long, and had been a burial place for Spiroans since the 1000s. In all, archaeologists reckon that the entire Craig Mound, all four lobes, had 189 separate burials containing over 500 bodies or body parts. It also held some of the most beautiful Mississippian-period works of art ever created.[74] Nevertheless, no matter how many priest-chief bodies or power goods were reburied there, nothing was going to change the weather. And over the next few years, disappointed Spiroans drifted away, hoping to find fertile lands with regular rainfall. Where they went makes up another part of the Spiro mystery. Nevertheless, by 1450, Spiro, the city of the dead, was completely abandoned. Even its outlying villages were rapidly losing people. Also abandoned were all the great Mississippian cities and ceremonial centers. Cahokia. Moundville. Etowah. Okmulgee. They became ghost towns when their inhabitants walked away, done in by changing weather and unpredictable crop yields. And Spiro, that once great chiefdom that had dominated the region for almost five hundred years, now sat powerless. Empty of all but the dead. Forgotten by the living.

7

An American King Tut's Tomb

Kansas City and Spiro, 1935–1936

Tuesday, December 3, 1935: Harry Trowbridge remembered that day for the rest of his life. After a day of work as office manager at the Abner Hood Chemical Company, he arrived at his home on Wigwam Road in Bethel, Kansas, a bedroom community of Kansas City, at about 6:15 P.M. Waiting for him were a couple of strangers. One of them carried a large cardboard box. They introduced themselves as Joe Balloun and his brother, Frank, explaining they'd just done a little business with Trowbridge's friend John G. Braecklein in nearby Kansas City. Braecklein was much impressed and suggested they come see Trowbridge. They had some things that might interest him.[1]

Trowbridge was always interested in things, particularly things having to do with Indian relics. His fascination with pre-Columbian Indians had gone from being a hobby to an avocation. Deep reading as well as getting his hands and knees dirty digging at Indian sites had made him a pretty good amateur archaeologist. He didn't have any university training, and he wasn't connected with any museum, but he read the literature and understood how to conduct an excavation. A proud Kansan, he'd devoted himself to the preservation of the early Indian history of Wyandotte County. In the meantime, he had become locally famous when he uncovered and excavated a Hopewell culture site in his own Kansas City backyard. Never so hard-headed as to believe he knew everything, he was quick to consult with professional archaeologists when he had a question. In turn, this gained him respect from the professionals, and he even co-authored some articles with Waldo Wedel, one of the most influential and respected Great Plains archaeologists of the day.[2]

However, like many archaeologists both amateur and professional, Trowbridge was an artifact collector. It was in his blood. His own excavations, particularly his backyard Hopewell experience, had provided him with a collection of very nice artifacts. His penchant for Indian history, archaeology, and relic collecting put him in contact with John Braecklein, a respected Kansas City architect and avid collector of Indian artifacts, whose assemblage numbered about a hundred thousand. That was the difference between Trowbridge and Braecklein: Braecklein wanted quantity, Trowbridge wanted quality.

Trowbridge got his wish that December evening. He never wrote what he felt when Joe and Frank Balloun began unwrapping relics fresh from the central chamber in Craig Mound. Excitement? Certainly, which no doubt increased with every artifact the Ballouns handed him. Amazement? Definitely. Huge engraved conch shells. Flint blades. Pieces of pottery. It was incredible! Sometime during the evening, Braecklein and his sister drove over from Kansas City and joined the party. All the while Joe Balloun told them the story of the Pocola Mining Company and how they had dug the guts out of Craig Mound. Most of Balloun's story was accurate, though he included himself as one of the diggers. It must have been a hell of an evening; the first meeting between Trowbridge and Joe Balloun lasted over six hours and didn't end until after 1:00 A.M.[3]

That night, Trowbridge made his first Spiro purchase: a large conch shell engraved with a rattlesnake. He never said how much he'd paid for it. While the conch shells were rare and spectacular, something else caught Trowbridge's eye: a small, brown, crumpled piece of cloth. Balloun handed it to him. "I rubbed my eyes several times," Trowbridge said. "It seemed unbelievable that Mound-Builders' fabrics should be in that box, and yet the mass of dirty, lime-bearing material had every indication of being genuine."[4] Pre-Columbian Indian cloth was very rare. Trowbridge had only heard of small bits ever being found anywhere in America. So this was big. "I thought I had a duty to perform right then, as it was plain that the relics would be scattered the next day, and few would have the interest to preserve them as they should. Consequently the risk was assumed, and as every inquiry made afterward, pointed to their genuineness, I bought all this vendor had."[5]

From that point on, acquiring and preserving the Spiro fabric became Trowbridge's mission. He was amazed to find he had pieces of a five hundred-year-old grass skirt as well as fragments of a cloak made almost entirely of feathers.[6] Over the next few months, Trowbridge bought all the cloth Balloun could get his hands on. Preserving it proved time consuming. He spent weeks, just about every evening after work and on weekends, unfolding and drying the larger pieces, "cleaning thousands of particles of decayed shell lime, removing wrinkles by shifting pins and slightly stretching the larger pieces each day, finally placing them between heavy sheets of glass in walnut frames."[7] Eight of these larger pieces were between thirty-six and fifty-three inches long. The smaller fragments were also cleaned and arranged in about a dozen glass-topped walnut trays.[8]

By February 1936, Trowbridge had acquired just about all the Spiro cloth available. Balloun informed him that the diggers had found only a little bit more cloth as well as a few feathers. "But they are not for sale reasonable. You were a lucky man to buy that blanket material now."[9] Having cornered the Spiro textile market, Trowbridge now had the premier collection of pre-Columbian Indian fabrics anywhere in North America. It was all safely tucked away behind glass in a fireproof, humidity-controlled display vault at his house in Bethel, Kansas.

Naturally, curiosity is a strong point in archaeologists, and Trowbridge had more than his share. Wanting to know more about his fabrics, he sent samples to various laboratories as well as to S. Stroock and Company, "Manufacturers of Fine Specialty Fabrics," in New York City. But doing this went beyond curiosity.

As Trowbridge pointed out, if a modern fabric company could gain some useful business knowledge from these pre-Columbian fabrics, then that would take archaeology out of the "luxury sciences" category and prove its usefulness to the world. It would make "hard-headed legislators probably swallow hard when voting appropriations for subjects dealing with a very dead past. The fact you personally are searching for helpful clues in these old Mound Builders fabrics . . . proves archaeology may be of value even in the realm of modern business."[10]

The company's president, Sylvan Stroock, thanked Trowbridge for the sample and wrote back that his chemists could not identify all the fibers in the cloth but did recognize fox, wolf, coyote, beaver, and muskrat. Other labs listed rabbit, jackrabbit, buffalo, and possibly dog and squirrel as well, all woven using a twined and twill-twined style.[11]

Although Trowbridge doted on his fabric collection, he did not neglect other Spiro artifacts. He, Braecklein, and other collectors, such as Lyle A. Stephenson and Frank E. Caffee, all became regular stops when Joe Balloun came calling in Kansas City.[12] In fact, Trowbridge and Balloun developed quite a correspondence, with Balloun trying to interest Trowbridge in some particular item and Trowbridge putting in orders for what he wanted. Not long after Trowbridge met the dealer, Balloun informed him that he had some Spiro pottery for sale, including three effigy statues as well as a three-legged painted bottle with one of its spout holes in the shape of a fish. He'd let all three go for thirty dollars. Not only that, Balloun had "all kinds of heads and two wooden faces and many common arrow heads at the right price. Let me here [sic] from you."[13] And Trowbridge bought. For as little as $22.80, he bought nineteen "war points," nine arrowheads, two carved stone ear spools, a stone pendant, and a hematite celt.[14] He also told Balloun he wanted one of the cedar poles from the central burial chamber, but he seems to have never gotten one.[15]

A problem for Trowbridge was that he faced fierce competition from other relic buyers in Kansas City and elsewhere in the Midwest. Trowbridge had hoped to get his hands on a large flint mace that Balloun was selling for $150, but was outbid by E. Lee Renno of St. Charles, Missouri.[16] "Joe, I was much disappointed that the maces did not come my way; please remember me if and when you get started again at the Temple Mound, and carved conch shells would fit into my collection nicely, as well as many other things."[17]

Balloun could not provide everything because the other Dardanelle dealers were also at work. Goodrich Pilquist also had contacts in Kansas City. H. I. Player, a member of the State Archaeological Society of Missouri who had made a visit to the mounds, expressed interest in acquiring some Spiro artifacts. Pilquist told him that many of his own pieces had already been sold, but he had others, such as an engraved shell breastplate for five dollars, and other pieces ranging from one dollar to five dollars. Pilquist knew Spiro artifacts and had written an early piece about Spiro for *Hobbies* magazine, which had appeared in the April 1935 edition. He also warned Player about Joe Balloun and that he should not believe everything Balloun said. Pilquist told him that Balloun made of habit of claiming to have been a digger on the mound but in reality had never been and was only a relic dealer.[18]

Nevertheless, if Balloun nor Pilquist could not or would not come through, Trowbridge would turn to other sources. He'd heard that Mrs. John Hobbs was in Kansas City on a visit, so he invited her to come by to see his collection. He'd hoped he could get an in with her husband and bypass middleman Balloun.[19] Within a short period, Trowbridge had a major Spiro collection consisting not only of fabrics but also of over sixty conch shell engravings, several stone maces and pipes, and many beads, pearls, lumps of galena, and other artifacts.[20]

When his sources could not come through with what he wanted, Trowbridge was willing to buy pipes, spearheads, crystals, and other Spiro artifacts from Braecklein, his friend and fellow collector.[21] Braecklein was one of the first people in Kansas City to see the Spiro artifacts. He had been at his office in early

December 1935 when in walked Joe Balloun with his box of Spiro relics. "'They tell me you are interested in things like this,'" Balloun said and unwrapped a sixteen-inch-long stone scepter made of translucent jasper.[22]

Braecklein almost fell out of his chair. "'Good heavens, a ceremonial mace! Where did you get it?'"

"'I've got six more almost exactly like that out in my car.'"

"'Six more you say? Like this. Why, there are only about a dozen of these in the whole world so far as I know.'"

"'There may have been only that many known until I found these. Wait, I'll bring them in.'"

Over the next few hours, Braecklein sat in awe, just as Trowbridge would later that same evening, as Balloun pulled out artifact after artifact. He laid the other six maces in front of the architect, who "stood, too much overcome with astonishment to speak." Each was about as long as the first. Then came a necklace of freshwater pearls, a twenty-six-inch-long flint spearhead "sharp as a needle at both ends, and of exquisite workmanship." Finally, Balloun unwrapped the prize: the Big Boy effigy pipe, standing eleven inches tall and weighing about ten pounds. The pipe depicted an Indian man "squatting on his haunches, his legs far apart and a hand on each knee. His head was bent and he was looking at the ground. He wore a head dress and a heavy necklace of beads around his neck, and in his ears were round plugs, such as the lost tribes of the ancient Mayans in Yucatan wore, and his hair was dressed in the Mayan fashion, too. Upon his back was a robe of feathers. A large hollow in his bent back, with a little hole for a stem at its base, showed that the figure was really a pipe."

Braecklein stared at the huge pipe. And it was much more than just a pipe. It was one of the great pre-Columbian archaeological finds of all time, because here was a statue that realistically showed what Indian people looked like six or seven hundred years ago. Braecklein looked up in wonder at the man in front of him.

The man smiled. "'My name is Balloun of Arkansas, and I and John Hobbs of Spiro, Ok. [*sic*], got all these things and thousands of others from a mound near Spiro.'"

"'I have been opening mounds and visiting mounds that were being opened for forty years,'" Braecklein declared. "'I have visited all the great collections of the relics of prehistoric men in this country and I never before saw such a fine collection of ceremonial maces as this you have.'"

Although he doesn't say, Braecklein probably bought the maces right then, before sending Balloun over to Harry Trowbridge's house in Bethel. But Braecklein's curiosity got the best of him, and he couldn't just let Balloun go without getting more information. After all, he'd paid a pretty penny for these artifacts, and he wanted to make sure they weren't fakes. They didn't look to be. Somehow, while Balloun was in Kansas City, Braecklein talked the dealer into taking him; H. I. Player, a member of the State Archaeological Society of Missouri; and A. B. Macdonald, a reporter for the *Kansas City Star*, down for a look at the Great Temple Mound at Spiro.

For Balloun, taking the trio down to Spiro just made good business sense. No use being secretive anymore; the Pocola lease was up, and Clements' antiquities bill had made sure they wouldn't be able to renew it. If Balloun and the other dealers could get the stamp of approval from an amateur collector like Braecklein and a professional archaeologist like Player, get it played up in a major newspaper by Macdonald, then the price of their artifacts would jump considerably. It was the same strategy Pilquist had used with the Carden Bottoms, Arkansas, relic rush back in 1924.

During the second week of December 1935, Balloun took the Kansas City trio down to Spiro. There they met John Hobbs and his wife, who told them of their early days relic hunting around the mound. They also got the whole Pocola Mining Company story. Balloun and Hobbs took the visitors over to Craig Mound and showed them where the company had tunneled in, what the men had found and where, then let the trio clamber all around and through the site. Braecklein, Player, and Macdonald were thrilled but also disappointed to see the destruction of the mound and the bits and pieces of artifacts, shells, and beads crushed underfoot. Macdonald seemed enamored with what he saw, and as they headed back toward Kansas City, he asked Braecklein who he thought had built the mounds.

This would become a major question about Spiro, and Braecklein pontificated. They were people of the Mound Builder culture, obviously, and the "Mound-Builders were immigrants from other shores, bringing their peculiar customs with them. In the course of time they flourished in the Mississippi valley and became a numerous people whose public works, from the grandeur and extent of their ruins, are as much a wonder today as the pyramids and ruins along the Nile. But, something happened, some grand holocaust, perhaps a plague or epidemic, and the Mound Builders fell a prey to neighboring barbarians who absorbed a part and drove the others way, perhaps to the south."

The headline blazing across the feature section of the Sunday, December 15, 1935, *Kansas City Star* made people put down their morning coffee and take notice. "A 'King Tut' Tomb in the Arkansas Valley—On a Negro's Farm in Eastern Oklahoma Are Unearthed Relics from the Mound Builders of Past Centuries." Macdonald's story took up most of that section's front page and a good part of the second. In column after column, Macdonald told of Joe Balloun's maces and his visit with Braecklein, their trip to Spiro, the meeting with John Hobbs and the pot-hunting history lesson, the digger's excavation of Craig Mound, the treasure found inside the central burial chamber, and finally of Braecklein's theory of who built the mounds. Several photographs on the front page spiced up the story. One showed Craig Mound, another John Hobbs and two unidentified diggers, but more important were photos of a fragment of engraved shell with a chief holding one of the ceremonial maces and a fourth photo showing the maces, a huge engraved conch shell, and the large Big Boy effigy pipe Joe Balloun had brought to Braecklein's office.

It was truly an amazing newspaper story and became the talk around Kansas City water coolers. Other newspapers picked up the story or parts of it, and suddenly Spiro Mounds went from a little backwater excavation to an international archaeological find.

And the rush was on as relic hunters and artifact collectors raced down to Le Flore County.

In reality, the rush was over before it ever began. When the Pocola Mining Company's lease ran out on November 27, 1935, the men hoped they might get it back somehow. But Clements and his antiquities act had ensured that would never happen. George Evans, the legal guardian of the children who owned the property, was willing to renegotiate, but he wanted more money. It didn't matter, though, for Evans soon discovered that the antiquities act tied his own hands. He could lease to Clements or no one.

So during the final days of their lease, the members of the Pocola Mining Company were angry men, bitter at being forced off their claim. So in a fit of spite, just to jab their finger in Clements' eye, they packed the central chamber of the Great Temple Mound with kegs of black powder and touched off a mighty explosion. Amazingly, Craig Mound didn't burst open, nor did it implode on itself. Still, the explosion broke many of the remaining items in the chamber, caused a moderate cave-in, and created a huge crack in the mound, which started on the southwest side and ran over the slope and down the north face.[23] The explosion also destroyed the Pocola men's reputations as down-home heroes fighting for their property rights, blowing them instead into the ranks of looters and destroyers.

With that explosive fit of pique, the Pocola Mining Company ceased to exist. The diggers' days at Spiro Mounds came to an end. The time had not been all that rewarding. Although the men of the Pocola Mining Company were good diggers, they were not good businessmen. Relic dealers like Balloun, Pilquist, and Daniel, men who could talk fast and flash cash, managed to separate the relics from the Pocola men at fire-sale prices. Huge engraved conch shells had gone for as little as two dollars each. One dealer packed his car full of artifacts and took them to Chicago, where "they were hawked on the street at a fraction of their value."[24] It was "purely a Depression-time business venture," another collector explained. "It is doubtful if the diggers received even the prevailing Depression-time wage for their efforts."[25]

As Guinn Cooper told it, hard times back then made people do anything to make a living. "Everybody was scratching to make a dollar any way he could. We tried to make a deal with the University of Oklahoma so all of the artifacts from the central chamber could be kept together, but didn't seem to have much luck. We were under tremendous expense and had to sell to anyone who was willing to buy. We spent the money almost as fast as it came. I don't think anyone of the group realized much more than a living from the operation."[26]

So as the black powder smoke cleared from the Great Temple Mound, John Hobbs went back to his farm. Bill McKenzie returned to his store in Pocola. For Guinn Cooper, the end of Spiro was bad. Nothing had panned out right. He tried to find his old gold-prospecting spot in the Kiamichi Mountains but could never locate it again. He bummed around the area for the rest of the decade, became a carpenter, and then joined the navy when World War II began.[27]

If the future seemed bleak for the Pocola partners, other people connected with Craig Mound had no future at all. Reverend R. W. Wall, the African American preacher who had helped the company lease the mound from George Evans, drowned in a stream so shallow that no one could figure out how it happened. His death was considered very suspicious, but there was no investigation. Down in the Le Flore County seat of Poteau, an attorney who had been the chief opponent of Clements' antiquities act mysteriously up and died. More tragically, tuberculosis finally caught up with twelve-year-old James Craig, one of the two child owners of the property.[28] The legend of the curse of Spiro Mounds had taken root.

Clements certainly seemed cursed. He gazed at the gutted Craig Mound in "shock and grief." Taking off to teach the 1935 summer quarter in California had given the Pocola Mining Company the chance to tunnel into the central burial chamber. Once he'd heard about it, he'd raced back to Oklahoma, but it was way too late. Here was firsthand proof of what he had been trying to prevent. "Sections of cedar poles lay scattered on the ground, fragments of feather and fur textiles littered the whole area; it was impossible to take a single step in hundreds of square yards around the ruined structure without scuffing up broken pieces of pottery, sections of engraved shell and beads of shell, stone and bone. The site was abandoned; the diggers had completed their work."[29]

Enraged, Clements went down to the Le Flore County Sheriff's Office and demanded that the diggers be arrested. He explained that the Pocola Mining Company, as the recently passed Oklahoma antiquities act stated, had been ordered to cease and desist from digging on the mound, despite their lease. They were not to dig on it again until they received a license from Clements. He stated that he had given the partners a license application form, but they had never filled it out and therefore never obtained a license to dig. The sheriff's office issued arrest warrants for Bill McKenzie, Kimball McKenzie, Jim Vandagriff, William Vandagriff, Guinn Cooper, John Hobbs, as well as hired diggers Hayden Vandagriff and Columbus Eubanks. The penalty, if convicted, was a fine of two hundred dollars, thirty days in jail, or both.[30]

According to Clements, the men were arrested, but after that the story gets sketchy.[31] It's not known whether the case made it to court, whether the diggers were convicted, nor whether they paid a fine or went to jail or both or neither. Thirty days in jail during the winter of 1936 might not have posed too big of a hardship on the men, but a two-hundred-dollar fine certainly would have.

In the end, it really did not matter if they got prosecuted or not. The damage had been done, and Clements could do nothing about it. The diggers did not have the artifacts, the dealers and collectors did, and there was no law against that. Even worse, by the spring of 1936, the Craig Mound relics were quickly spreading across the country, even across the Atlantic.

And Clements could no more retrieve them than Guinn Cooper could bring back his Kiamichi gold or dead wife.

Although Clements' knees sagged whenever he thought about the destruction that went on at Craig Mound, he firmly believed there were more artifacts to be found. He needed to lead a slow, thorough scholarly excavation. He had been planning it for months. It could still be done. Still needed to be done. But first, he had to get his hands on the Craig property, and that was not going to be easy. The December 15 "'King Tut' Tomb" article in the *Kansas City Star* had sent hordes of relic hunters down to Spiro in hopes of leasing the mound from George Evans.

A few weeks after the *Kansas City Star* article ran, Clements wrote an angry letter to Braecklein, deploring the seemingly positive light the article cast on the diggers and their "archaeological vandalism." Braecklein should not be taken in by the diggers, Clements warned. They were a shady bunch, not above forging artifacts or taking relics from other sites and attributing them to Spiro to boost their price. Even worse, Clements complained, the article had stirred up considerable interest in Spiro, and now an army of out-of-state collectors had descended on Le Flore County in hopes of leasing the mound. Clements believed some of the original Pocola men were again involved in this, trying to get a new lease not so much to dig again, but to resell it to unsuspecting relic hunters. Nevertheless, Braecklein should understand that the Oklahoma antiquities act had not been repealed and was still in effect, despite rumors to the contrary. So while it was perfectly legal to sell a lease and perfectly legal to purchase one, "the moment such a lessor begins to excavate for specimens without a permit the law will be invoked against him. Such a person acquiring a lease under the impression that his operations would be let would merely be a victim of a swindling proposition."[32]

While trying to stave off nosy relic hunters, Clements began working on George Evans, who still hoped to re-lease the property. In addition, Clements wanted to see three other mounds on the property excavated. However, Evans had seen what had come out of the central chamber of Craig Mound, and now he upped his price. Too high, it seems, and with Clements telling every potential lessor that they could lease but not dig, nobody stepped forward to close the deal. That gave Clements time to get his own finances in order. Finally, in the spring of 1936, Evans decided to sell the property. Since so many people were interested in buying it, an auction was held in the Le Flore County judge's chamber.[33]

By then Clements had managed to get some financial backers. He cut a deal with the Oklahoma Historical Society in which they would actually purchase the land, but he, as head of the Department of Anthropology at the University of Oklahoma, would take physical possession of the mound and excavate it. Clark Field, a wealthy Tulsa contributor to Tulsa University and the Philbrook Museum, announced that he would make up any additional costs. So with a final bid of $450 for the purchase of the Craig property and the mounds on it, the judge was just ready to award it to Clements and the Oklahoma Historical Society when in walked Joe Balloun.[34]

Balloun had made some nice money off the Spiro artifacts and wanted more. He certainly despised Clements and hated to see him get his hands on Spiro. He well knew that if Clements got control of the mounds, then independent dealers like him and Pilquist would never see another Spiro artifact. Instead, they would all go to rich men like Clark Field, who funded university excavations and were then rewarded with the very same artifacts the dealers had been buying themselves. It was just the flip side of the same coin. Clements was going to do what the diggers and dealers had been doing all autumn, only he got his money in the form of excavation grants. Meanwhile, Clark Field, unlike Trowbridge and Braecklein, would not have to compete for artifacts with other collectors. Nor would he have to dirty his hands negotiating with relic dealers. Besides, Balloun did not think the antiquities act would hold up in court, and if he got title to the property, he'd be willing to fight it.[35]

Balloun really did not have much of a chance against the single-minded Clements. Whatever amount Balloun bid on the property was quickly topped by Clements and the Oklahoma Historical Society, but Balloun had managed to raise the selling price to $600. Once again, the judge was just ready to award the property to the Oklahoma Historical Society when a telegram arrived from a Jack Reed of Fayetteville, Arkansas. Reed, the telegram said, was then in New York but wanted to bid on the property and requested a week's delay for him to get his money together. No one knew who Jack Reed was, but he had a right to make a bid, so over Clements' protests, the judge agreed to wait a week.[36]

The mounds had been there for maybe a thousand years, so what was a week? For Clements, a week meant everything, and he wanted the process over as quickly as possible. The boy, James Craig, co-owner of the property, was very sick with tuberculosis and might not last the week. Because he owned the land jointly with his sixteen-year-old sister, his death before the sale could go through had the potential to snarl the legal technicalities with intestate court rulings. Who knew what would happen to the deal then. Clements' bad luck seemed to be holding steady. A mere three hours after the judge postponed the sale, Clements "watched little James Craig die as he lay in bed on the porch of his grandfather's cabin, almost in the evening shadow of the great Spiro Mound."[37]

While Craig's death was a personal tragedy, it posed none of the problems Clements anticipated. By the end of the week, all legal matters that Craig's death may have raised with the sale had been cleared up. Even better, Jack Reed never submitted his bid, so for $600 the Oklahoma Historical Society, the University of Tulsa, and the University of Oklahoma received title to the property. Maybe his luck was changing after all, because not only did Clements get access to the mounds, but Clark Field; Frank Phillips, founder of Phillips Petroleum; and Alfred Reed (no relation to Jack Reed)—all wealthy philanthropists—along with the federal government's Works Progress Administration (WPA) agreed to help finance Clements' excavation of Craig

Mound. Of course, any artifacts found would be fairly divided between Clements' University of Oklahoma museum; Phillips' own Woolaroc Museum in Bartlesville, Oklahoma; and Field's favorite, the Philbrook Art Center at Tulsa.[38] Clements walked out of the judge's chambers a conflicted man. Sour over the destruction of Craig Mound, he could at least take assurance that the pot hunters had been excised from the mound. It was his now, and whatever remained would be excavated by him and his team. Clements didn't know it, but his problems were only just beginning.

8

Dividing the Loot

1936–1960

If Clements imagined that purchasing Craig Mound would end all controversy, he was sadly mistaken. Too many diggers, dealers, and collectors disagreed with his tactics and felt his antiquities act was unfair. Using the sheriff's office to run off legitimate leaseholders seemed arrogant. Besides, purchasing the land was not going to stop relic hunters from getting their hands on Indian artifacts.

Glen Groves of Chicago, a member of the North American Indian Relic Collectors Association (NAIRCA), took Clements to task. Having visited the Spiro excavation, where he met "the boys," as he termed the Pocola partners, Groves concluded that the destruction at Spiro should be laid at Clements' feet. Putting a fanciful spin on the story, Groves gave the impression that a couple of kids wandering around the countryside had just stumbled across Craig Mound. They had picked up a few artifacts and tried to interest the scientific community in what they had found, but had been rebuffed. Ignored by the academics, the boys invested their own money, did the hard work, opened the mound, and hit it big. While Groves regretted that Craig Mound had not been excavated in a scientific manner, he still supported the boys' actions. Had it not been for them, Groves said, "perhaps another thousand years would have passed before the mound would have been excavated in accordance with the wishes of the Oklahoma professors."[1]

But what Groves really detested was the boys being thrown off their lease. As he saw it, Clements had had his chance to lease Craig Mound but had not acted on it. The boys did what Clements' should have done, so they alone should reap the profits. It was only when the State of Oklahoma realized there was something valuable in the mounds that it passed the antiquities act, which cut the boys off from their hard-earned profits. And just because they had to ignore the act in order to take what was rightfully theirs, they should not be prosecuted by the state. "The archaeologists and officials seem to be taking revenge for their own lack of interest by prosecuting the parties making the discovery. This is remindful of the fate of Columbus and his Spanish prosecutors."[2]

While he wished that some accord between Clements and the Pocola men could have been reached, Groves felt the diggers had done the right thing. "The finer details are perhaps lost, but on the whole, it is better for this generation to know it as it is now, than never to have realized the treasures it contained."[3]

Groves' version of events had many supporters and was taken as gospel for years to come. As late as 1960, an editorial in *Hobbies* about the Craig Mound excavation gave credence to it. As the writer saw it, the academics had been asleep at the wheel on Craig Mound. Instead of peacefully resolving the issue with the diggers, Clements had overreacted with the antiquities act once relics began to be hauled out of the central chamber. "The moral is that had informed professionals spent a little time cultivating public relations as intelligently as they did rivaling each other's scientific achievements, they might have saved the story told by this structure. . . . Meanwhile the numerous artifacts from the Spiro Mound still in collections or in circulation have become somewhat mournful souvenirs, like relics from a battlefield whose story has been completely lost to history."[4]

In the 1930s, Groves' idea seemed compelling. Even *Time* magazine picked up the story and sent a *March of Time* news-reel crew to the area. The editors had heard that a couple of Indian boys had made the discovery. Using their own pluck and grit, they had managed to find the central chamber only to have the state step in and take it away from them. When Clements explained that it was not kids but a well-organized mining operation of adults, *March of Time* dropped the story.[5]

Still, on a certain level, the criticism held water. Clements could be his own worst enemy and probably took a condescending tone when dealing with the working-class Hobbs, Cooper, and crew. And as one of the "new" archaeologists, Clements was unwilling to compromise. He detested pot hunters and saw them as looters. Nothing would ever change his mind that only academically trained professionals should excavate Spiro.[6] Clements did not just want the artifacts; he wanted to study the entire site. And besides, he had tried to save the mounds and would have if he had only had the money back in 1933 that Clark Field, Frank Phillips, and the Oklahoma Historical Society were providing in 1936.

Naturally, the Pocola men wholly agreed with Groves' indictment of the professor. They despised Clements, seeing him as a manicured coat and tie, backed by crooked politicians and Big Money men, who rode roughshod over the little man's property rights. After all, a man had the right to do with his property as he wanted. If they had struck oil, it would have been theirs. Why not the relics? Even the Smithsonian Institution recognized that. When questioned about the pillaging of Craig Mound, its director replied, "but what can we do about it? The mounds in question were doubtless on private land and the diggers had permission from the owner. We have in the United States no law of eminent domain; there is nothing to prevent a property owner from doing what he will with prehistoric remains on his own land. And just so long as pot-hunters can get $750 for one pipe and $1000 for six chert maces, there will be inducement for such operations as that before us."[7] So there was really no way Clements and the Pocola Mining Company could have ever reached a compromise by the time the lease had run out in November 1935.

By late spring 1936, Clements was much too busy to worry about what collectors thought of him. He was preparing his first excavation of Craig Mound, slated for that summer. But what seemingly kept him busiest was dealing with the crush of relic hunters and curio dealers descending on Spiro thanks to the *Kansas City Star*'s "'King Tut' Tomb" story. Rumors only spurred it on. Word had it that Tiffany's of New York had received a quart of Spiro pearls, which they valued at five hundred thousand dollars. Another rumor was that a new scientific process had been developed that would rejuvenate the "dead" powdery pearls. With all these stories about, itinerant pot hunters were meeting with locals and offering cash for the right to dig on their property. And locals were taking them up on it.[8]

While Clements could now rely on the governor to help protect Craig Mound, there was not much he could do about the pot-hunting excavations going on at nearby sites. Diggers tunneled into Skidgel Mound, about a mile west of Craig Mound. They tried digging at Round Mountain, but that outcrop aligned two miles southeast of Craig was solid rock, not dirt, and they quickly gave up. Pot hunters attacked the village sites all around Le Flore County, such as Littlefield, Moore, Fort Coffee and many others that had once been satellite communities of Spiro. As always, locals raked through the area in search of relics, and word was that John Hobbs was planning another mound excavation somewhere, but he would not say where. There were even rumors about the Pocola Mining Company reforming to excavate other sites. This time investors could buy stock in the company to reap even greater profits.[9] Everyone seemed to forget that only the dealers, not the Pocola men, had been the ones to profit. The folks at the Smithsonian Institution just shook their head over the entire frenzy. "I doubt that there is any possibility of stemming the tide of curio collecting. And I presume there is nothing to do but let the work go on until the supply is exhausted as it eventually will be."[10]

While trying to discourage all the pot hunters and lease-hopers drove Clements crazy, John Hobbs was also getting a lot of attention. Pot hunters and collectors contacted him incessantly. By late summer 1936, Harry Trowbridge's curiosity got the best of him, and he drove down to Spiro. He met with Hobbs and Guinn Cooper and talked them into drawing maps for him, detailing where they had found certain relics inside the central chamber.[11]

Even worse, people were pestering Hobbs for artifacts. When he had earlier stated that he might do other excavations in the area, collectors took him at his word and got angry when he did not come through. In May 1938, John Maff complained that Hobbs was not moving fast enough on a new excavation. It had been two years since he had heard from Hobbs, and he guessed the former Pocola man had not done anything. Still, Maff wanted more Craig Mound relics, though "money is not as plentiful in the last six months as it was previously. I am sure you missed a good many sales since I last wrote you."[12] Others did the same, asking Hobbs for a list of items he had and their prices.[13] Some just sent him a letter and put in an order. Carl Clausen of Pennsylvania wrote that he could "use about 200 gem points and the same number of war points, also any other fine pieces. I'd like to have the quartz discoidal if you can get it for me . . . I have several collector friends that could use fine material, so send any you can get along and you'll have the check within a few days."[14]

Though Clements had outmuscled him with the antiquities act, Hobbs never seemed to get over Spiro. He more than likely was involved with illegal excavations, illegal according the dictates of the antiquities act, of village sites surrounding Spiro. Certainly the Dardanelle, Arkansas, dealers kept in touch with him, still asking if he had anything else to sell.[15] By the end of the decade, Hobbs was recognized as the leader of the Pocola Mining Company and the man to see for Spiro artifacts. In March 1941, the board of trustees of the Houston Museum of Fine Arts invited Hobbs to attend the reception and preview of their recently acquired collection of Spiro artifacts donated by philanthropist A. T. McDannald.[16] It's not known whether Hobbs attended. Probably not. But the McDannald Collection of Spiro items can still be seen in the Museum of Natural Sciences in Houston.

As late as December 1943, Hobbs was involved with Colonel Fain White King, a major artifact collector from Wickliffe, Kentucky, in a scheme to purchase three acres of Spiro property from Mamie Brown. This would have given them ownership of Brown Mound. They were also to lease what was left of the smaller lobe of Craig Mound from Percy Brewer. As the contract between Hobbs and King clearly stated, "these mounds are being purchased to excavate for an equal partnership." They would split the proceeds fifty-fifty, but King got first rights on buying anything they found. To get things going, King paid Hobbs thirty-five dollars for securing the Brown property, five dollars for getting the lease from Percy Brewer, and another twenty dollars to hire laborers to begin excavating.[17] For Percy Brewer, repeatedly leasing his property was an old tactic, especially because no one could dig on it once they leased it. Back in December 1939, Z. J. Harrison of Poteau, Oklahoma, was overjoyed to lease Brewer's property for ten dollars but never got to dig.[18] Apparently for Colonel King, it was not money well spent. By mid-May 1944, King was requesting Hobbs to "advise if you will be excavating by that time. Have you found anything yet?"[19] It didn't look good. And though Hobbs would still be asked for more artifacts, it appears he never had the chance to do any additional excavations at Spiro proper.[20]

Driving all the pot hunters and leaseholders was that now Spiro items were in great demand. After the "'King Tut' Tomb" story, everybody wanted something from Spiro. Dealers, old and new, just fanned the flames. Pilquist got in first, and in the December *Hobbies*, he ran a small ad selling "Long Rare Heavy Prehistoric Shell Amulet" for one dollar, which he claimed came from the Great Temple Mound.[21] He ran another in January 1936, but now, since the "'King Tut' Tomb" story, prices had gone up. Copper needles went for as much as seven dollars each.[22] Glen Groves, the relic dealer from Chicago, ran the first ad headline in *Hobbies* that hawked "Great Temple Mound Relics." He pitched the goods to "museums and advanced collectors who want only the finest prehistoric relics." He offered stone axes for anywhere from $10 to $25, and copper axes with parts of a breastplate attached for $125. Engraved shells went for $10. Beads were anywhere from $1.50 to $3.50 per hundred.[23]

And people bought. In quick order, Spiro artifacts spread across the country and into Europe, often changing hands several times over. E. Lee Renno, a St. Charles, Missouri, collector, acquired a good stock of Spiro goods. When he died in August 1940, Colonel King bought Renno's collection and sold it off piece by piece, offering some of it directly to Harry Trowbridge.[24] And prices only went up. A. W. Pendergast of Fairbury, Illinois, had bought a ten-inch white flint Spiro blade from Pilquist soon after the Pocola Mining Company had broken open the Great Temple Mound. Not five years later, Pendergast sold the blade to E. K. Petrie of Chicago for an eye-popping $640.[25] And once anyone got a nice collection, it was not long before he tried selling it. Frank Phillips of Phillips Petroleum and founder of his personal Woolaroc Museum was deluged by sellers offering spectacular Spiro goods, maybe authentic, maybe fake. Sometimes Phillips bought, but mainly he waited for Clements' excavation, knowing he would then benefit.[26]

As Spiro artifacts spread to the cardinal points, one man realized that some type of photographic record should be made before everything disappeared into private vaults and got mixed in with other collections. Henry Hamilton and his wife Jean Tyree Hamilton of Marshall, Missouri, were amateur archaeologists fascinated by Mississippian mound builders. After reading about the Great Temple Mound, they went down to see it in June 1936, long after the Pocola men had done their work. The Hamiltons hit upon the idea of producing a book that would show off the Spiro artifacts and even received encouragement from Clements and other archaeologists. So throughout the first half of the 1940s, Henry and Jean contacted people and places that owned Spiro artifacts, then traveled across the country to beg the opportunity to photograph the items. In all, they took almost four hundred photographs of Spiro artifacts. Although a book never panned out, they published an article in *The Missouri*

Archaeologist in October 1952. To this day, Hamilton's "The Spiro Mound" is considered the best, if not the only, photographic record of what came out of the Great Temple Mound at Spiro. In the Hamiltons' photographs we see the effigy pipes, copper plates, conch shell engravings, stone maces, and many other wonders of the central chamber.[27]

The Hamiltons' efforts to document the Spiro artifacts proved to be a true odyssey. They contacted just about everyone involved with Spiro: collectors of Spiro items, academics who pondered Spiro, even museums that were beginning to get hold of Spiro items. First, the Hamiltons went back to Le Flore County and interviewed Hobbs and his wife, as well as the two McKenzies and Jim Vandagriff. R. W. Wall was dead by this time, and Guinn Cooper was in the navy and at war.[28] The Hamiltons photographed all they were allowed to and got the Pocola men's version of the story.[29] Later, the couple tracked down Pilquist, Balloun, and Daniel and talked them into letting them snap a few pictures. They went on to see the assemblages of as many collectors as they could, including William C. Barnard of Seneca, Missouri; Raymond Blake of Independence, Missouri; Ralph J. Duerr of Clinton, Missouri; Glen Groves; Albert Hansen of Kansas City, Missouri; Richard K. Meyer of Peoria, Illinois; H. I. Player; E. Lee Renno; B. W. Stephens of Quincy, Illinois; Lyle A. Stephenson; and, of course, Braecklein and Trowbridge. These last two provided most of the photos Hamilton made.[30]

The Hamiltons' efforts were not easy. Many collectors were protective of, if not secretive about, what they had. "In one case I had to sign a long and detailed contract. This was after much correspondence and about 5 hours of continuous discussion concerning the manner of use of the photographs, the stipulation that the negatives would become the property of the collector as soon as they were snapped, that we would be permitted to retain only 2 copies of each print, as well as specifying the number of prints which had to be given the collector." Although not all collectors were like this, Henry Hamilton found that all too many of them had stringent demands with which he had to comply.[31]

On the other hand, some collectors saw the benefits of Hamilton's pictures. Barnard welcomed Hamilton's visit and encouraged him to photograph not only his Spiro collection, but also many non-Spiro pieces, such as some Arkansas pottery and even a fake stone ax. When Barnard died in 1945, the Hamiltons went back to try to convince his wife to donate his collection to the University of Oklahoma Museum. Instead, the Hamiltons discovered that Barnard had used their pictures to sell off his collection to the famous Heye Museum of the American Indian in New York City. Virtually every bit of Barnard's Spiro collection was gone. "Every single piece that we had photographed is now missing from the collection," Henry Hamilton bemoaned.[32]

If Hamilton felt used by Barnard, the Heye Museum might also have felt a little handled. Certainly, museums had long been in the practice of purchasing artifacts. The display of exotic artifacts had been the mainstay of museums since museums had come about. Thomas Hoving, director of the Metropolitan Museum of Art in New York from 1967 to 1977, which had its own show of Spiro artifacts in 1941, summed it up this way, "the lifeblood of the great Metropolitan was collecting. Pure and simple. Every other function of the institution—conservation, exhibition, scholarship, teaching—evolved from that basic act. It was chase and capture, one of the most invigorating endeavors in life, dramatic, emotional, fulfilling as a love affair."[33]

This attitude put many academics on a collision course with the new professionalism of archaeology that had been emerging over the last few decades. Many professional archaeologists were taking a dimmer view of robbing graves for relics. But the thrill of the chase and the need for dramatic artifacts pushed many professionals into doing things they might have thought twice about. Like their colleague Clements, many archaeologists despised pot hunters and did not like to do business with them. Buying artifacts just encouraged the destruction of ancient sites. The ravaging of Craig Mound was testament to that. But they also wanted Spiro artifacts for their museums. They could wait for Clements to finish his upcoming excavation, but that could take years. Even then, most of the artifacts he found, if he found any at all, were going to the University of Oklahoma or into the private museums of his backers, Frank Phillips and Clark Field. So other museums could just watch as some of the most beautiful pre-Columbian artwork ever found in the United States got sucked into private collections, or they could join the buying frenzy. Most joined.

From the very first, while the Pocola men were still potting around the top of Craig Mound, museum archaeologists had shown up and found themselves faced with the choice of buying and thereby supporting pot hunting or not buying and missing out on great finds. Sam Dellinger, curator of the University of Arkansas Museum at Fayetteville as well as founder of the Arkansas Archaeological Survey, visited Spiro several times during the summer of 1935, when the men were cleaning out the central chamber. Awed and distressed by what he saw, Dellinger began buying whatever he could for the University of Arkansas. He acquired some amazing items, including two human skulls, one with patches of human hair and bits of cloth still adhering to it as well as engraved shell pieces, copper breastplates, and beads. These quickly went on display at the museum. Other Arkansans, proud of what their university museum was acquiring, began pitching in to help. Jack Reed of Fayetteville, who had managed to hold up Clements' purchase of the Spiro tract, loaned many of his own Spiro acquisitions to Dellinger's museum through an arrangement made by Colonel T. H. Barton of El Dorado, Arkansas, president of the Lion Oil Company.[34]

Robert Bell, who later became the chair of the University of Oklahoma's Department of Anthropology, was a graduate student when he visited the pot-hunting excavations at Spiro. He kept a sharp eye on what the Pocola men were doing and even took photographs of some of the items coming out of the mound. Fearing the relics would disappear before scholars could get a look at them, Bell, like Dellinger, purchased some of the artifacts directly from the diggers. Years later, he gladly shared them and his knowledge with other academics. When Hamilton toured the country to photograph Spiro material, Bell provided him with sketches of points, beads, and shell carvings. Henry C. Shetrone, director of the Ohio State Museum, also allowed Hamilton to photograph some beautiful embossed copper figures as well as some thin copper feathers, copper snakes, and ear spools. These, Shetrone explained, were items he had received from Bell.[35]

Of course, the academic to benefit most from all this should have been Clements himself. Well, he and his backers: the University of Oklahoma, Tulsa University, the Oklahoma Historical Society, and several wealthy Oklahoma patrons. Since Clements was going to take over the Spiro site and actually dig for the artifacts, these museums realized that all they really had to do was sit back and wait for him. Other museums would have to continue dealing with pot hunters, But they also knew that time was on their side. Eventually, thousands of Spiro goods would come to them, if not donated outright then offered for purchase. The McDannald donation to the Houston Museum of Fine Arts was proof of that.

Nevertheless, the Heye Museum, as Hamilton discovered, went on the offensive early and began purchasing artifacts from Joe Balloun, Goodrich Pilquist, Glen Groves, and anyone else who would sell.[36] So did the Smithsonian Institution.[37] Dellinger's initial purchases directly from Craig Mound provided the foundation for an incredible Spiro collection at the University of Arkansas. In 1947, Arkansas purchased part of the collection of Colonel King, who had been so hungry for Spiro goods. In time, the University of Arkansas acquired some of the most spectacular Spiro items, such as the Big Boy effigy pipe, a woven cane burial box, some engraved conch shells, and several sheets of copper repoussé.[38]

Eventually, though, the biggest contributors to the museums were the collectors themselves. Many collectors had built their collections from scratch, knew the literature and history of the Mississippian culture, and were experts on what they had and what it was worth. When they died, their heirs, either not interested or just not familiar with what the collection contained, often sold it off or donated it. Some collectors saw profit in a museum's interest. As early as 1936, Guinn Cooper, one of the original Pocola partners, and Jack Reed, the collector from Arkansas, offered to sell their collection to the Smithsonian. But nothing came of it. That's what may have made Reed turn to the University of Arkansas.[39] Others truly possessed a historical and archaeological bent and really wanted their collections to be seen. One of these was Harry Trowbridge.

Trowbridge, one of the first major collectors of Spiro artifacts, who had begun buying personally from Joe Balloun in December 1935, was approached by other dealers and collectors to buy their stock. As he later admitted, "within a short time I purchased here and there such items as opportunity and means would permit, so that they might be salvaged for scholars and others to study over the years ahead."[40] Pretty soon these included several shell carvings, maces, pipes, ear spools, and beads, but his real prize was the only collection in the world of pre-Columbian North American Indian fabrics.[41]

With his own collection, Trowbridge developed a small private museum in Bonner Springs, near Kansas City, Kansas. In fact, when he heard about Cooper and Reed offering to sell their collections to the Smithsonian, Trowbridge wrote to ask if they would instead donate them to his little museum. He understood that they wanted to make money, but since he already had Spiro cloth, their donation would keep the collection together. If things could be worked out, he would buy their collection outright for a moderate price or bit by bit over a short period. It seems Cooper and Reed turned Trowbridge down.[42]

At times, museums approached Trowbridge to donate his collection, but he was angered at their stinginess. In a letter to a friend, Trowbridge summed up the complaints collectors had with museums and the apparent double standard they applied to collectors. "Museums have now and then, asked what disposition was planned for the collection. Most of them doubtless hoped it would be presented as a gift or sold for a song. If I were wealthy I would be glad to give it to an institution which in location or aims, appealed to me as a suitable depository. But I am not rich; I have done about all I could to rescue from certain destruction these rare fabrics, and also to assemble more than sixty shells carvings and maces, etc. from Spiro. I have spent money freely, and given an enormous amount of time to the work. It was done without any thought of reward. But as I get older I am more inclined to think some of my friends are right in urging me to sell the collection sometime, like one might offer art treasures. I fully realize professionals are not all given to following that line of reasoning, and yet there are not many professionals who donate their services to archaeology for the love of the science. Museums often spend thousands of dollars sending expeditions out, but are reluctant to assign comparable amounts to acquire material probably a hundred times more valuable than their 'digs' will develop." In the end, Trowbridge swore never to sell to anyone who would not preserve his collection.[43]

Still, Trowbridge was proud of his collection and wanted it seen. During the late 1940s he lent it to the Kansas City Museum for a ten-year period.[44] Over time, he became closely associated with Spiro artifacts by collectors and laypeople alike. Some wanted to sell him artifacts.[45] Others wanted his opinion on Spiro and other mysteries. In some cases, he was off base. He figured the peak of Spiro culture had been about 1492, when actually it had been about 1250.[46] At the same time, he was quick to admit when he was out of his league. In December 1954, a Mrs. D. E. Jones of Garden City, Kansas, wrote him a series of questions, including whether the Spiro shell engravings had been deciphered, but also, "Have the Morock Tablets been found? Who do you think is the best author on the subject of the Lost Continent of Mu?"[47] Trowbridge wrote back explaining what he knew of the Southern Cult, but "I regret to say I am not familiar with the 'Morock Tablets.' And I am equally lacking in data about the Lost Continent of Mu."[48]

His passion for preservation and his knowledge about archaeology and Spiro also gained him the respect of academics and
professional archaeologists. Trowbridge even published two
articles on Spiro: "Analysis of Spiro Mound Textiles" in the
1938 edition of *American Antiquity* and "The Trowbridge Collection of Spiro Mound Artifacts" in the 1944 edition of the
Journal of the Illinois Archaeological Society. Others wanted to see
his cloth collections, and he corresponded with professionals
throughout the field.[49] However, not everyone seemed to think
his collection so special. In 1958, he tried to get *Life* magazine
interested in doing a full-color story on his Spiro fabrics. *Life*
turned him down.[50]

Although *Life* might ignore his Spiro fabric collection, the
professionals did not. Trowbridge finally got his wish. In 1959,
the Smithsonian Institution purchased Trowbridge's entire Spiro
collection, fabrics, shells, coppers and all, for twenty thousand
dollars.[51] Over the next decade, Trowbridge remained active in
local archaeology and history. He served as curator and director
for the Wyandotte County, Kansas, Museum. When he died on
July 1, 1969, at the age of eighty, the museum honored him by
naming its library wing the Trowbridge Memorial Library.[52]

Of course, with all this Spiro material floating about and
changing hands, one of the biggest worries was that of fakes
and forgeries. From the very first days of Spiro, fakes had been
a concern. In fact, when the first Spiro pieces hit the market in
December 1933, they were so amazing and exotic that most
collectors thought they were fakes. It was their appearance and
high quality that piqued the interest of Carl Guthe and got him
on the phone to Clements.[53]

At first, there was so much Spiro material hitting the curio
markets, particularly after the opening of the central chamber,
that there was no need for fakes. As Henry Hamilton pointed
out, so much material was found "as temporarily to break the
market for such objects."[54] But after the "'King Tut' Tomb"
story hit and everyone wanted something from the Great Temple
Mound, prices climbed, and fakes began appearing. The most

common way to fake a find was merely to take something from another Mississippian site and claim it came from Spiro's Great Temple Mound. Pipes and pottery were often the bait. Once these got mixed in with large collections, and if good records had not been kept, it was difficult to tell what was and was not from Spiro. This mixing of artifacts particularly angered archaeologists because it skewed their data and could create wrong conclusions. Along with general site destruction, this mixing was the most serious charge academics made against pot hunters.[55]

However, it was not long before clandestine workshops of forgers began turning out Spiro fakes, and no one was safe from being taken. When Frank Phillips first began buying Spiro artifacts, he appealed to Clements for guidance.[56] The archaeologist immediately warned him about Spiro fakes then making their appearance.[57] But the damage had already been done. A stone pipe in the shape of a frog that Phillips bought from a dealer in Hodgens, Oklahoma, for twenty-five dollars turned out to be a complete forgery and had to be removed from the Woolaroc Museum display.[58] A few years later, when Clements offered to provide some Spiro artifacts for Woolaroc, Phillips' secretary wrote that the oilman would be delighted to receive them "because they are indisputably authentic."[59] Even Trowbridge got suckered into buying some fake pipes and drills, possibly even some forged beads and hairpins.[60]

Henry Hamilton, who took pictures of many Spiro artifacts, realized several of his photographs were of Spiro fakes. He discovered that some decorated stone plummets "not only [are] not from Spiro, they are not even genuine."[61] He soon spotted fakes in numerous collections.[62] Pipes became a favorite of some forgers. In later years, Hamilton provided a list of rather prestigious museums that he believed possessed fake Spiro artifacts. These included the Witte Museum of San Antonio, Texas, which had a carved sandstone pipe in the shape of a mother with twins as well as a carved sandstone snake bowl. The museum at the School of the Ozarks in Point Lookout, Missouri, had a number of large human effigy pipes, all fake. The A. T. McDannald Collection at the Houston Museum of Fine Arts, Hamilton believed, also had several fake effigy pipes, as did the Gilcrease Museum in Tulsa. "It would be interesting to know if all of these originated with the same man," Hamilton wondered.[63] Since then, all these museums have recognized these specific pipes as fakes and labeled them as such.[64]

Matter of fact, one man, or maybe a couple of them, might have been responsible for many Spiro fakes. Not long after Spiro artifacts began hitting the curio market, *Hobbies* began running stories and editorials railing against forgeries. It was one thing if people wanted to duplicate Indian artwork, but it was something else to try to pass off these duplicates as originals.[65] There was also a debate over whether even restoring broken artifacts counted as forgery.[66] H. T. Daniel, one of the Dardanelle, Arkansas, relic dealers who had bought so much from the Pocola men, took exception to the tone in *Hobbies*. In a letter to the editor in the December 1935 edition, Daniel wrote that *Hobbies'* sky-is-falling attitude toward fakes only scared people off from buying authentic artifacts from reputable dealers. "While some publicity is necessary on the subject, it should be handled in such a way as to not reflect on the whole bunch of us, and the hobby in general."[67]

Daniel's letter was the height of hypocrisy because Daniel himself was the source of many forgeries. B. W. Stephens of Quincy, Illinois, bought a Spiro copper hairpin from Daniel. Whether he was suspicious or just curious, Quincy had the hairpin tested at the University of Illinois chemical laboratory, where it turned out to be just a piece of number 6 gauge copper wire. Soon others reported that artifacts they had bought from Daniel turned out to be fakes, including Trowbridge's drills and pipes. Eventually, Braecklein confronted Daniel about the forgeries. The dealer apparently admitted it and agreed to quit selling them, but not before selling his remaining fake drills "to suckers."[68] Nevertheless, when *Hobbies* found out about it, they refused to run his ads. From then on, things went bad for Daniel. His reputation was ruined, his business suffered, and his wife divorced him. Nevertheless, Daniel was still trying to palm off Spiro artifacts as late as the 1960s. After that, he faded from the Spiro story. As for Trowbridge, Braecklein commiserated with him. "I hate to see your fine collection have those fake drills. They are like a rotten apple in a barrel of fine ones."[69]

Other forgers were also at work. The name of John C. Pfalzgraf of tiny Poteau, Oklahoma, just a stone's throw from Spiro, often came up in connection with fakes. Pfalzgraf had sold Frank Phillips the fake frog pipe.[70] Whether sale of a forgery had been accidental or on purpose, it made Phillips suspicious enough of Pfalzgraf that when the dealer later offered other Indian items for sale, Phillips' secretary politely told him that her boss was not interested.[71] Suspicion trailed Pfalzgraf. Hamilton believed it was he who had sold the Witte Museum in San Antonio their fake sandstone pipes and bowls.[72]

In the long run, collectors and museums could do little about fakes other than try to chase down the originators and spread the word, maybe get the law on them if they could. The Pocola boys had looted the site without making many notes of what they had found or where. Then there had been so many side deals and individual selling sprees by diggers, partners, dealers, collectors, visitors, passersby, and locals that no one was sure who had sold what to whom. That meant no one knew exactly what came out of Spiro. And that made it easy for fakes to proliferate. After all, who could say what they had was not from the Great Temple Mound?

Therefore, Clements' dig would be all the more important. Whatever he found would be, as Phillips' secretary had exclaimed, "indisputably authentic."[73] Come the summer of 1936, Clements gathered his team and equipment to begin the excavation of what remained of Craig Mound.

9

The WPA Excavations

1936–1941

Archaeology is a tough mistress. Great finds make exciting headlines, but they come only after long, hard, often dull work. And it is not just braving the cold and the heat and the rain, knees and back aching from hunching over some half-buried artifact, that makes archaeology difficult. Paperwork, approvals, and legal niceties can take years before the first shovel ever cuts the ground. But Clements had done that part. He had fought the Pocola Mining Company, and though he had lost out on discovering the central chamber, what was left was to be his, at least his and his backers'. And he had done well in that too, getting some serious support from Frank Phillips, Clark Field, Alfred Reed, the Oklahoma Historical Society, even the federal government. Now the summer of 1936 would bring his reward. Craig Mound, what was left of it, was his to excavate.

Still, this was to be a major project, and Clements was a busy man. He was still chair of the Department of Anthropology at the University of Oklahoma, with classes to teach, meetings to attend, and other projects that needed guidance. At the same time, he had to oversee the Spiro excavation. In this respect, he served as a sort of army general. He assembled the crew, and then let them take over. He lived in Norman and would only periodically show up at the site, do a little excavation, see what was being found, show it off to the backers, buck up the troops, and be the front man for Spiro when the press came calling. His real work would come when all the artifacts had come back to his lab, where he and his students could study and interpret them.

To oversee the actual excavation, run the crew, decide where and how to dig, and basically know what was and was not important, Clements needed an officers corps of trained archaeologists to serve as project supervisors. He got most of these from the graduate schools at the University of Oklahoma. These were young, hardworking, earnest men and women, with a smattering knowledge of Mississippian Indian history and archaeological excavation techniques. They were not completely trained archaeologists at the time; none had a PhD or much excavation experience. Still, Clements used six thousand dollars from Frank Phillips to pay them and to purchase equipment.[1]

From 1936 until 1941, when Clements' excavation of Spiro ended, he utilized several different supervisors, including Fred Carder, J. J. Finklestein, Carl Ball, Lynn Howard, Kenneth G. Orr, Phil J. Newkumet, David Barreis, Rodney Cobb, and Sarah White, who later became Clements' wife.[2] However, Orr, who supervised from January 1938 until May 1939, and Newkumet, who served from 1938 to 1941, served longest and were most closely associated with the Spiro excavation. World War II interrupted the lives of both men, but after the war, they would work awhile together to analyze and interpret the Spiro artifacts. Orr would go on to receive his PhD in archaeology from the University of Chicago and would come back to the University of Oklahoma to teach. In later years, Orr's relationship with Clements soured, and he accused his boss of forcing him to kick back fifty dollars from every paycheck for "field expenses," a total of fifteen hundred dollars in Orr's case.[3] Newkumet would do his stint in the military and come back to the University of Oklahoma to finish his master's degree. He'd make his home in Norman, and eventually he would marry a Caddo woman, Vynola Beaver. Both would become very involved in Caddo cultural affairs.[4]

Beneath the project supervisors were a band of foremen, essentially the noncommissioned officers of the project. According to

Clements' rules, "foremen must be able to read and write and perform ordinary arithmetic operation and calculation. Must be able to handle a surveyor's level, stadia rod and tape. Must be able to intelligently fill out archaeological field data sheets and must understand technic [*sic*] of archaeological excavation. Must be able to write daily field reports. Must have had a least one year's experience on an archaeological excavation."[5]

Orr instructed his foremen to keep good records of their finds, particularly of complete or restorable pots, points, *manos*, *metataes*, bone awls, pipes, beads, flint knives, decorated sherds, and the like. They were not necessarily to worry too much about every piece of wattle, bone, or charcoal. Still, they were to provide date, site, grid number, feature number, square, location north and east from a southwest stake, location related to the ground's surface, and description of the artifact.[6] While there may have been more or others, seven men are recorded as foremen on the Spiro excavation at one time or another: Jess Jones, W. T. "Woody" Miles, C. R. "Roll" Mahar, J. E. "Bud" Hunter, Marvin Bradbury, Jim Tibbotts, and Cornelious "Fats" Shoates.[7]

These foremen oversaw a crew of about seventy excavators. "Excavators" might be overly romantic because these men were, for the most part, laborers. Using picks and shovels, they moved tons of dirt in wheelbarrows and mule-drawn carts. Most came from the local communities and had been what was termed "farm to market laborers," essentially hired farmhands or sharecroppers. Few had more than an eighth grade education, and many had less. As they worked, the foremen or supervisor noted if any displayed special skills, such as carpentry, rock masonry, painting, the ability to work survey chains, or the "ability to locate [archaeological] material and record it."[8] As the excavators worked on Spiro, they gained valuable experience, and many became very good at doing methodical archaeological excavations.

Seventy or more jobs in 1936, when the Great Depression had a chokehold on that part of Oklahoma, made the Spiro excavation a boon to many out-of-work men. Hundreds of men, white, black, and Indian, tried to hire on, and most came through the Works Progress Administration (WPA). Begun in 1935 under the auspices of President Roosevelt, the WPA was a government agency that put paychecks in the pockets of men and women by creating jobs for them. Unemployed Americans built roads, hospitals, and schools, cleared firebreaks and planted trees. They did whatever the government would pay them to do so that they could put food on the table. Spending their government money also meant getting the economy running again. Clements' Spiro excavation seemed a perfect WPA project.

Although the supervisors selected which men would dig on the project, the crew was actually hired through the WPA office in McAlester, Oklahoma, and government regulations often interfered. In those days, when racial segregation was the norm, white men received thirty-two dollars a month, black men only twenty-two dollars. Both could work for only eighteen months before they were dismissed from the rolls so that another person could be hired. That meant supervisors often had to fire some of their best men just when they finally knew what they were doing. Still, supervisors and the hired men found ways of manipulating the system, and many worked longer than eighteen months.[9] In the initial WPA Spiro excavations that went from May 1936 to February 1937, the federal government spent about eighteen thousand dollars, while local sources contributed between two and three thousand dollars.[10]

By June 1936, Clements had his crew together and was ready to begin moving dirt. A bunkhouse for his supervisors and a mess hall for the workers had been built on-site.[11] Once under way, the men worked five days a week, from early morning to late afternoon, eating lunch at the mess hall. Since Clements spent most of his time in Norman, his supervisors lived on-site during the week. Newkumet spent many evenings trying to glue broken artifacts back together.[12] On weekends he would take off to court Vynola. To watch over the site and storehouse and prevent further looting, he hired Cornelious Shoates, a large, amiable African American local.[13]

Since Clements had managed to acquire rights only to the Craig tract, he had his men concentrate on the north and largest lobe of Craig Mound, which had contained the central chamber. All could see the destruction left by the Pocola men, the gaping tunnels, even the jagged crack blasted open by the black powder explosion. Since the mound had already been looted and pretty much ruined, Clements realized it was useless to try to preserve it. He ordered his crew to excavate the mound using the profile system.

The profile system was a common method of archaeological excavation, but there was some controversy surrounding it. Some called it "slice and dice" archaeology.[14] Essentially, the Great Temple Mound would be sliced away, north to south, in ten-foot-wide row after ten-foot-wide row, just the way a loaf of bread was sliced. As they cut away the mound, any artifacts would temporarily be left in place on small pedestals of earth while work continued around them. Eventually the artifacts would be brushed clean, photographed in place, logged into the books, carefully removed to a storage area, and then later hauled to the University of Oklahoma archaeological laboratory in Norman. While the profile system meant Clements would find just about every remaining artifact, it would also completely destroy Craig Mound. Cut away slice by slice, there would be nothing left of it when finished. This type of archaeology was "not designed to recover stratigraphic relationships or large-scale features," explained archaeologist James Brown. Rather it "had as its objectives a systematic discovery of finds only."[15]

Though Craig Mound would be destroyed, it was not wanton destruction in the way the Pocola boys had gone at it. Each row had its own profile sheet, which indicated what had been found in it and where. Also, the excavators were careful, or as careful as they could be at that time, and had been instructed to look for burials, cache pits, specific artifacts, and such. They could tell the difference between buried material and surface material, even material that had come out of already disturbed areas.[16]

On the other hand, they were not as thorough as they could have been. In search of tiny artifacts and fragments, they screened some of the dirt the Pocola miners had left behind, but apparently Clements' crew members did not screen their own dirt. This they just hauled away and later used to refill excavated areas. Even then, WPA excavators sometimes just filled sacks with potsherds and left them in storage. This meant the diggers lost all context to their work as well as many small items that could tell much about Spiro's history.[17]

Amazingly, after two years of continual looting by the Pocola Mining Company, Craig Mound still contained a considerable number of artifacts. Skeletons, some large effigy pipes, a few pieces of feather fabric, engraved conch shells, copper breastplates, flint arrow points, pottery, cedar litter poles, beads, and much more turned up.[18] Again, this is testament to just how rich Spiro actually was. For his backers, the investment paid off. Clements found so much Spiro material that he gladly spread the wealth around to their museums. A Spiro exhibition opened at the University of Tulsa on January 28, 1938.[19] He donated a skeleton, some pearls, a large polished stone celt, and a carved wooden rattle to Frank Phillips' Woolaroc Museum.[20] The University of Oklahoma loaned several Spiro pieces for a show at the Museum of Modern Art in New York City in early 1941.[21] Many artifacts given to Clark Field eventually wound up in Tulsa's Philbrook Museum of Art and later at that city's famed Gilcrease Museum.

Overall, the dig did not go badly, but problems often cropped up. Rain could turn the mound into a quagmire, which could be especially destructive to artifacts awaiting removal, items that had not seen sunshine or rain for over five hundred years.[22] Summers in Oklahoma were always bad, and malaria took out several men for days, including supervisor Newkumet.[23] Winter brought its own bad weather, and the excavations usually came to halt.[24] In the five years Clements conducted excavations at Craig Mound, from June 1936 to October 1941, only about two years of actual digging took place.[25]

It was only a matter of time before the monster of race reared its head. Clements, Orr, and Newkumet insisted that the crew be integrated, and they had no qualms about mixing white and black laborers in their work crews. Photographs of the 1936 excavation show whites and blacks digging together, and Shoates was a foreman.[26] However, the archaeologists had no control over the WPA's pay differential for white and black laborers.

Nor could they always control local prejudice. Although the early 1936–1937 excavations seemed pretty trouble free, racial prejudice got worse during the 1939 excavations. In August 1939, some of the white members of the excavation crew began complaining about working with blacks. Even local community leaders visited Supervisor Newkumet at the site and insisted on a "no negroes allowed" policy.[27] Newkumet negotiated as best he could and came up with a plan. Whites would continue work around Spiro, while the black excavators would dig on Skidgel Mound. Shoates was reassigned as a cook and guard and kept at Spiro, as was another black man, Buster Bunch. Newkumet was determined that Shoates and Bunch be allowed to stay with him at Spiro, even "if I have to use artillery."[28] The community leaders agreed as long as the other blacks were sent to Skidgel. Still, the racially colorblind Newkumet noted in his field diary how upset the whole controversy made him. "Am very sorry [I] can't use a little force on this question. Both whites and Indians appear to be agin [sic] the Negroes here now that we have settled. Am sure that I can keep things smooth. Can't afford to have any trouble in this situation."[29]

Most men worked hard, but digging through burial mounds, opening graves, and uncovering skeletons could get a little unnerving. Shoates, before being reassigned to cook, dug into a grave of skeletons and was appalled, after all these years, at the stench of death.[30] For months, superstitious George Baxter would not step over a skeleton. Although he later grew used to it, he never joked about the burials the way some men did, believing that to be bad luck.[31] When Mrs. Edison Barnes visited her husband at Spiro, she was shocked to see him working among the skeletons. "They had 32 of them skeletons dug. His job was he picked the dirt out from under their teeth . . . Oh, 32 of them. They'd dig down around them, you know. Oh, I'd never went to sleep that night."[32] It got worse for Iva Mayhar Chelf, whose husband worked on the site. One Christmas, needing a place to store a skeleton encased in plaster of Paris before sending it to Norman, her husband brought it home and put it in their bedroom. Iva was not sleeping in her bedroom that night. "That thing's likely to crawl in bed with me," she wailed.[33]

Although the excavators probably did not have to worry too much about spooks or ghosts, cave-ins were real dangers. On January 12, 1939, the collapse of a dirt wall at Skidgel Mound, where most black excavators were working, killed one man and crippled another. Pot hunters had tunneled into the mound during the great artifact rush, but the tunnel had been concealed, and excavators did not realize it was there. As they cut close to the tunnel, it collapsed, and a part of the mound toppled over. Bill Harris was killed instantly when three feet of dirt crashed down on him, crushing his skull and breaking his neck. Sam Reynolds was severely injured in his back and hips and apparently crippled for the rest of his life. A third man, John Collins, just managed to throw himself clear.[34] Later, an excavator named Richard Eubanks became ill and died on the site.[35] Of course, this just got everyone talking about the curse of Spiro Mounds and spooked the workers all over again.

Still, fatalities, ancient curses, and decaying skeletons did not seem to keep anyone away. Locals quickly realized that the Spiro excavation could be prime Sunday afternoon entertainment. Crowds of onlookers often drove down to see the dig and what was coming out of it. With Orr or Newkumet gallivanting around the countryside on weekends, it often fell to Shoates, left guarding the place, to interpret things. "The new people would like you to sit and explain to them," Shoates recalled. "They wants to know what is this stuff, and what do you think about it, and how long it's been here, and I don't know."[36]

Just as bad, stray archaeologists often showed up, and every now and again, Clements would bring his backers. Clark Field of Tulsa, the wealthy philanthropist who was also chair of the Oklahoma State Archaeological Society, would come down to take pictures of the excavation. He would usually bring along friends and family, particularly his daughter Dorothy, who was fascinated by Spiro. When they came out, they did a little light digging and artifact brushing.[37] Frank Phillips and Alfred Reed made their own trips to Spiro.[38] Usually a few days before Clements' backers showed up, he would send a menu down to Cornelious Shoates so that he could have a big dinner cooked up.[39]

Clements' visits could cause headaches for the workers. In late 1938, the archaeologist decided to make a film of the Spiro excavation, which would feature some of his backers. Titled *The Spiro Mound*, Clements believed it would be great to show to archaeological clubs as a fundraiser.[40] Reality did not meet expectations. The film turned out to be more of a home movie, twelve hundred reel feet made with a handheld sixteen-millimeter camera. According to George Baxter, one of the workers at Spiro, the movie caused the diggers all sorts of problems. Excavating at Spiro was already hard, sweaty work, but when Clements began rolling the film, "everyone was required to work twice as hard to impress the film audience." So everyone loaded up on water before filming because they knew there would not be any water breaks during the shoot.[41] Clements' film would have been a great archaeological treasure, but over the past seventy years, it was not properly stored and is now too fragile to be viewed.

Although Clements had the right to dig the main part of Craig Mound, he realized that to understand Spiro, he needed to excavate other parts of the site and surrounding locations as well. While getting things together for the 1936 Craig Mound excavation, Clements also managed to talk Bill and Mamie Brown into leasing him Brown Mound for two years, the lease to expire in March 1938.[42] The Brown Mound excavation proved difficult from the start. Seems the Brown's property line ran directly across the mound, but they owned only the south one-third of the mound. The north two-thirds was owned jointly by seven people, but only three would agree to let Clements excavate it. So while Clements sliced and diced the south third of Brown Mound, finding only a few graves and a temple, the north two-thirds remained relatively untouched.[43]

Still, the Browns had high expectations from the lease. In April 1938, Newkumet recalled a visit from Mamie Brown. She'd been drinking and was "six sheets in the wind, mad as a flock of wet turkeys." She was "wanting to know 'when is ah going to git my third of all that valuable stuff you is been hauling out of my mound.?!!!'"[44] She never would.

The first round of excavations on the Great Temple Mound and Brown Mound ended in spring 1937. The site was left guarded to prevent the return of the Pocola men or any other pot hunters. The next push began in spring 1938, and by the end of that year, Craig Mound would be completely leveled. Once that was done, Clements and his crew turned to further excavations around the Spiro site itself while expanding their search to surrounding settlements. On the Spiro site, Clements now searched for houses, using test trenches several feet deep and about five feet wide. Many were found, showing the sheer size of Spiro in its heyday.[45]

As the Spiro excavations wound down in 1938, Clements concentrated on surrounding sites. Newkumet often drove around the area looking for them. And he found plenty. Sometimes he might be tipped off about the location of a village site, and sometimes it would be a wild-goose chase; other times something was actually there.[46] Like the Browns, landowners saw Clements's interest as a profit-making opportunity. If the WPA boys wanted to excavate, they were going to have to pay for it.[47] Landowners usually had their price list ready. Louis Jones, who had ten acres near Skidgel Mound, wanted one dollar for every ten-foot-square hole and ten dollars for every hundred-foot-square hole. Whether Jones got that or not is another question.[48]

Naturally, once Clements, Newkumet, and their WPA crew showed an interest in any area, schemes cranked into motion. Now there were offers to lease the land, not so it could be pot hunted, but so it could be rerented to the WPA. At other times, landowners would try to entice the WPA to their property. During an initial inspection of one bit of land, they found the owner, Copeland, very cooperative but wanting some money for the lease. While Newkumet was walking the tract, Copeland's neighbor whispered that Newkumet should forget digging on Copeland's land and come rent his own.[49]

In all, Newkumet and his crew excavated scores of sites between 1938 and 1941. Skidgel Mound was sliced into nonexistence by mid-December 1939.[50] Many other villages were found and burials uncovered. In one, Newkumet found a skeleton with an arrowpoint broken off in the bone.[51] Then, after they were finished, the WPA crew had to refill their diggings so that the farmers could plant their crops.[52] It was a big job for Newkumet. As a short biographical sheet on him detailed, he "was responsible for surveying, mapping, photography, public relations, artistic work, and some basic analysis of the material." Nevertheless, "he approached his work with the idea of simply salvaging as much material as possible in the limited time span afforded by the leases, in order that the trained archaeologists could later return to the material and perform a formal analysis."[53]

Of course, the biggest problem Clements and Newkumet faced during the excavations was the same one that they had faced from the very beginning: pot hunters and relic dealers. Clements' excavation of Spiro, as well as the earlier "'King Tut' Tomb" story, all focused attention on the area as a place where Indian relics abounded. Pot hunters continued to descend on Le Flore County and on the Poteau River Valley, digging for artifacts, searching along the rivers and tributaries for any that might have been washed up. It became a continual hunt, and pot hunters' holes scarred the land like smallpox.[54] Long before it was leveled by Clements and the WPA, Skidgel Mound had been tunneled into by pot hunters, which resulted in the death of Bill Harris.[55] Other sites got destroyed the same way.[56] Though Clements had Craig Mound, and he might have the antiquities act on his side, he was way too busy to do anything about the illegal digs.

The area really was a treasure trove of Mississippian artifacts. At Spiro, and just about everywhere else within a several-mile radius, artifacts could almost be kicked up out of the ground.[57] Shoates, who farmed just a mile or so away from Craig Mound, found all sorts of artifacts on his property. Besides arrowheads on the ridges, Shoates "plowed up a body. I plowed up a skull. I plowed up a conch shell with some of this same engraving." He even discovered a method to finding buried artifacts by searching for the lighter, paler earth, where the darker topsoil had eroded away.[58] That so many sites were being potted attested to Spiro's great size and the influence it wielded seven hundred years earlier.

For the more experienced local pot hunters, why dig for artifacts when the government was digging them up for you? No matter how hard Clements, Orr, Newkumet, and the foremen tried to keep an eye on the artifacts, many of the items secretly wound up in the pockets of their laborers. Virtually everybody associated with the Spiro digs walked away with a collection of artifacts. For some, these became personal keepsakes, kept in shoeboxes, something to show the grandkids. Still, there was always pressure on them to give away something, especially to the Sunday visitors. They would see an arrowhead or a clay pot on Cornelious Shoates's desk, and as Shoates remembered, they would say "'Boy, I sure would like to have it,' and I'd just give it to you." While friends always benefited from Shoates's generosity, he drew the line at professional relic hunters. "I would never try to take advantage and try and sell that stuff, because I was responsible, and I had it in my charge."[59]

Other workers were not so scrupulous. They pocketed artifacts for the sole purpose of selling them. With that attitude floating around Spiro, John Hobbs, Columbus Eubanks, who had been one the diggers for the Pocola Mining Company, and others began prowling the edges of the excavation.[60] Often they would buy what they could from willing laborers. Other times, they outright stole from the excavation site. And there was no honor among thieves. Edison Barnes, one of the diggers at Spiro, recalled finding a very nice clay pot. He and some fellow conspirators covered it up with the idea of retrieving it that evening and selling it to the relic dealers. But John Hobbs had already spotted them. When Barnes went back that night, the pot was gone, and Barnes knew Hobbs had taken it. "He gathered up a lot of stuff," Barnes said. "He found a stone pipe that didn't have a chip knocked out it no where. It was perfect."[61] Even after Craig Mound was totally flattened, Hobbs picked over its bones, looking for anything that might have been overlooked.[62] Columbus Eubanks also gained a reputation as man getting his share of Spiro goods.[63]

By October 1941, Clements' and the WPA's digging around Le Flore County came to an end. Craig, Skidgel, and much of Brown mounds had been flattened. Other sites had been investigated. Thousands of artifacts and skeletons had been hauled back to the University of Oklahoma for analysis. But it was also an end to an era. When the United States entered World War II in December 1941, excavations and interpretation of the Spiro material came to a halt. With a war to win, people associated with the Spiro story scattered across the world. Clements left the University of Oklahoma to take a job in the war effort. The military called away Orr, Newkumet, Cooper, and many of the WPA diggers as well. Except for relic hunters who might pot around the site in hopes something might turn up, it was the last real Spiro excavation for decades. The artifact rush was over.

Ever since, archaeologists have been unsure what to think of Clements' Spiro excavation. In some ways, it was too big and too ambitious. Like so much early archaeology, it focused on the finds and not on relationships of the items to the site. But who could blame him? The site had been savagely looted, so there was little time, money, and trained labor to do it right.

And with the added pressure of the pot hunters and relic dealers snapping at his heels, it was amazing Clements got what he did.[64] Still, after the war, Spiro would enter a new era, not only for the site itself, but for its interpretation as well.

10

The Spiro Mysteries

1941–Present

From the moment John Hobbs and company dug out their first artifact from Craig Mound, questions began swirling about Spiro and its people. Essentially, all were the same question Thomas Jefferson had asked so many years ago: Who built the mounds? Many rightly attributed them to Indians. Forrest Clements certainly did. He believed everything that came out of Spiro was Indian. The *Oklahoma City Times* agreed, marveling that "while Charlemagne was receiving the crown of the Holy Roman Emperor in Europe, this weird race of Indians was carving their remarkable beads, chipping stone knives, and erecting mounds."[1] But what Indians? And could the Indians who lived in Oklahoma in the twentieth century—the Caddos, Wichitas, Cherokees, Choctaws, Comanches, or whoever—could any of their ancestors have really been the ones who built Spiro?[2] Many thought not.

When a reporter asked Braecklein who built Spiro, the collector pointed out that "you will find similar pictographs or hieroglyphic inscriptions on the ruins of the ancient Egyptians along the Nile and on the ruins of the Mayans of Yucatan. . . . When you ask who built this mound, the only answer is the echo of your own question within the vault that has been hidden in darkness within this mound for no one knows how many centuries. The dead past has surely buried its dead within this mound."[3]

A Maya and Aztec connection to Spiro soon became a popular theory. Professional archaeologists and others in the know believed it. Paul Nesbitt, head of Beloit College's Department of Anthropology, studied a Spiro pipe and announced it was of Maya or Inca origin.[4] Glen Groves, president of the NAIRCA and defender of the Pocola miners, certainly thought so, terming Spiro "a colonization project." In his mind, Spiro became a sort of Maya candle in the darkness. "It seems just as logical that they may have dispatched expeditions in to the unknown, for scientific reasons, and that they made their last stand here against the savage tribes of the unknown."[5] The *Kansas City Star* certainly agreed, commenting that the engravings on the conch shells "look decidedly like those of Maya art, depicting men paddling a canoe, priests conducting a religious ceremony, etc."[6]

Until fairly recent times, a Maya or Aztec connection to the great Mississippian cities was accepted by many archaeologists and historians. The spread of corn, the pyramid temple mounds, the priest-chiefs and their rituals, it all seemed similar to the ancient Indian societies of Mexico and Central America. And the spectacular artwork with similar images coming out of Spiro just reinforced the idea. As late as 1993, the renowned historian Francis Jennings wrote that "it would seem that groups of the Mesoamericans established themselves as trading elites among hunting peoples, teaching the wonders of horticulture to the hunters and acquiring prestige in the process. Whereupon they put up pyramids and placed themselves on top to make their superiority unquestionable."[7]

By the turn of the twenty-first century, the Mexican invasion idea had lost favor. Archaeological studies across the Southeast just did not turn up much of a Maya, an Aztec, or a Valley of Mexico influence. It seems the great Mississippian cities of the American Southeast were home grown. Nevertheless, back in the 1930s, '40s and '50s, Spiro artwork seemed to drive the theories. The shell engravings and embossed copper sheets reminded people of other cultures, and made some think Mayan.

However, still others said only white people had the knowledge and ability to build these mounds. One newspaper, attributing the idea to Dellinger of the University of Arkansas, declared that Spiro proved "the existence of white men here before 1492."[8]

And there was one particular piece of Spiro artwork that made some people point toward Roman Catholic Europe. The bishop plate, as a large piece of engraved conch shell came to be called, fell into the hands of Jack Reed, that proud Arkansan who funneled so much Spiro artwork to the University of Arkansas. To Reed, the bishop plate clearly depicted the coronation of a Roman Catholic bishop. The engravings show a man seated on what looks like a throne, holding a staff, the kind Catholic bishops carried as symbols of office. The figure seems to be dressed like a bishop, complete with a long robe and maniple. A halo appears about his head, and incense wafts from an altar. Reed showed the bishop plate to Fayetteville, Arkansas, monsignor Walter Tynin. The monsignor, speaking only for himself and not for the Church, said he thought it looked a lot like a Catholic bishop, too.[9]

Reed could put it all together in his head, and he wove an incredible story. As he saw it, a colony of Catholic Danish Vikings left Iceland in the tenth or eleventh century and came to America. They sailed down the eastern seaboard into the Gulf of Mexico, up the Mississippi, up the Arkansas, and finally settled at Spiro. There they built the Great Temple Mound. The engraved shell commemorated the consecration of the first Catholic bishop in America. Later on, when a rune stone with apparently Scandinavian writing on it was found at nearby Heavener, Oklahoma, many thought Jack Reed might be on to something.[10] Others thought the shell depicted a Spanish bishop, even identifying him as Friar Padilla of the 1540s.[11] The Masonic Order chimed in and said the bishop plate proved that Masons were in America as early as the 1500s.[12] Though many wanted to buy it, the shell eventually wound up in the collections of the University of Arkansas.[13] Unfortunately, a recent search by museum personnel could not match any of their shells with Reed's description.

It did not matter that Forrest Clements went out of his way to convince people that Spiro was Indian. They wanted to see white and could not believe Indians could do this sort of work.[14] Countering Reed's Catholic Viking bishop, the Latter Day Saints saw Spiro as proving the Book of Mormon. Charles B. Woodstock, who said he was from the Department of Religious Education of the Reorganized Church of Jesus Christ of Latter Day Saints, saw Spiro artifacts as having a Hebrew origin but strongly influenced by Egypt and Syria. This fit in nicely with Mormon beliefs that Indians were descended from the Lost Tribes of Israel. According to Woodstock, the Book of Mormon "also gives an account of a former colony from Bible lands which came from 2200 B.C." Could Spiro be it?[15]

In later years, Gloria Farley, a historian from the Le Flore County area, discovered a small engraved stone tablet from Spiro at a local museum. She believed she recognized the inscription as being ancient Libyan hieroglyphics. It told a story from ancient Egyptian mythology, of how every day a boat carried the god Ra across the sky, and at the end of his day journey, he was attacked by the serpent Aapep, which he defeated. The boat then carried him back through the night to his dawn starting point. Of course, the Libyan inscription made it thousands of years older than the time of Spiro. So how did it wind up in the central chamber? From ancient Libyan traders or explorers who came to Oklahoma thousands of years ago, Farley wrote. "Apparently it had been handed down through the centuries as a sacred object, from Libyan to Indian to Indian, to be preserved as a special treasure with the bodies of Spiro's great personages."[16]

Of course, all this speculation might have been put to rest once the artifacts at the University of Oklahoma could be studied. However, World War II had not only put an end to excavations, it also delayed study of the material. Clements left the University of Oklahoma for war work, and it does not seem that he ever got his job back at the university. Kenneth Orr and Phil Newkumet went off to the military. But as the war wound down and the Allied victory was just a matter of time, archaeological interest in Spiro artifacts picked up again. Now the question was, Who would get to study them? After all, interpreting Spiro could make an academic career.

Naturally, Clements thought he should be the one; after all, it had been his project from the start. However, his former righthand man Kenneth Orr, who had received his PhD from the University of Chicago before the war and was then serving as a sergeant in the army, made his own claim in late 1944. Still smarting from having to kick back fifty dollars every payday to Clements, Orr wrote J. Willis Stovall at the University of Oklahoma that he, not Clements, was the most qualified to undertake the study. Orr spelled it out. Clements was not a real archaeologist but really a physical anthropologist who had never published anything in archaeological publications. Not only that, Clements had never really been involved in the excavation of Spiro. He had just shown up every four or five months and gotten most of his information from his site supervisors, like Orr. Finally, Clements just wanted to restore pottery and create show pieces. He was not really interested in researching the site or its people.[17]

Orr then ticked off his own qualifications. He had been project superintendent at the Spiro excavations from January 1938 to February 1939. He had done the lab work on Spiro and had excavated other mounds around Spiro and in other counties as well. He had already published articles on Spiro and mounds in general, and his PhD dissertation at the University of Chicago dealt with Spiro. Now he wanted to write a series of articles on the site, as well as conduct future excavations and research.[18] Orr's reasoning must have swayed Stovall because even before Orr was discharged from the army in 1945, he had been named an assistant professor at the University of Oklahoma and chair of its Department of Anthropology. He had even received a scientific demobilization award of nineteen hundred dollars, which was given to certain scientists whose work had been interrupted by the war.[19]

In 1946 Orr published the first real scholarly work on Spiro, "The Archaeological Situation at Spiro, Oklahoma: A Preliminary Report," in *American Antiquity*. Clements, other than his "Historical Sketch of Spiro Mound" in 1945, published nothing else on Spiro. Not a member of the University of Oklahoma faculty anymore, he did not have access to the artifacts. Where he went after this is unclear. He seems to have truly faded from history. Even the University of Oklahoma archives cannot seem to locate a picture of him. For the man who fought for the mounds, who had saved and excavated what was left of Craig Mound, this was a hard personal defeat and a sad end to a major participant in the Spiro story.

In his article, Orr was one of the first to state that Spiroans were Caddoan peoples. The archaeological record and location of Spiro in the middle of a Caddo area indicated this. However, "Caddoan" is a term for a language spoken by peoples along the margins of the prairies and Great Plains. It also designates a distinct culture with certain ways of making pottery and conducting their lives. In a way, "Caddoan" could be equated with a term like Scandinavian. Though Scandinavians might share a similar language and culture, they eventually became Danes, Norwegians, Swedes, Icelanders, and Finns. In that same light, after 1450, Caddoans eventually became the Caddo proper who lived along the Red River and its tributaries in northwestern Louisiana, northeastern Texas, southeastern Oklahoma, and southwestern Arkansas. But Caddoans also included the Wichitas and Kichais of the Texas panhandle, western Oklahoma, and Central Kansas; the Pawnees of Kansas and Nebraska; and the Arikaras along the Missouri River. But which of these Indian nations, if any, were the descendants of Spiroans?

And that became the new mystery and controversy. When Spiroans walked away from Craig Mound around 1420, they walked away for good. Skidgel Mound and many other sites remained occupied for another hundred years, maybe less. Then during the sixteenth century, the Spiro region and eastern Oklahoma seemed to shed itself of people. All the small communities that had once existed around Spiro were abandoned as well. By the mid-1500s, certainly by 1600, nobody lived in the Spiro region anymore. And nobody would reside there permanently until the Choctaws arrived in the 1830s. So the mystery of Spiro continued. Where did the Spiroans go? What became of them? Whom did they become?[20]

Orr strongly associated Spiro with the Caddo proper along the Red River. Their pottery and pipes were very similar, as were their tools, mounds, burials, social system, and economy.[21] As Orr and others saw it, when the unpredictable climate finally caused the Spiro center to collapse in the early 1400s, many Spiroans, culturally similar to the Red River Caddos, and long involved in trade with them, naturally migrated south and joined them. Spiro refugees helped form the Kadohadacho chiefdom at the Great Bend of the Red River near Texarkana as well as the Hasinai chiefdom in the river valleys of East Texas. For years, this remained the chief interpretation concerning what became of the Spiroans.[22] Today's Caddo Indians, with their tribal headquarters near Binger, Oklahoma, certainly believe this. They claim Spiro as an ancient homeland and its artwork, wherever it may sit, as their own.

During the 1970s, archaeologist Don Wyckoff of the University of Oklahoma introduced a different theory. As Spiro broke down and the weather made farming in eastern Oklahoma tenuous at best, Spiroans migrated west and began hunting buffalo. They took their knowledge of farming with them and planted gardens of corn, beans, squash, and sunflowers along the rivers and streams cutting across the plains. Their many years of trade relations with the buffalo-hunting peoples on the plains helped facilitate this, and Spiro shell breastplates, pipes, and ear spools show up in village sites around the Washita River in western Oklahoma.

As Wyckoff saw it, there on the plains, the Spiroans and the Plains peoples melded to form the Wichita and Kichai peoples.[23] In his own archaeological investigations around Oklahoma and Kansas, Wyckoff noted many similarities, such as tools, houses, and burials, between Spiroans and Wichitas. At one site in central Kansas, Wyckoff saw burials and pottery that very much reminded him of Spiro. He believed this site "could represent a situation in which people living in the Arkansas Valley region of Oklahoma had moved further west out onto the plains. There, they might have attempted to establish and maintain the kind of political and social system that they had had in eastern Oklahoma."[24]

Today, most scholars go with either the Caddo or Wichita interpretation. Many accept that at least some Spiroans, as the chiefdom collapsed, moved south to the Caddos or west to the Wichitas. In 1540, the Spanish conquistador Francisco Vázquez de Coronado and his men crossed the plains and passed through Wichita villages that meandered for miles along river valleys, surrounded by great fields of beans and corn. In many ways, Wyckoff's Wichita theory has carried the day. Part of this may stem from Wyckoff's positions on the Oklahoma Archaeology Survey and at the Sam Noble Oklahoma Museum of Natural History. Being one of Oklahoma's most renowned archaeologists, his authority and reputation certainly enabled him to popularize and entrench his theory, which shows up in books and articles on Spiro. The official slide show and pamphlet on Spiro says they became Wichitas. The Wichita Indians of Oklahoma accept it, though their tribal leaders rarely comment about the Wichita connection to Spiro.[25]

Since the Caddos and the Wichitas are both Caddoan peoples, does it really matter which one claims Spiro? Potentially yes, because there could be millions of dollars worth of artifacts at stake. In 1990, Congress passed the Native American Grave Protection and Repatriation Act, an attempt to return human remains, burial goods, and sacred objects held in federally funded museums and universities to the Indian peoples to whom they belong. Could either the Caddos or the Wichitas prove to these institutions' satisfaction that they are the indeed the legitimate descendants of Spiroan peoples, they could potentially receive a windfall of all Spiroan goods now being held in American museums, particularly the Smithsonian's Museum of the American Indian and the University of Oklahoma Sam Noble Museum. There are thousands of Spiro objects worth millions of dollars in museums across the United States.

This does not mean either the Caddos or the Wichitas are demanding an immediate return of Spiro artifacts. Both Indian nations understand the value of these goods, and both realize that they do not have a museum or security system in place to protect the artifacts. Right now, the artifacts are safer in the custody of the museums. However, the day may come when the Caddos or Wichitas or both build a secure museum, and then we will see which nation can make the best claim to Spiro. Of course, keeping the argument going about which tribe is descended from Spiro and who should possess the artifacts works to the museums' and universities' favor. If archaeologists or government officials cannot determine whether they should go to the Caddos or Wichitas, then the artifacts remain with the museum.[26]

This continuing argument has even affected the archaeological research of Spiro material. For example, at the Sam Noble Oklahoma Museum of Natural History on the University of Oklahoma campus at Norman, for a researcher to examine Spiroan skeletal material and virtually any item considered a burial object, he or she must get written permission from both the Caddos and the Wichitas. On one hand, the Caddos, wanting to prove their connection to Spiro, often give permission for research. However, Wichita tribal officials hardly ever grant research permission and rarely will even talk about Spiro. This goes even for publishing pictures of some Spiro items, and many photos were not allowed to be used for this book. This rule certainly prevents the Caddos from proving they are Spiro descendants and at the same time prevents the Wichitas from being excluded.

If the contest between the Caddos and Wichitas for Spiro were not enough, in the 1990s, Frank Schambach, an archaeologist at Southern Arkansas University at Magnolia, roiled the waters even more. Schambach claimed that neither the Caddos nor the Wichitas were heirs to Spiro. Its real descendants were the Tunica Indians who presently live on a small tract of land near Marksville, Louisiana. The way Schambach saw it, as the unpredictable weather broke down the chiefdom, Spiroans moved east, down the Arkansas River into western Arkansas. There they grew crops and continued trading for buffalo hides and tools with their old trading partners in central Oklahoma, around the Nagle site. Those plains buffalo hunters were then in the process of becoming Wichitas. When the remnants of Hernando De Soto's expedition moved up the Arkansas River in 1541, they got within a hundred miles east of Spiro, where they met the Tula people whom the Spanish described as possessing thousands of buffalo hides and having long, tapered cone-like heads. These tapered-skull Tulans, says Schambach, were the descendants of Spiro.[27]

By the late seventeenth century, the Tula had moved down the Arkansas and across the Mississippi River to the Yazoo River basin in western Mississippi. As the French settled Louisiana in the early eighteenth century, the Tula moved to the mouth of the Red River to trade with both the English colonies to the east and the French in Louisiana. Now called the Tunica, which sounds rather similar to Tula, their Spiro history made them avid traders in the area. The Tunicas acquired guns and merchandise from the French along the Mississippi River, then carried these goods into East Texas to trade with the Wichitas and Caddos for horses, bois d'arc bows, and buffalo hides to carry back to the French.[28] As Schambach saw it, it was the same old Spiro trade network that had been running for centuries, just the new prestige goods were not shells and pipes but European guns and kettles.

Schambach associated Spiro with the Tunica for several reasons. First, he believed Spiroans relied more on hunting and gathering than on growing corn. So did the Tunicas, who often spent a month with their families in the woods gathering things like persimmons. Among the Tunica, the men, not the women, were tanners of buffalo hides and were considered masters of it, but they earned this reputation even though there were not any buffalo in western Mississippi or central Louisiana. To Schambach, this knowledge must have passed down to them from their Spiro ancestors who had long been involved in the buffalo hide trade. Salt trading was another connection. Spiroans had acquired salt from a site near Russellville, Arkansas. As the Spiroans moved downriver, they took over this site. In later years, the Tunica dominated this salt works, even trading salt to Plains peoples for buffalo hides. The Tunica origin myth says they came from a more mountainous area, but there are no mountains in the Yazoo River Valley, which scholars had long considered to be the Tunica ancestral home. Schambach says the mountainous area was more than likely the Ouachita or Ozark mountains of eastern Oklahoma near Spiro. Finally, the Tulans' tapered, conelike heads suggest a connection. The Tulans were the descendants of Spiroans, and this type of head molding, Schambach said, was characteristic of Spiro traders.[29]

Schambach's Tunica argument caused a row among those doing Spiro studies. It was met with skepticism by those who advocated a Wichita or Caddo connection. And Schambach himself routinely gets panned by colleagues in the field. Mention Schambach and his Tunica thesis, and you will likely get a heavy sigh, a snort of derision, a shrug of the shoulders, or a roll of the eyes. Naturally, the Caddos do not like his argument, and the Wichitas, though they are not talking, certainly cannot agree with him either. However, despite their criticism, his detractors have never disproved his argument, so he soldiers on, taking a whole new angle on the Spiro story.

Though the Caddos, Wichitas, and even Tunicas might maintain that their descent from Spiro gives them control over Spiro artwork, nineteenth-century treaty rights might make the Choctaws into Spiro players. The land on which the Spiro

Mounds sits was guaranteed to the Choctaws in the removal treaties they negotiated with the United States government in the 1830s. Though the Atoka Agreement of 1897 broke up Choctaw lands, and the Curtis Act of 1898 disbanded the Choctaw government for years, the Choctaw Nation has fought for the restoration of treaty guarantees ever since. It would not be surprising for the Choctaws to demand some type of say on the disposition of artifacts found on land they claim as their own. So even the Choctaws might find themselves part of the Spiro story.

But what was the Spiro story? No one is really sure. The twentieth-century arguments about who the Spiroans were and what became of them indicated that real research needed to be done. However, many academics felt the looting and WPA excavations had compromised the site to such an extent that it was useless to try for any interpretation. World War II did not help, delaying for years any research at just the time when the artifacts were coming out of the ground. And as the artifacts got taken off the market, bought up by museums and collectors, most people forgot about Spiro. After Orr's article in 1946, with a few other minor ones in the late forties, and Henry Hamilton's pictorial essay on the artifacts published in the *Missouri Archaeologist* in 1952, most researchers paid no more attention.[30]

Even the site of the once great city itself was abandoned and ignored. With Craig Mound flattened, Brown Mound severely scarred, and other mounds just as wounded, the place was deserted. A pot hunter might show up every now and again and hope for the best. As late as 1964, H. T. Daniel and others were still selling Spiro artifacts, both originals and fakes.[31] But most people had just forgotten about the place. Though the Oklahoma Historical Society still owned the Craig Mound tract, the forest was slowly reclaiming it.

Then in mid-1960s came a renewed interest in Spiro and Spiro archaeology. Sparking both was a potential threat to the site itself. In the 1960s, the federal government initiated a huge Arkansas River project. The Army Corps of Engineers planned on building a series of locks and dams that would control flooding, provide irrigation, and make the river more conducive to boat traffic and recreation. One of the locks, W. D. Mayo Lock and Dam 14, was to be located near Spiro, and the river terraces on which Spiro sat were slated to be used as fill.

Concerned locals protested the move, believing that making the site into a park would draw tourists. Fortunately, Robert Black, a regional planner for the corps of engineers, once he heard about the ancient chiefdom, became a strong supporter of saving Spiro. He not only agreed to move the lock and dam to spare the site but had the corps purchase additional land around the mounds, then lease it to the State of Oklahoma so that the site could be made into a park.[32] The corps could only do so much, though, and a citizen's committee would have to come up with the money for paving, grading, and building any park facilities.[33]

Even before the Arkansas River project was under way, some archaeologists had rediscovered Spiro. Once again, it was the fantastic artifacts that caught their eyes. Most new archaeologists had been graduate students going through the Heye Museum collections in the 1960s, where they had been amazed at Spiro's engraved conch shells and effigy pipes. James A. Brown, Jon Mueller, Jeffrey Brain, Philip Phillips and others became very interested in Spiro.[34] However, they were a new breed of archaeologists. Like Clements before them, they believed that sites should be left to academically trained professionals, but they were not necessarily interested in finding an amazing artifact. They saw archaeology, along with the cross-disciplines of anthropology and history, as providing a means of explaining the people who had lived at Spiro. They wanted context and interpretation more than they wanted a big ticket item to put on display. In this, they were much more like Kenneth Orr than like Clements. So are most modern archaeologists. Though they differ on interpretation, Don Wyckoff and Frank Schambach certainly fall into this same new breed, to whom understanding culture is the key. The shells and coppers are beautiful and interesting, but only in what they can tell us about the Spiro people.

Of all those recent archaeologists, James A. Brown of Chicago's Northwestern University has become most associated with Spiro. He's written extensively on the mounds and was one of the first since Kenneth Orr to try to interpret the artifacts. In early 1964, Brown received a thirty-thousand-dollar grant from the National Science Foundation for a two-year study of Spiro. He would work with University of Oklahoma anthropology professor Robert Bell, the same man who as a young graduate student saved some of the relics being excavated by the Pocola Mining Company. Now, Brown and Bell, along with a host of University of Oklahoma archaeology graduate students, planned on studying seventy-six thousand Spiro artifacts dug up by the WPA workers. From this, Brown hoped to develop a picture of Spiroan life and culture, how the artifacts were used, and how Spiroan life changed over time.[35] From their work, Brown and his team were able to show the complexity of the site, particularly of the elites who were able to control trade and be buried in the mounds.[36]

Between 1973 and 1983, Phillips and Brown co-authored the six-volume now-classic *Pre-Columbian Shell Engravings from the Craig Mound at Spiro, Oklahoma,* published by Harvard University's Peabody Museum. It was the first great study of Spiro artifacts since Henry and Jean Hamilton had roamed the country in the early 1940s, snapping pictures of Spiro items. Phillips, Brown, Mueller, Brain, and artists Eliza McFadden and Barbara Page tracked down Spiro shells in museum collections across the country. They found that photography would not show the curves of the shells, so McFadden and Page made line drawings and rubbings of the engraved shells.[37] In 1996, Brown published the multivolume *The Spiro Ceremonial Center: The Archaeology of Arkansas Valley Caddoan Culture in Eastern Oklahoma.* Together, these works make up the most comprehensive archaeological study and interpretation of the Spiro Mounds.

Brown encouraged other archaeologists to come work at Spiro. From 1978 to 1982, Brown worked with J. Daniel Rogers of the Oklahoma Archaeological Survey to take samples around the site to find activity areas. The archaeological team concentrated on the great plaza but also completed the excavations on Brown Mound. This was to be a major four-year excavation, and Rogers brought American Indian groups on board to ensure respect for the artifacts and customs. Along with Brown, other members of Rogers' team included soil expert Frank L. Hardy of the University of Iowa and paleoethnobotanist Gayle Fritz from the University of North Carolina. The excavations were a huge success, with Rogers and company proving that Spiro did not have a protective palisade around its sacred mounds. They also discovered other mounds built over demolished structures, did extensive excavation on House Mound 5, and test-trenched Brown and Copple mounds. Rogers was one of the first to conclude that the city of Spiro was abandoned by its population in order for it to become a ceremonial center of the dead.[38]

Rogers' was the last major excavation at Spiro. Lack of funds has prevented others from taking place. Nevertheless, in the summer of 1993, a team of Japanese and American scientists from the Smithsonian, Miami University, and the Nara National Cultural Properties Research Institute of Nijo-cho in Nara City, Japan used state-of-the-art ground-penetrating radar on House Mound 6. Using the radar, as well as a soil-resistivity meter and a proton magnetometer, they found that House Mound 6, which had never been excavated, contained the remains of three house structures, two of them having been burned, buried, and the mound built over them. This new technology was touted as a way of studying mounds without having to destroy them.[39]

While archaeologists studied and interpreted it, Spiro was slowly transforming itself into one of Oklahoma's most popular tourist attractions. After the corps of engineers saved it in 1964, archaeologists and Oklahoma state officials spent the remaining years of the 1960s and into the 1970s working on a plan to transform the site into an archaeological park. Back then, what with Craig Mound flattened, Brown and Copple mounds scarred, and the other mounds too shallow or grown over, there really was not much to see. The most logical, but also most controversial, part was the plan to reconstruct Craig Mound as it had been before the pot hunters had gotten to it. After all, this was Spiro Mounds, and visitors had to have a mound to look at. Oklahoma even appropriated three hundred thousand dollars for the restoration project.[40]

Once again, an archaeologist taking off for an extended absence posed a challenge. In 1973, just when the whole Spiro Mounds park and restoration project seemed ready to go, Oklahoma state archaeologist Don Wyckoff, who had been heading the project, took a year's leave of absence. With Wyckoff gone, acting state archaeologist Ronald Corbyn objected to the sizes and location of several of the structures planned for the park, especially plans "to build mound-like features which . . . were not there originally."[41] Corbyn's objections brought all work to a halt and threatened the loss of the three hundred thousand-dollar appropriation. Angry locals and infuriated state senator James Hamilton protested Corbyn's actions. "It would seem to me that if one person can hold up progress when so many agencies and citizens have been involved for such a long time, that agency who is obstructing the project should be abolished or the power reduced by appropriate legislation."[42]

Corbyn's objections were overcome, and in 1973 the Oklahoma Tourism and Recreation Department took control of Spiro Mounds. Immediately a six-foot-high chainlink fence went around the 135-acre site to keep out pot hunters and vandals. Over the next five years, the Craig and Ward mounds were rebuilt. An interpretive center was constructed, and in June 1978 the Spiro Mound Archaeological Park opened to the public, with James Bruner as park superintendent.[43] Soon after, in 1980, during Rogers' excavation, his team, with the help of Oklahoma high school and university students, reconstructed a Spiro mud-and-wattle house. Again, this was new archaeology, focused on trying to understand the problems Spiroan people faced so long ago. "We'll learn the practical problems of building a house," Rogers explained. "Such as how much mud should be used for the walls, how to tie grass in bundles for the roof and how to place wood posts on top of each other without using nails."[44]

It was one thing to create the Spiro Mound Archaeological Park; it was something else to maintain it. Walking paths needed to be graded, trees cut back, the visitor's center maintained and expanded. Money was always needed, though the park benefited from small grants and gifts from supporters. One Spiro supporter even urged that inmate labor be used for Spiro projects.[45] Personnel changes brought Dennis Peterson in as park superintendent in the 1980s, and about that time, the site caught the imagination of the state. Soon politicians and businesspeople were visiting Spiro.[46] In 1991, the park was transferred from the Oklahoma Department of Tourism back to the Oklahoma Historical Society. Money was slated for more walking paths, building the Spiro house replica, as well as future archaeological work.[47] As Peterson said, the park is "the only prehistoric site in Oklahoma people can visit. . . . It could be the number one teaching tool in the state on American Indians."[48]

While Spiro was being picked over by archaeologists, and the site itself becoming Oklahoma's only archaeological park, museums were acquiring the last of the major Spiro artifacts. In 1967, Guinn Cooper donated his entire collection of Spiro artifacts to the Poteau Chamber of Commerce. The chamber was not really sure what to do with these hundreds of extremely valuable points, engraved shell cups, copper pieces, pottery, beads, and such. So the chamber, along with the Eastern Oklahoma Historical Society, decided to start a museum. Oklahoma senator Robert S. Kerr had started his own unofficial museum on his family estate in Poteau. When he died in 1963, his children took over the estate. In the late 1960s, they allowed the chamber and historical society to combine their holdings with Kerr's, creating the basis for the Robert S. Kerr Museum. In 1979, the family donated the estate to the state and in the early 1980s turned it into a conference center. Later a new Kerr Museum was built at the conference center, which became the home for Guinn Cooper's astounding collection of artifacts.[49] Cooper lived several more years, dying in a Booneville, Arkansas, nursing home on August 20, 1992. He was probably the last Pocola man alive and one of the few who remained known to history in later years.[50]

In 1975, William Clay Beach, a retired teacher in the Bureau of Indian Affairs, donated his extensive collection of Spiro artifacts to the Kerr Museum. Beach had begun collecting Spiro items back in the thirties, when he was teaching Indian students at nearby Tucker, Oklahoma. Many of his artifacts had been those thrown away by the Pocola men because they were chipped or broken and believed to be worthless. Others he found himself as he pot hunted around the area. Beach became interested in Spiro Mounds and the artifacts when one of his students brought him an engraved conch shell. The student had broken the shell in half in order to fit it inside his pocket.[51]

The Beach Collection consisted of three thousand beads, three hundred different arrow and spear points, some stone ear spools, as well as some shell-faced effigies and bone awls. He also included a 1930s relic hunter's catalog, which offered such buys as "100 authentic Spiro Indian arrowheads, regularly 84 cents, for 64 cents." Beach's collection was shown along with Cooper's, and suddenly the tiny Robert S. Kerr Museum possessed a major Spiro artifact collection.[52]

Spiro artifacts still exerted a tremendous pull. There was just something about Spiro and the treasure it gave up that made people do things they might not normally do. Though Spiro artifacts had been acquired by collectors and museums large and small, people still hungered for them. By the 1960s, not many Spiro artifacts were available for purchase, and those that were put on the market went for very high prices. Now theft became a key method of acquiring them. Actually, thefts had always been a problem with Spiro artifacts. As early as 1938, collectors reported Spiro artifacts disappearing from their assemblages. Collector Lyle Stephenson reported that a string of seventy-five Spiro shell beads had been stolen from his desk. He said he had planned on giving the beads to a local Kansas City museum and begged the thief to return them.[53]

Thefts had haunted Clements' WPA excavations, with items often stolen directly out of the warehouse on-site. They continued to plague archaeologists. During his excavations in the 1960s, archaeologist James Brown was notified that Joe Haines had photos of the Clements' excavation, which Brown dearly wanted to see, but Haines refused to lend them to the University of Oklahoma. As a friend explained it to Brown, Haines believed "some Spiro material has been stolen from your storage area and he does not want to take a chance." Instead, Brown and a photography crew visited Haines at his home, but during the photo shoot, one of the crew accidentally broke a Spiro pendant. They "squared things by giving him a small string of Spiro beads."[54] Haines may have actually had reason to worry because the Stovall Museum on the University of Oklahoma campus, which held most of Clements' Spiro finds, did have a large flint blade stolen sometime in the mid-1950s.[55]

As the value of Spiro goods skyrocketed, larger museums increased their security and tracking measures. Now, smaller museums became targets. And often the thefts were not by bands of high-tech thieves but were inside jobs done by people who just coveted the artifacts or the money they could bring. In September or October 1991, officials at the Robert S. Kerr Museum in Poteau noticed several Spiro pieces donated by Guinn Cooper missing from their collection. These included almost ninety arrow points and knives; a large number of beads, as well as a complete necklace of stone beads; a stone ornamental pipe; a couple of engraved conch shells; a shell breastplate; and a by-then-famous "long-nosed God maskette."[56]

Kerr officials contacted the Poteau Police, the Oklahoma Bureau of Investigation, and Harvard's Peabody Museum, which had published Phillips and Brown's *Pre-Columbian Shell Engravings from Craig Mound.* One of the Kerr shells had been featured in the book, and the officials hoped the Peabody

Museum might provide them with an estimate of the value of the missing items, particularly the shell items.[57] The engraved conch shell was valued at a conservative twenty-five thousand dollars.[58]

However, the spectacular nature and rarity of Spiro goods worked against the thieves because it made buyers suspicious. In early 1992, a professor at the Pacific University College of Optometry in Forest Grove, Oregon, was offered a Spiro shell cup for one thousand dollars. She contacted James Brown at Northwestern to ask if it was real. About the same time, Brown received word of the Kerr Museum theft. Brown wrote the museum that he thought the shell being offered to the Oregon professor was the stolen Kerr Museum shell. The museum contacted the Federal Bureau of Investigation, and the Oregon shell did in fact turn out to be the stolen shell. It was quickly returned to the museum.[59] The Museum of the Red River in Idabel, Oklahoma, purchased a Spiro shell and sent it to Greg Perino, who had worked with the Brown excavation in the 1960s, for authentication. This also turned out to be one of the stolen shells, and Perino, who valued the shell at twenty thousand dollars, returned it to the Kerr.[60]

It did not take too long for authorities to put the story together. Seems that a young man who had often volunteered to work at the Kerr Museum just could not resist the Spiro artifacts. Trusted by the staff and using keys to the display cases, over time he pocketed the Spiro items, covering his theft by rearranging the remaining artifacts in the cases in order to hide the holes left by the missing items. The volunteer would sell the goods to an artifact dealer in Anadarko, Oklahoma, who would then resell them on the curio market. The Anadarko dealer bought the conch shell from the museum volunteer for $350, then turned around and offered it to the Oregon professor for $1,000.[61]

The volunteer was later brought in by the police for questioning. At first he claimed that he'd found the Spiro goods in a box at Mary's Swap Meet in nearby Spencer, Oklahoma, bought them, and then resold them to the Anadarko dealer. He later changed his story, saying his grandfather had collected the items during the 1930s. But it did not take long for the authorities to get the truth. The volunteer was charged with grand larceny. What made the story even more interesting is that the volunteer, as a boy, had gained national fame as one of the discoverers of the Poteau rune stone, another of those mysterious Scandinavian-carved rocks found in the vicinity. Apparently the volunteer received a fairly light sentence, because he continued living in the area and went on to become a public school teacher. All items were later recovered and sent back to the Kerr Museum, which immediately upped its security measures.[62] Somehow, it seems appropriate that the Spiro story ends with a theft. After all, theft seems to be the Spiro legacy.

Epilogue

Today, six hundred years after Spiroans buried their elites in the central chamber of Craig Mound, Spiro is a changed place. The once bustling chiefdom is long gone. The gods-on-earth priest-chiefs are forgotten. We will never know their names or their lives. Still, Spiro is a beautiful place. The reconstructed mounds are there, sitting across meadows of waving grass bordered by hickories and oaks. Boy Scouts, rather than Indian commoners or WPA laborers, are more likely to work on paths. And kite fliers rather than pot hunters are the norm. Though far off the main road, getting there is not too difficult. Over fifty thousand tourists a year visit Spiro from across the United States, Germany, Japan, China, and Argentina. Since 1988, it has been one of the top tourism destinations in Oklahoma.[1] Now visitors can take footpaths around the mounds, while interpretative signs and booklets explain the site. A special presentation is given every solstice and equinox, and visitors can stand on Brown Mound and watch the sunset. But it can be a lonely place, too. The great ceremonial center is no more, its graves robbed, its riches taken.

And what of those riches? Today, Spiro artifacts from Craig Mound are found around the world. The Sam Noble Oklahoma Museum of Natural History at the University of Oklahoma in Norman has an extensive Spiro collection, as does the University of Arkansas at Fayetteville; the Gilcrease and Philbrook museums in Tulsa; Frank Phillips' Woolaroc Museum in Bartlesville, Oklahoma; the Museum of the Red River in Idabel, Oklahoma; the Oklahoma Historical Society Museum in Oklahoma City; the Robert S. Kerr Museum in Poteau, Oklahoma; the Witte Museum in San Antonio, Texas; the School of the Ozarks Museum in Point Lookout, Missouri; UCLA; the University of Chicago Museum; the Houston Museum of Natural Sciences; and the Ohio State Museum. Some of the world's great museums also own Spiro material, including the Louvre in Paris and the British Museum in London. The largest collection is at the Smithsonian Institution, which acquired the world-famous Heye Museum in New York in the early twenty-first century, making it the Smithsonian's Museum of the American Indian, on the Washington, D.C., Mall. Though some Spiro goods might go on display every now and then, most, because they are considered funerary objects, will sit in storage rooms at the Smithsonian's Suiteland, Maryland, facility.

Although the big museums eventually got the bulk of the Spiro artifacts, pieces were still being sold throughout the remainder of the twentieth century. Spiro gained a sort of mythological aura, and collectors still want a piece of it. They would buy if any artifacts ever came on the open market.[2] And sometimes they did and still do. A check on the Internet auction house Ebay turns up a Spiro artifact for sale every now and again.

In the end, almost everybody today considers the looting of Spiro Mounds to be one of the great archaeological tragedies of all time. So much knowledge was lost, never to be regained. We will never fully and truly know what was happening at Spiro during the Mississippian years. But the looting of Spiro Mounds did have an effect. After Spiro, antiquities acts became common in most states. In fact, many states require an archaeological survey before roads can be built or factories constructed. A find can put a halt to all work. Pot hunting also fell out of public favor. This does not mean that the desire to own Indian artifacts ceased. There are still many nonacademic relic dealers and collectors involved in finding, buying, and selling artifacts. Many of these folks are very professional, knowledgeable people similar to Trowbridge. Some advertise on the Internet, usually stating up front that all their items are authentic and come from isolated finds, and that they would never sell anything illegally obtained or associated with Indian burials. Others might not have such high standards. Plenty of men and women still go out with iron rods to prod the earth in hopes of finding a skull or a pot or whatever. Site vandalism is one of the biggest problems the National Park Service and historical places face. But now grave robbing and pot hunting are furtive, criminal, and not nearly so open as they once were. Even the North American Indian Relic Collectors Association went out of business. And about 1970, so did *Hobbies: The Magazine for Collectors*.

Spiro was a necessary coming of age for archaeology. By its nature, an archaeological excavation is destructive, but now professionals rely much more on trenching, slow, painstaking excavation, and returning sites to the way they were once the excavation is finished. There is also more use of nonintrusive technology, like ground-penetrating radar. And in the same vein as Clements, archaeologists have become even more forceful in trying to protect sites from pot hunters. Sometimes they have been successful, sometimes not. Museums have certainly become more sensitive about displaying American Indian artifacts. It is rare that a person will see skeletons or burial artifacts displayed anymore. Because most Spiro artifacts are considered sacred grave goods, many museums refuse to show them out of respect to Indian people. And since the passage of the Native American Graves Protection and Repatriation Act in 1990, many skeletons and sacred objects held in museum vaults have been returned to Indian tribes for burial.

Today, Spiro is a synonym for archaeological destruction. The pot hunters are viewed as the villains, and Clements and the archaeologists, the heroes. But in 1935, the lines were not so clear. This was a battle over property rights; one could almost say mineral rights. Who had the right to excavate and gain custody of the artifacts at Spiro? The Pocola Mining Company, who had a legal lease? Or did the items belong to the State of Oklahoma, regardless of whose land they were on or who held a legitimate lease? There was also a little class conflict taking place here; at least, the men of the Pocola Mining Company believed so. These were hard-pressed men trying to make it through the Great Depression. They had found a way, and it was snatched from them by someone who could manipulate the state legislature in his favor. They certainly did not believe Clements represented the state or that he should have any more standing with it than they did. Of course, Clements scorned the Pocola men and refused to see any part of their situation or arguments.

So both the Pocola Mining Company and Forrest Clements saw Spiro as a treasure trove. Each wanted what was in it. While Clements might have been more careful in his excavations, he wanted the artwork just as the pot hunters did. And in that way, both the Pocola boys and Clements were similar, grave robbers, just differing on who should have the goods: academia or free enterprise. Is it better to rob a grave in order to preserve the artifacts so that the public will one day get to see them, or do property rights endorse robbing a grave in order to sell the artifacts? Certainly many modern-day American Indians, such as the late author and professor Vine Deloria, Jr., have criticized archaeologists for their cavalier attitude toward Indian remains.[3] And in many ways, during the 1930s, everyone's attitude toward Spiro Mounds was rather cavalier. Unfortunately, we, Spiro, and history as a whole are the less for it.

Notes

Abbreviations

Chapter 1

1. Groves, NAIRCA Report, 5; A. B. Macdonald, "A 'King-Tut' Tomb in the Arkansas Valley: On a Negro's Farm in Eastern Oklahoma are Unearthed Relics from the Mound Builders of Past Centuries," *Kansas City Star*, December 15, 1935.

2. Clements, "Historical Sketch," 48.

3. *Hobbies*, August 1935, 105; *Hobbies*, November 1935, 99.

4. Tallant, "The 'Bug' of Archaeology."

5. Daniel to Hobbs, August 29 (no year provided, but could be 1940 or 1941), Spiro Folder, RSKM; *Hobbies*, June 1935, 96; *Hobbies*, July 1935, 96; *Hobbies*, August 1935, 97; *Hobbies*, November 1935, 99; Groves, NAIRCA Report, 19.

6. Newspaper clipping, *Tulsa Daily World*, n.d., Braecklein Collection.

7. Trowbridge to Balloun, January 5, 1936, Archaeology–Spiro Mound Folder, Balloun Collection.

8. *Hobbies*, July 1935, 92; *Hobbies*, August 1935, 104–105; *Hobbies*, October 1935, 93; *Hobbies*, November 1935, 99.

9. Cooper, *Lest We Forget*, 68.

10. Iva Mayhar Chelf, interview, March 16, 1979, transcript, Spiro Collection, SNOM.

11. M. R. Harrington, "A Pot-Hunter's Paradise," 85–86.

12. Ibid.

13. Cooper, *Lest We Forget*, 68.

14. Clements, "Historical Sketch," 48.

15. Clements to Otto Spring, September 17, 1934, minor box S-35, Spring Collection; Clements to Mrs. Don Zuhlke, November 21, 1936, FPF.

16. Hamilton, "Spiro Mound," 26–27; Phillips and Brown, *Pre-Columbian Shell Engravings*, 1:2–3.

17. Hamilton, "Spiro Mound," 26–27; [Don] Wyckoff, transcripts of Wyckoff's tape on Spiro Mounds, 1973, C-4, OAS, 10–11, hereafter cited as Wyckoff, "Transcripts," 10–11; Groves, NAIRCA Report, 4–5.

18. Brown, *Spiro Ceremonial Center*, 1:12, figure 1-4.

19. Ibid., 105.

20. Ibid., 112.

21. Ibid., 12, figure 1-4; Peterson, "A History of Excavations," 114–115; Hamilton, "Spiro Mound," 27.

22. Thoburn, "Prehistoric Cultures," 224–25; Peterson, "A History of Excavations," 114–15; Brown, *Spiro Ceremonial Center*, 1:115, 117–18; Wyckoff, "Transcripts," 14–15.

23. Thoburn to Col. Patrick J. Hurley, August 8, 1927, photocopy of original letter in Spiro Collection, SNOM.

24. Peck, *Le Flore County*, 155–161.

25. Phillips and Brown, *Pre-Columbian Shell Engravings*, 1:30; J. A. Brown to Forrest Clements, March 15, 1965, Spiro Correspondence Folder, Spiro Collection, SNOM; Groves, NAIRCA Report, 8.

Chapter 2

1. Peterson, "A History of Excavations," 114.

2. Brown, "Arkansas Valley Caddoan," 241–42, 245–46; Paul W. Parmalee to James Brown, May 11, 1965, Spiro Correspondence Folder, Spiro Collection, SNOM; Brown, *Spiro Ceremonial Center*, 1:11–12, 29–31.

3. Joutel, *The La Salle Expedition*, 172–73, 270.

4. Schambach, "Spiroan Traders," 26; Brown, *Spiro Ceremonial Center*, 1:198; Thomas, *Exploring Ancient Native America*, 166.

5. Wyckoff, "Transcripts," 2.

6. "Introduction to the Arkansas Basin Caddoans," no author, n.d., pamphlet, OAS.

7. Thomas, *Exploring Ancient Native America*, 174–75; Brown, "Arkansas Valley Caddoan," 245–46.

8. Thomas, *Exploring Ancient Native America*, 174–75; Brown, "Arkansas Valley Caddoan," 245–46.

9. Thomas, *Exploring Ancient Native America*, 167–68; Brown, *Spiro Ceremonial Complex*, 1:131; Wyckoff, "Transcripts," 20–21; Thoburn, "Prehistoric Cultures of Oklahoma," 221–26.

10. Kenneth Gordon Orr, "A Pictographic Survey of the Spiro Mounds, Leflore County, Oklahoma," Spiro Mounds Information and Photographs Box, 1–3; Brown, "Arkansas Valley Caddoan," 241.

11. Fiedel, *Prehistory of the Americas*, 69–75; Thomas, *Exploring Ancient Native America*, 20–35; La Vere, *Texas Indians*, 5–8, 32.

12. La Vere, *Texas Indians*, 8–9.

13. Gibson, *Ancient Mounds*.

14. Wyckoff, "Transcripts," 3–4.

15. Peterson, "A History of Excavations," 117; Brown, *Spiro Ceremonial Center*, 1:11–12, 29–31; Wyckoff, "Transcripts," 4–5; Early, "Prehistory of the Western Interior," 561–63.

16. Shaffer, *Native Americans Before 1492*, 24–25, 56–57; Hudson, *Southeastern Indians*, 80; Brown, *Spiro Ceremonial Center*, 1:29–31, 198; Early, "Prehistory of the Western Interior," 563–64.

17. Pauketat, *The Ascent of Chiefs*, 40; Thomas, *Exploring Ancient Native America*, 153–54.

18. Schambach, "Osage Orange Bows," 212; Pauketat, *The Ascent of Chiefs*, 40–41.

19. Thomas, *Exploring Ancient Native America*, 151–52; Wyckoff, "Spiro," 54–56.

20. La Vere, *Texas Indians*, 5–9, 32.

21. Ibid., 31–33.

22. Webb, "Functional and Historical Parallelisms," 289; DePratter, *Late Prehistoric and Early Historic Chiefdoms*, 8, 77–78.

23. Hudson, *The Southeastern Indians*, 365–75.

24. Emerson et al., "Sourcing and Interpretation," 303.

25. Brown, "Arkansas Valley Caddoan," 254.

26. Pauketat, *The Ascent of Chiefs*, 9–11, 16–22, 40.

27. Brose, "From the Southeastern Ceremonial Complex," 29–30; DePratter, *Chiefdoms*, 77–78; Smith, *Archaeology of Aboriginal Culture*

Change, 3–4; Thomas, *Exploring Ancient Native America,* 162–63; Peebles and Kus, "Some Archaeological Correlates," 422.

28. Hultkrantz, *Native Religions of North America,* 32–34; Hudson, *Southeastern Indians,* 171–72.

29. Fiedel, *Prehistory of the Americas,* 10, 72–75; Newcomb, Jr. *The Rock Art of Texas Indians,* 39–40.

30. Turpin, Henneberg, and Riskind, "Late Archaic Mortuary Practices," 296–305; Hester, "The Prehistory of South Texas."

31. Brown, *Spiro Ceremonial Center,* 1:188.

32. Kniffen, Gregory, and Stokes, *Historic Indians Tribes of Louisiana,* 244–45.

33. Brown, *Spiro Ceremonial Center,* 1:23, 184; Kupperman, *Roanoke.*

34. Brown, *Spiro Ceremonial Center,* 1:115, 117–118, 188–89, 194, 222.

35. Ibid.; Wyckoff, "Transcripts," 14–15; Kniffen, Gregory, and Stokes, *Historic Indian Tribes of Louisiana,* 245.

36. Brown, *Spiro Ceremonial Center,* 1:115, 117–18, 122, 133; 166, 190–91; Orr, "Pictographic Survey," 1–3.

37. Brown, *Spiro Ceremonial Center,* 1:122, 196.

38. Brown, *Spiro Ceremonial Center,* 1:71, 75, 83, 133, 190–91; Wyckoff, "Transcripts," 10–11.

39. Brown, *Spiro Ceremonial Center,* 1:75; 190–191, 197; Thomas, *Exploring Ancient Native America,* 162; Frank Schambach to author, July 12, 2004, personal communication.

40. Wyckoff, "Transcripts," 7–10; Wyckoff, "Spiro," 51.

41. Brown, *Spiro Ceremonial Center,* 1:105, 108–112, 167, 197; Wyckoff, "Transcripts," 7–10.

42. Brown, *Spiro Ceremonial Center,* 1:112–13, 165–167; "Japanese Scientists Bring 'Toys' to Mounds," *Poteau Daily News and Sun,* September 5, 1993.

43. Brown, *Spiro Ceremonial Center,* 1:123, 197; Brown, "Arkansas Valley Caddoan," 257.

44. Brown, *Spiro Ceremonial Center,* 1:16

45. Ibid., 16–17, figure 1-6.

46. Thomas, *Exploring Ancient Native America,* 157.

47. Brown, *Spiro Ceremonial Center,* 1:16.

Chapter 3

1. Bruner, "They Found Oklahoma's Greatest Treasure," unpublished manuscript, n.d., Spiro Collection, SNOM, 1–3; Wilmont Stumpff, IPH,

58:362; "Spiro Indian Mounds Yield Archeological Treasure," *Southwest Times-Record*, May 9, 1937.

2. Bruner, "They Found Oklahoma's Greatest Treasure," 1–3.

3. Ibid.

4. Phillips and Brown, *Pre-Columbian Shell Engravings*, 1:1–2; Schambach, "Spiro and the Tunica," 179–80, 188; Brown, *Spiro Ceremonial Center*, 1:27.

5. Peck, *Le Flore County*, 12–14; Faiman-Silva, *Choctaws at the Crossroads*, 19.

6. Peck, *Le Flore County*, 80–81; Debo, *Choctaw Republic*, 66; Hamilton, "Spiro Mound," 26; Morris, Goins, and McReynolds, *Historical Atlas of Oklahoma*, map 38.

7. Debo, *Choctaw Republic*, 60–61.

8. Morris, Goins, and McReynolds, *Historical Atlas of Oklahoma*, maps 17, 24, 27, 39; Peck, *Le Flore County*, 50–51, 57–59, 80–81; Debo, *Choctaw Republic*, 60–61; James L. Avant, IPH, 77:48; Fredericka Fannin Hale, IPH, 4:227; J. R. Fields, IPH, 3:451; William M. Conaway, IPH, 20:375–76; Grant Foreman, *The Five Civilized Tribes*, 93.

9. Debo, *Choctaw Republic*, 74–76; Foreman, *Five Civilized Tribes*, 140–41.

10. Phillips and Brown, *Pre-Columbian Shell Engravings*, 1:1.

11. Debo, *Choctaw Republic*, 84, 99–109.

12. B. M. Palmer, IPH, 8:42; Peck, *Le Flore County*, 63.

13. Peck, *Le Flore County*, 63, 182–83, 188–89; Brown, *Spiro Ceremonial Center*, 1: 13.

14. Clements, "Historical Sketch," 51; Debo, *Choctaw Republic*, 259, 262, 275–277.

15. Clements, "Historical Sketch," 51.

16. Ibid.; Brown, *Spiro Ceremonial Center*, 1:167.

17. Phillips and Brown, *Pre-Columbian Shell Engravings*, 1:2.

18. Clements, "Historical Sketch," 51; Phillips and Brown, *Pre-Columbian Shell Engravings*, 1:3.

19. Clements, "Historical Sketch," 51.

20. Ibid.

21. "Relic Hunters Found 'Gold Mine' in Indian Mound; Didn't Realize It." *St. Louis Post-Dispatch*, December 13 1952; Hamilton, "Spiro Mound," 25; Trowbridge Catalog, p. 2618, n.d., scrapbook 4, Spiro Folder, Spiro Mounds Collection, HTRL.

22. Macdonald, "'King Tut' Tomb"; Peck, *Le Flore County*, 331; Phillips and Brown, *Pre-Columbian Shell Engravings*, 1:3.

23. Clements, "Historical Sketch," 51.

24. Hamilton, "Spiro Mound," 25, 27–28; Peck, *Le Flore County*, 203.

25. Phillips and Brown, *Pre-Columbian Shell Engravings*, 1:3; Brown, *Spiro Ceremonial Center*, 1:41.

26. Clements, "Historical Sketch," 54; Hamilton, "Spiro Mound," 27–28.

27. Bruner, "They Found Oklahoma's Greatest Treasure," 4–5.

28. Hamilton, "Spiro Mound," 26–27, 29; Phillips and Brown, *Pre-Columbian Shell Engravings*, 1:4.

29. Macdonald, "'King Tut' Tomb."

30. Groves, NAIRCA Report, 5; Pilquist, "Along the Arkansas," 101–102.

31. "Hobbies Became Livelihood." *Dardanelle Post Dispatch* (Arkansas), August 5, 1981.

32. Harrington, "A Pot-Hunter's Paradise," 84.

33. "Hobbies Became Livelihood."

34. G. E. Pilquist to H. I. Player, December 30, 1935, Scrapbook 4, Spiro Folder, Spiro Mounds Collection, HTRL.

35. "Local Ornithologist to Add to Collection." *Dardanelle Post Dispatch*, May 31, 1923.

36. "Hobbies Became Livelihood."

37. Ibid.

38. Pilquist, "Along the Arkansas," 101–102.

39. Pilquist Obituary, January 3, 1963, *Dardanelle Post-Dispatch*, 5.

40. Peterson, "A History of Excavations," 115–116.

41. Clements, "Historical Sketch," 63.

42. Hamilton, "Spiro Mound," 19.

43. Clements, "Historical Sketch," 54–55.

44. Joseph Thoburn to Doctor Kidder, August 19, 1938, photocopy of original letter, Spiro Collection, SNOM.

45. Clements, "Historical Sketch," 55.

46. Phillips and Brown, *Pre-Columbian Shell Engravings*, 1:4; Clements, "Historical Sketch," 55.

Chapter 4

1. Peterson, "A History of Excavations," 118; Brown, *Spiro Ceremonial Center*, 1:29–31, 36–38; Brown, "Arkansas Valley Caddoan," 245–46; Wyckoff, "Spiro," 50; "Introduction to the Arkansas Basin Caddoans," OAS.

2. La Vere, *Texas Indians*, 33–35; Hamilton, "Spiro Mound," plates 13, 14, 15.

3. Creel, "Bison Hides," 40–49; Schambach to the author.

4. La Vere, *Texas Indians*, 33–37.

5. Ibid.

6. Wyckoff, "Transcripts," 24–25; Hamilton, "Spiro Mound," plates 9, 10, 11, 12, 14, 15.

7. Thomas, *Exploring Ancient Native America*, 160–61.

8. Dillehay, "Disease Ecology and Initial Human Migration," 234–43; Turpin, Henneberg, and Riskind, "Late Archaic Mortuary Practices," 306; Schambach, "Spiroan Traders," 26–27.

9. Thomas, *Exploring Ancient Native America*, 160–61; Wyckoff, "Transcripts," 24–25; Schambach, "Osage Orange Bows," 221.

10. Wyckoff, "Transcripts," 24–25; Turpin, Henneberg, and Riskind, "Late Archaic Mortuary Practices," 306; Schambach to the author, July 12, 2004.

11. Crosby, *The Columbian Exchange*.

12. Wyckoff, "Transcripts," 17.

13. Hamilton, "Spiro Mound," plates 9, 10, 11, 12; H. M. Trowbridge to Dr. Henry C. Shertone, December 25, 1936, Scrapbook 6, Spiro Mounds Collection, HTRL.

14. Thomas, *Exploring Ancient Native America*, 156; La Vere, *Texas Indians*, 104–105, 130; Frank Schambach to Jay C. Blaine, June 18, 2000, letter provided to author by Schambach; Brown, "Arkansas Valley Caddoan," 249–50.

15. Derrick and Wilson, "Cranial Modeling," 139–144; Lawson, *A New Voyage to Carolina*, 39–40; Schambach, "Spiroan Traders," 25–26.

16. Schambach, "Spiroan Traders," 25–26; Schambach to Blaine, June 18, 2000; Schambach, "Osage Orange Bows," 222; Brown, "Arkansas Valley Caddoan," 259; Hamilton, "Spiro Mound," plates 10, 11, 12, 14, 26, 27.

17. Iva Mayhar Chelf, interview, March 16, 1979, Spiro Collection, SNOM; Brown, *Spiro Ceremonial Center*, 1:98, 102–103; La Vere, *Caddo Chiefdoms*, 18–19.

18. "Introduction to the Arkansas Basin," OAS.

19. Brown, *Spiro Ceremonial Center*, 1:32–33, 197–98.

20. Pauketat, *Ancient Cahokia*, 106.

21. Hodge, *Spanish Explorers*, 129–272; La Vere, *Texas Indians*, 143.

22. Wyckoff, "Spiro," 56–58.

23. Peterson, "A History of Excavations," 114; Brown, "Arkansas Valley Caddoan," 255.

24. Hudson, *Southeastern Indians*, 243.

25. Brown, *Spiro Ceremonial Center*, 1:23; Brown, "Spiro Art," 19–23.

26. Hamilton, "Spiro Mound," plates 1 and 12; Emerson et al., "Sourcing and Interpretation," 303.

27. Emerson et al., "Sourcing and Interpretation," 303.

28. Schambach, "Spiro and the Tunica," 171–173.

29. Knight, "Mississippian Religion," 677, 680, 684.

30. La Vere, *Texas Indians*, 50–53

31. Hudson, *Southeastern Indians*, 239–40.

32. Ibid., 240–45.

33. Ibid., 244–51.

34. Wyckoff, "Transcripts," 5–7, 8–9, 22–23; Wyckoff, "Spiro," 52; Brown, *Spiro Ceremonial Center*, 1:32–33.

35. Wyckoff, "Transcripts," 5–7, 8–9, 22–23; Wyckoff, "Spiro," 52; Brown, *Spiro Ceremonial Center*, 1:32–33; "Mounds Magic," *Spiro Graphic*, November 17, 1988, RSKM; Clements, "Historical Sketch," 64; Dennis Peterson, site manager of Spiro Archaeological Park, interview by author, September 21, 2002; Brown, "Arkansas Valley Caddoan," 242–43.

36. Barreis, "Southern Cult," 23.

37. Thomas, *Exploring Ancient Native America*, 167. Thomas gives the number of villages in thrall to Spiro. Dennis Peterson provided the number 250,000, interview by author, September 21, 2002.

38. Wyckoff, "Transcripts," 6.

39. Brown, "Arkansas Valley Caddoan," 252–54; Schambach, "Osage Orange Bows," 223–33.

40. Wyckoff, "Spiro," 56.

41. Peterson, "A History of Excavations," 118–19. See also Martin, *Wonderful Power*.

42. Schambach, "Spiroan Traders," 7, 25–26; Wyckoff, "Transcripts," 18–19; La Vere, *Caddo Chiefdoms*, 48.

43. Brown, *Spiro Ceremonial Center*, 1:31–33; Schambach, "Osage Orange Bows," 217–23.

44. Schambach, "Spiroan Traders," 7–27; Schambach, "Osage Orange Bows," 217–32.

45. Schambach, "Spiroan Traders," 7–27; Schambach, "Osage Orange Bows," 217–32; Schambach to author, July 12, 2004.

46. "Indian Legends of 'Firebringer' Similar," *Spiro Graphic*, February 2, 1989, RSKM; Schambach to Blaine, June 18, 2000; Schambach, "Osage Orange Bows," 223.

47. Wyckoff, "Spiro," 53–54; Thomas, *Exploring Ancient Native America*, 156.

48. Wyckoff, "Spiro," 53–54; Brown, "Arkansas Valley Caddoan," 252–54.

49. Bell, "Trade Materials at Spiro Mounds," 181–84.

50. Brown, *Spiro Ceremonial Center*, 1:194, 199; Emerson et al., "Sourcing and Interpretation," 303; Brown, "Exchange and Interaction," 681.

51. Brown, *Spiro Ceremonial Center*, 1:183.

52. Brain, "Great Mound Robbery," 25.

53. "Relic Hunters Found 'Gold Mine' in Indian Mound"; Trowbridge to Dr. Ganier, December 15, 1947, Spiro Mounds Collection, HTRL; Wyckoff, "Spiro," 58–59.

54. Prentice, "Marine Shells as Wealth Items," 199.

55. Barreis, "Southern Cult," 24.

56. Thomas, *Exploring Ancient Native America*, 169.

57. Barreis, "Southern Cult," 24; Emerson et al., "Sourcing and Interpretation," 303.

58. Brain, "Great Mound Robbery," 25.

59. Wyckoff, "Transcripts," 18; Wyckoff, "Spiro," 59; Brown, "Spiro Art," 13–17.

60. "Relic Hunters Found 'Gold Mine' in Indian Mound"; Barreis, "Southern Cult," 25–26; Brown, *Spiro Ceremonial Center*, 1:137.

61. Wyckoff, "Spiro," 59; Hamilton, "Spiro Mound," plates 6–22; Brown, "Arkansas Valley Caddoan," 255; Emerson et al., "Sourcing and Interpretation," 289–90.

62. Big Boy effigy pipe from Spiro, Oklahoma, was viewed by the author on September 24, 2002, at University Museum, University of Arkansas, Fayetteville; Hamilton, "Spiro Mound," plates 9, 10; Emerson et al., "Sourcing and Interpretation," 287–313.

63. Hamilton, "Spiro Mound," plates 11, 12; Groves, NAIRCA Report, 9.

64. Groves, NAIRCA Report, 7–8; Macdonald, "'King Tut' Tomb"; Hamilton, "Spiro Mound," plates 6–11.

65. Emerson et al., "Sourcing and Interpretation," 303–305, quotation on 305.

66. Brown, *Spiro Ceremonial Center*, 1:136–37, 142, 183, 194; Tests of Fibrous Materials, May 6, 1937, National Bureau of Standards, Spiro Mound Textiles, Trowbridge Collection Folder, Spiro Mounds Collection, HTRL; Wyckoff, "Transcripts," 23–24; Moorehead, *Archaeology of the Arkansas River Valley*, 73; Orr, "Pictographic Survey," 4–5.

67. Wyckoff, "Transcripts," 18–19; Wyckoff, "Spiro," 54.

68. Brown, "Arkansas Valley Caddoan," 246–48.

69. Brain, "Great Mound Robbery," 25.

70. Ibid.

71. Phillips and Brown, *Pre-Columbian Shell Engravings*, 2:v; Wyckoff, "Spiro," 61–63.

72. Barreis, "Southern Cult," 25–26; Wyckoff, "Spiro," 61–63; Brown, *Spiro Ceremonial Center*, 1:20; Brown, "Arkansas Valley Caddoan," 246; Brown, "Spiro Art," 23–28.

73. Brown, Spiro Ceremonial Center, 1:199.

Chapter 5

1. Thomas, *Skull Wars*, 38–41, 52–63, 119–120.
2. Ibid., 33–34.
3. Ibid., 133–34.
4. De Mézières, *Athanase De Mézières and the Louisiana-Texas Frontier*, 2:263.
5. Thomas, *Skull Wars*, 33.
6. Ibid., 124–32.
7. Ibid., 136–38.
8. Clements to Otto Spring, September 17, 1934, Spring Collection.
9. Bruner, "They Found Oklahoma's Greatest Treasure," 5–7; Brown, *Spiro Ceremonial Center*, 1:19.
10. Phillips and Brown, *Pre-Columbian Shell Engravings*, 1:3
11. Ibid., 4.
12. "Seeks to Save Indian Mounds from Looting," *St. Louis Post-Dispatch*, April 28, 1929; Thoburn to Kidder, August 19, 1938, Spiro Collection, SNOM; Phillips and Brown, *Pre-Columbian Shell Engravings*, 1:4.
13. Clements, "Historical Sketch," 55–56.
14. Ibid., 56.
15. Ibid.
16. Phillips and Brown, *Pre-Columbian Shell Engravings*, 1:4.
17. Bruner, "They Found Oklahoma's Greatest Treasure," 5–7.
18. Phillips and Brown, *Pre-Columbian Shell Engravings*, 1:4.
19. Clements, "Historical Sketch," 63.
20. Hamilton, "Spiro Mound," 33–34.
21. Ibid., 29–30, 33–34; Brown, *Spiro Ceremonial Center*, 1:89.
22. Brain, "Great Mound Robbery," 21.
23. Macdonald, "'King Tut' Tomb"; Groves, NAIRCA Report, 6; Peck, *Le Flore County*, 331–33; Phillips and Brown, *Pre-Columbian Shell Engravings*, 1:6; Hamilton, "Spiro Mound," 29–30.
24. Hamilton, "Spiro Mound," 29–30.
25. "Spiro Indian Mounds Yield Archeological Treasure." May 9, 1937, *Southwest Times-Record*; "Relic Hunters Found 'Gold Mine' in Indian Mound."
26. Hamilton, "Spiro Mound," 33.
27. Groves, NAIRCA Report, 6–7.
28. Ibid.; Hamilton, "Spiro Mound," 33.
29. Clements, "Historical Sketch," 60.
30. Macdonald, "'King Tut' Tomb"; Hamilton, "Spiro Mound," 30, 34.

31. Hamilton, "Spiro Mound," 31, 34; "Spiro Indian Mounds Yield Archeological Treasure."

32. Hamilton, "Spiro Mound," 31–32.

33. Clements, "Historical Sketch," 60.

34. Peck, *Le Flore County*, 333; Groves, NAIRCA Report, 7; "Relic Hunters Found 'Gold Mine' in Indian Mound"; Hamilton, "Spiro Mounds," 31.

35. Macdonald, "'King Tut' Tomb."

36. Bruner, "They Found Oklahoma's Greatest Treasure," 8.

37. "Relic Hunters Found 'Gold Mine' in Indian Mound"; Macdonald, "'King Tut' Tomb"; Hamilton, "Spiro Mound," 31–33; Groves, NAIRCA Report, 8.

38. "Relic Hunters Found 'Gold Mine' in Indian Mound"; Trowbridge to Dr. Ganier, December 15, 1947, Spiro Mounds Collection, HTRL; Wyckoff, "Spiro," 58–59; Macdonald, "'King Tut' Tomb"; Hamilton, "Spiro Mound," 31–33; Groves, NAIRCA Report, 8.

39. "Relic Hunters Found 'Gold Mine' In Indian Mound"; Hamilton, "Spiro Mound," 30; Groves, NAIRCA Report, 8.

40. Groves, NAIRCA Report, 8.

41. Hamilton, "Spiro Mound," 29–30; Wyckoff, "Transcripts," 16; Clements, "Historical Sketch," 63; Philips and Brown, *Pre-Columbian Shell Engravings*, 1: 6–7.

42. Newkumet, interview by author, September 17, 2002.

43. Phillips and Brown, *Pre-Columbian Shell Engravings*, 1:3; Brown, *Spiro Ceremonial Center*, 1:61.

44. Macdonald, "'King Tut' Tomb."

45. Clements, "Historical Sketch," 62–63.

46. Brain, "Great Mound Robbery," 21.

47. Groves, NAIRCA Report, 5; "Relic Hunters Found 'Gold Mine' in Indian Mound"; Hamilton, "Spiro Mound," 31–33.

48. Brown, *Spiro Ceremonial Center*, 1:89; Hamilton, "Spiro Mound," 31.

49. Phillips and Brown, *Pre-Columbian Shell Engravings*, 1:4; Clements, "Historical Sketch," 55; Photo, June 1936, Spiro Mound Views, Clark Field Papers; Orr, "Pictographic Survey," Photo 4.

50. "Relic Hunters Found 'Gold Mine' in Indian Mound.'"".

51. Hamilton, "Spiro Mound," 27, 31; Brown, *Spiro Ceremonial Center*, 1:105–108; Preliminary General Report on Archaeological Work in Oklahoma, August 1938, "Le Flore County," folder 1, box 1, minor box I-21, WPA Archaeological Survey Project Files, 120.

52. "Indian Burial Mound Yields Many Relics"; Hamilton, "Spiro Mound," 27–28.

53. Macdonald, "'King Tut' Tomb"; "Lost Civilization in Oklahoma May Be Related to the Mayas," *Kansas City Star,* October 10, 1938.

54. Peck, *Le Flore County,* 331–32.

55. Hamilton, "Spiro Mound," 18–34.

56. Phillips and Brown, *Pre-Columbian Shell Engravings,* 1:4.

57. Collins, "'On Land Where the Indians Lived,'" 2.

58. Zula Welch to Trowbridge, September 29, 1948, Spiro Folder, Spiro Mounds Collection, HTRL.

59. "Mound Yields Indian Relics Centuries Old.".

60. Brain, "Great Mound Robbery," 22.

61. McWade interview report, n.d., Spiro Reference File Folder, Spiro Collection, SNOM.

62. Hamilton, "Spiro Mound," 32.

63. Phillips and Brown, *Pre-Columbian Shell Engravings,* 1:7; Clements, "Historical Sketch," 62–63.

64. Scrapbook 4, Spiro Mounds Collection, HTRL.

Chapter 6

1. Pauketat, *Ancient Cahokia,* 9–12, 67–71, 79.

2. Emerson et al., "Sourcing and Interpretation," 303.

3. Pauketat, *Ancient Cahokia,* 152–55.

4. Emerson et al., "Sourcing and Interpretation," 303–304; Schambach, "Spiroan Traders," 7–27; Schambach, "Osage Orange Bows," 217–32.

5. Brown, *Spiro Ceremonial Center,* 1:142–43.

6. Brain, "The Great Mound Robbery," 21; Knight, " Mississippian Religion," 675–85; Thomas, *Exploring Ancient Native America,* 168–69; Barreis, "The Southern Cult," 23–38; Ford and Wiley, "An Interpretation of the Prehistory," 325–63; Emerson et al., "Sourcing and Interpretation," 303–304.

7. Gunning, *Prehistoric People of Oklahoma,* 30–31; La Vere, *The Caddo Chiefdoms,* 14–16; Pauketat, *The Ascent of Chiefs,* 33.

8. Brown, "Arkansas Valley Caddoan," 256–58; "Indians of the Southeast Had Same System of Worship," *Kansas City Star,* April 22, 1945.

9. Thomas, *Exploring Ancient Native America,* 162–65; Wyckoff, "Spiro," 51; Barreis, "Southern Cult," 24; Knight, "Mississippian Religion," 675–85; Fundaburk, *Sun Circles and Human Hands,* 38–59; Peterson, "A History of Excavations," 118–19.

10. Brown, *Spiro Ceremonial Center,* 1:189; Wyckoff, "Spiro," 53–54; Orr, "Pictographic Survey."

11. Emerson et al., "Sourcing and Interpretation," 305.

12. Wyckoff, "Spiro," 53.

13. "Indian Legends of 'Firebringer' Similar," *Spiro Graphic*, February 2, 1989, RSKM.

14. Ibid.; Wyckoff, "Spiro," 53–54; Brown, "Arkansas Valley Caddoan," 254–55.

15. Thomas, *Exploring Ancient Native America*, 165.

16. John Sibley to Dearborn, April 10, 1850, bound vol. 3, Melrose Collection; Sibley, "Historical Sketches of the Several Indian Tribes,"66–68.

17. Peterson, "A History of Excavations," 120–21; "Indian Legends of 'Firebringer' Similar"; Margare Dornaus, "A Town of Buried Treasures," *Poteau Daily News and Sun*, Sunday Supplement, n.d., RSKM; Wyckoff, "Spiro," 61–63; Barreis, "Southern Cult," 23–38.

18. Swanton, *Indian Tribes of the Lower Mississippi Valley*, 104.

19. Ibid., 100–106.

20. Ibid., 154–57.

21. Ibid.

22. Ibid., 149 (quotation), 157.

23. Ibid., 149.

24. Ibid., 146.

25. Ibid., 149 (quotation), 157.

26. Ibid., 149.

27. Hudson, *Southeastern Indians*, 332; Swanton, *Indian Tribes of the Lower Mississippi Valley*, 143.

28. Swanton, *Indian Tribes of the Lower Mississippi Valley*, 103.

29. Schambach, "Spiroan Traders," 25–26; Derrick and Wilson, "Cranial Modeling as an Ethnic Marker," 143–45; Schambach, "The Significance of the Sanders Site," 1.

30. Brown, *Spiro Ceremonial Center*, 1:23–24, 186–87, 198–99; Brown, "Spiro Art," 13–17.

31. Brown, *Spiro Ceremonial Center*, 1:24.

32. Ibid., 1:186–88, 195–96; Iva Mayhar Chelf, interview, March 16, 1979, Spiro Collection, SNOM.

33. Brown, *Spiro Ceremonial Center*, 1:23, 75–79, 133, 183–84, 190–91; Orr, "Pictographic Survey," photos 18 and 20; Kniffen, Gregory, and Stokes, *Historic Indian Tribes of Louisiana*, 244–45.

34. Brown, *Spiro Ceremonial Center*, 1:75–79.

35. Ibid., 1:79, 83; Wyckoff, "Transcripts," 12–13.

36. Wyckoff, "Transcripts," 13.

37. Brown, *Spiro Ceremonial Center*, 1:134, 187–88; 190–91; Pauketat, *Ancient Cahokia and the Mississippians*, 91–92.

38. Brown, *Spiro Ceremonial Center*, 1:188.

39. Kniffen, Gregory, and Stokes, *Historic Indian Tribes of Louisiana*, 244–45; Pauketat, *Ancient Cahokia*, 91–92.

40. Brown, *Spiro Ceremonial Center*, 1:167.

41. Emerson et al., "Sourcing and Interpretation," 303–304; Brown, *Spiro Ceremonial Center*, 1:134, 167, 199.

42. Brown, *Spiro Ceremonial Center*, 1:196, 198; Current Work Report by Dan Rogers, November 1979, Spiro Collection, SNOM; Brown, *Spiro Ceremonial Center*, 1:195.

43. Brown, *Spiro Ceremonial Center*, 1:195–97; Thomas, *Exploring Ancient Native America*, 166.

44. Brown, *Spiro Ceremonial Center*, 1:3, 7, 195, 197–98.

45. Peterson, "A History of Excavations," 118; Brown, *Spiro Ceremonial Center*, 1:196.

46. Orr, "Field Notes and Laboratory Analyses of Sites in the Spiro Area, Le Flore County, Oklahoma," microfilm, University of Chicago, 1950, Spiro Collection, SNOM; Newkumet, "Quarterly Field Report of Le Flore County Archaeology Project," Spiro Collection, SNOM; Newkumet, WPA Field Diary, April 23, 1938, to May 8, 1939, Spiro Collection, SNOM; Orr, "The Eufaula Mound," 2–15; Hester A. Davis to James Brown, February 3, 1965, Spiro Correspondence Folder, Spiro Collection, SNOM; "Prehistoric Site Purchase Talks OK'd" n.d., newspaper unknown,clipping in Spiro Folder, RSKM; Brown, *Spiro Ceremonial Center*, 1:3, 7; Peterson et al., *An Archeological Survey of the Spiro Vicinity*; Brown, "Arkansas Valley Caddoan," 242–43; Holmes and Hill, *The Spiro Mounds Site*, 10.

47. Brown, *Spiro Ceremonial Center*, 1:197

48. Barreis, "Southern Cult," 23.

49. La Vere, *Caddo Chiefdoms*, 14–16, 35

50. "Introduction to the Arkansas Basin Caddoans," OAS

51. Brown, *Spiro Ceremonial Center*, 1:38, 200; Will Dunham, "Climate Drove Southwest Native Cultural Changes." Daily News, Yahoo.com, October 5, 2001, http://dailynews.yahoo.com/htx/nm/20022004/sc/science_stalagmites_dc_1.htm.

52. Creel, "Bison Hides," 42.

53. Creel, "Bison Hides," 40–49; Wyckoff "Transcripts," 23; Krieger, "The Eastward Extension of Puebloan Datings," 141–48; Krieger, "The First Symposium," 203; "Naturally Speaking."

54. Brown, *Spiro Ceremonial Center*, 1:31–33; 199.

55. Brown, *Spiro Ceremonial Center*, 1:199; Lintz, "Texas Panhandle-Pueblo Interactions," 143–46; Krieger, *Cultural Complexes and Chronology*, 207.

56. Brown, *Spiro Ceremonial Center*, 1:196–97; Peterson, "A History of Excavations," 118.

57. Brown, *Spiro Ceremonial Center*, 1:194, 196, 199.

58. Ibid., 1:194–95.

59. Peterson, "Mounds Magic," *Poteau Daily News and Sun*, n.d., RSKM; Brown, *Spiro Ceremonial Center*, 1:195.

60. Brown, *Spiro Ceremonial Center*, 1:167.

61. Peterson, "Mounds Magic."

62. Brown, *Spiro Ceremonial Center*, 1:21

63. Ibid., 1:98; 2:306–307, 309.

64. Ibid., 1:22, 79–84, 87, 94–98, 102, 134, 194–95.

65. Ibid., 1:79–84, 87, 93–98, 102, 184; Hamilton, "Spiro Mound," 31.

66. Brown, *Spiro Ceremonial Center*, 1:22, 93–94, 98, 102.

67. Hamilton, "Spiro Mound," 30–32; Brown, *Spiro Ceremonial Center*, 1:87, 94–102, 166; Wyckoff, "Spiro," 48.

68. Brown, *Spiro Ceremonial Center*, 1:87, 94–102, 166; Wyckoff, "Spiro," 58; Hamilton, "Spiro Mound," 30–32; photos, April 1937, Spiro Mound Views, Clark Field Papers; Macdonald, "'King Tut' Tomb"; Orr, "Pictographic Survey," GM.

69. Hamilton, "Spiro Mound," 31; Duffield, "Oklahoma Craig Mound," 5–9.

70. Brown, *Spiro Ceremonial Center*, 1:66, 83, 85–87, 94, 96; Hamilton, "Spiro Mound," 29–31.

71. Brown, *Spiro Ceremonial Center*, 1:103.

72. Ibid., 1:79–84, 134, 196.

73. Ibid., 1:134, 187–88.

74. Wyckoff, "Transcripts," 11–14.

Chapter 7

1. Trowbridge Catalog, p. 2613, n.d., scrapbook 4, Spiro Folder, Spiro Mounds Collection, HTRL; Kansas City, Kansas, Planning and Zoning (website), Trowbridge Archaeological Site c. A.D. 200–600, http://www.kckplanning.org/trowbrid.htm, accessed July 17, 2003.

2. Collins, "'On Land Where the Indians Lived,'" 1, 5.

3. Trowbridge Catalog, p. 2618, n.d., scrapbook 4, Spiro Folder, Spiro Mounds Collection, HTRL; G. E. Pilquist to H. I. Player, December 30, 1935, scrapbook 4, Spiro Folder, Spiro Mounds Collection, HTRL.

4. Quote from Trowbridge to Moorehead, July 31, 1937, scrapbook 6, Spiro Folder, Spiro Mounds Collection, HTRL; Collins, "'On Land Where the Indians Lived,'" 2–3.

5. Trowbridge to H. C. Shertone, director of the Ohio State Museum, December 25, 1936, scrapbook 6, Spiro Folder, Spiro Mounds Collection, HTRL; Collins, "'On Land Where the Indians Lived,'" 3.

6. Trowbridge to Shertone, December 25, 1936; A. C. Whitford, "Fibres Contained in Samples sent by Mr. H. M. Trowbridge," April 11, 1939, scrapbook 6, Trowbridge Collection, HTRL.

7. Trowbridge to Andrew Heiskell, publisher, *Life* magazine, February 28, 1958, Spiro Folder, Spiro Mounds Collection, HTRL.

8. Trowbridge to Dr. Paul Martin, August 24, 1936, Spiro Folder, Spiro Mounds Collection, HTRL; Trowbridge to Heiskell, February 28, 1958.

9. J. W. Balloun to Trowbridge, February 10, 1936, Archaeology–Spiro Mound Folder, Balloun Collection.

10. Trowbridge to Sylvan Stroock, January 10, 1941, scrapbook 6, Spiro Folder, Spiro Mounds Collection, HTRL.

11. Stroock to Trowbridge, March 7, 1941, scrapbook 6, Spiro Folder, Spiro Mounds Collection, HTRL; Collins, "'On Land Where the Indians Lived,'" 3; National Bureau of Standards Report on Tests of Fibrous Material submitted by Smithsonian Institution, May 6, 1937, scrapbook 6, Trowbridge Collection, HTRL; Trowbridge, "Analysis of Spiro Mound Textiles," 51–53.

12. "Lost Civilization in Oklahoma May Be Related to Mayas," *Kansas City Star,* October 10, 1938.

13. Balloun to Trowbridge, February 10, 1936, Archaeology–Spiro Mound Folder, Balloun Collection.

14. Trowbridge to Balloun, September 9, 1936, Archaeology–Spiro Mound Folder, Balloun Collection.

15. Trowbridge to Joe [Balloun], April 19, 1936, Archaeology–Spiro Mound Folder, Balloun Collection.

16. Renno to Balloun, January 16, 1936, Archaeology–Spiro Mound Folder, Balloun Collection; Balloun to Trowbridge, August 18, 1936, Archaeology–Spiro Mound Folder, Balloun Collection.

17. Trowbridge to Joe [Balloun], April 19, 1936, Archaeology–Spiro Mound Folder, Balloun Collection.

18. Pilquist to H. I. Player, December 30, 1935, scrapbook 4, Trowbridge Collection, HTRL.

19. Trowbridge to Mrs. John Hobbs, April 20, 1936, Spiro Folder, Trowbridge Collection, HTRL.

20. Trowbridge to Heiskell, February 28, 1958; Hematite Rubbing Stone photo, Spiro, Okla., Mound, December 30, 1935, scrapbook 4, Spiro Mounds Collection, HTRL.

21. Catlinite pipe, Spiro, Okla., Mound, December 11, 1935, scrapbook 4, Trowbridge Collection, HTRL; hematite rubbing stone, Spiro, Okla. Mound, December 30, 1935, scrapbook 4, Trowbridge Collection, HTRL; Trowbridge to Braecklein, December 30, 1935, Trowbridge Collection, HTRL.

22. Macdonald, "'King Tut' Tomb." Subsequent details and quotations in the text are all from this source, unless otherwise specified.

23. Bruner, "They Found Oklahoma's Greatest Treasure," 10; Phillips and Brown, *Pre-Columbian Shell Engravings*, 1:5; Hamilton, "Spiro Mound," 28; Brown, *Spiro Ceremonial Center*, 1:88–89.

24. "Relic Hunters Found 'Gold Mine' In Indian Mound."

25. Hamilton, "Spiro Mound," 24.

26. Bruner, "They Found Oklahoma's Greatest Treasure," 14.

27. Ibid., 10; Guinn Cooper obituary, newspaper unknown. Clipping in Correspondence—Inquiries and Appreciative Letters Folder, RSKM.

28. Phillips and Brown, *Pre-Columbian Shell Engravings*, 1:7; "They've Dug into Middle Ages in an East Oklahoma Indian Mound," *Oklahoma City Times*, October 28, 1936,

29. Clements, "Historical Sketch," 56.

30. "Warrants Are Issued for Mound Diggers," *Poteau News*, January 9, 1936.

31. Clements to J. G. Braecklein, January 7, 1936, Archaeology—Oklahoma Folder, Trowbridge Collection, HTRL.

32. Ibid.

33. Clements, "Historical Sketch," 57–58.

34. Ibid.; Spiro Mound Views, Clark Field Papers; Clark Field to Robert E. Bell, February 3, 1965, Spiro Correspondence Folder, Spiro Collection, SNOM.

35. "Scientists Buy Right to Explore," May 8, 1936, photocopied clipping, newspaper unknown, Spiro Collection, SNOM; Clements, "Historical Sketch," 57–58.

36. Clements, "Historical Sketch," 57–58.

37. Ibid., 58.

38. Ibid., 57–58; Hamilton, "Spiro Mound," 23; "Scientists Buy Right to Explore"; L. S. Zuhlke to Dr. Forrest Clement, October 27, 1936, FPF.

Chapter 8

1. Groves, NAIRCA Report, 3.

2. Ibid., 4.

3. Ibid.

4. Miles, "Indian Relics," 112.

5. Clements, "Historical Sketch," 53.

6. Clements to Mrs. Don Zuhlke, November 21, 1936, FPF.

7. Neil M. Judd to J. G. Braecklein, February 13, 1936, Spiro Folder, Spiro Mounds Collection, HTRL.

8. Clements, "Historical Sketch," 57; Newkumet, Field Notes, 1938, Spiro Collection, SNOM; Newkumet, WPA Field Diary, May 1939 to July 1940, Spiro Collection, SNOM.

9. Newkumet, WPA Field Diary, December 18, 1939, Spiro Collection, SNOM; Phillips and Brown, *Pre-Columbian Shell Engravings*, 1:5; Bruner, "They Found Oklahoma's Greatest Treasure," 5–7; John Maff to John Hobbs, May 25, 1938, Spiro Folder, RSKM; Iva Mayhar Chelf, interview, March 16, 1979, Spiro Collection, SNOM; Judd to Braecklein, February 13, 1936.

10. Judd to Braecklein, February 13, 1936.

11. Collins, "'On Land Where the Indians Lived,'" 3.

12. Maff to Hobbs, May 25, 1938.

13. Merritt C. Masen to Hobbs, March 20, 1939, Spiro Folder, RSKM; H. T. Daniel to Hobbs, August 29, no year (c. 1940 or 1941), Spiro Folder, RSKM.

14. Carl Clausen to Hobbs, n.d. (c. 1939), Spiro Folder, RSKM.

15. H. T. Daniel to Hobbs, August 29, 1941, Spiro Folder, RSKM.

16. Ibid.

17. Contract of J. O. Hobbs, Fain White King, and Blanche Busey King, December 22, 1943, Spiro Folder, RSKM.

18. Newkumet, WPA Field Diary, December 18, 1939, SNOM.

19. Fain White King to Hobbs, May 19, 1944, Spiro Folder, RSKM.

20. H. T. Lawrence to John Hobbs, January 29, 1945, Spiro Folder, RSKM.

21. Pilquist, "Long Rare Heavy Prehistoric" ad, *Hobbies*, December 1935, 99.

22. Pilquist ad, *Hobbies*, January 1936, 93.

23. Groves, "Great Temple Mound Relics" ad, *Hobbies*, January 1936, 91.

24. Trowbridge to Miss Bertha M. Renno, July 4, 1941, Spiro Folder, Spiro Mounds Collection, HTRL.

25. A. W. Pendergast to Harry Trowbridge, n.d., Spiro Folder, Spiro Mounds Collection, HTRL.

26. Secretary to Mrs. D. O. Boudeman, January 15, 1950, FPF.

27. Hamilton, "Spiro Mound," 17–88; "Relic Hunters Found 'Gold Mine' In Indian Mound."

28. Hamilton, "Spiro Mound," 24–25.

29. Ibid.; Hamilton to Hobbs, May 11, 1938, Spiro Folder, RSKM.

30. Hamilton, "Spiro Mound," 18–21.

31. Hamilton to Orr, September 25, 1945, Orr Correspondence Folder, Spiro Collection, SNOM.

32. Hamilton to Orr, March 14, 1946, K. G. Correspondence Folder, Spiro Collection, SNOM.

33. Hoving, *King of the Confessors*, 41; "Called Meeting of the Board of Directors," 411.

34. Hamilton, "Spiro Mound," 32–33; "Spiro Indians Yield Archeological Treasures," *Southwest-Times Record*, May 9, 1937, typed copy in Spiro Collection, SNOM.

35. Hamilton, "Spiro Mound," 19, 22.

36. Frederick J. Dockstader to Stephen Borhegyi, November 6, 1956, Spiro Correspondence Folder, SNOM; Hamilton, "Spiro Mound," 21.

37. Brain, "Great Mound Robbery," 22.

38. Hamilton, "Spiro Mound," 21–22; *Federal Register*, 64, no. 141 (July 23, 1999): 40041; notices in http://www.cast.uark.edu/products/NAGPRA/DOCS/nic0283.pdf (accessed March 19, 2004).

39. Trowbridge to Jack Reed, September 17, 1936, Spiro Folder, Spiro Mounds Collection, HTRL.

40. Trowbridge to Prof. W. F. Linklater, January 31, 1955, Spiro Folder, Spiro Mounds Collection, HTRL.

41. Trowbridge to Warren King Moorehead, July 31, 1937, scrapbook 6, Spiro Folder, Spiro Mounds Collection, HTRL; Col. Fain White King to Trowbridge, January 4, 1942, Spiro Folder, Spiro Mounds Collection, HTRL; King to Trowbridge, July 29, 1941, Spiro Folder, Spiro Mounds Collection, HTRL.

42. Trowbridge to Reed, September 17, 1936, Spiro Folder, Spiro Mounds Collection, HTRL.

43. Trowbridge to Dr. John C. McGregor, November 2, 1946, Spiro Folder, Spiro Mounds Collection, HTRL.

44. Trowbridge to Lawrence Mills, July 29, 1959, Spiro Folder, Spiro Mounds Collection, HTRL.

45. Braecklein to Trowbridge, June 24, 1938, Spiro Folder, Spiro Mounds Collection, HTRL; George F. Coates to Trowbridge, January 13, 1946, Spiro Folder, Spiro Mounds Collection, HTRL; Coates to Trowbridge, January 14, 1947, Spiro Folder, Spiro Mounds Collection, HTRL; Willard Elsing to Trowbridge, March 12, 1950, Spiro Folder, Spiro Mounds Collection, HTRL.

46. Trowbridge to Welch, October 4, 1948, Spiro Folder, Spiro Mounds Collection, HTRL.

47. Mrs. D. E. Jones to Trowbridge, December 5, 1954, Spiro Folder, Spiro Mounds Collection, HTRL.

48. Trowbridge to D. E. Jones, December 7, 1954, Spiro Folder, Spiro Mounds Collection, HTRL.

49. Collins, "'On Land Where the Indians Lived,'" 5.

50. Trowbridge to Heiskell, February 28, 1958, Spiro Folder, Spiro Mounds Collection, HTRL; Mabel H. Schubert to Trowbridge, March 6, 1958, Spiro Folder, Spiro Mounds Collection, HTRL.

51. Trowbrigde to Lawrence Mills, July 29, 1959, Spiro Folder, Spiro Mounds Collection, HTRL; Collins, "'On Land Where the Indians Lived,'" 3.

52. Trowbridge Archaeological Site. http//www.wycokck.org/planning/trowbrid.htm (accessed March 19, 2004).

53. Clements, "Historical Sketch," 54–55.

54. Hamilton, "Spiro Mound," 24.

55. Phillips and Brown, Pre-Columbian Shell Engravings, 1:3–5; Hamilton, "Spiro Mound," 23–24.

56. John C. Pfalzgraf to Frank Phillips, September 14, 1936, FPF; L. S. Zuhlke to Clements, September 16, 1936, FPF.

57. Clements to L. S. Zuhlke, October 7, 1936, FPF.

58. Pfalzgraf to Phillips, September 14, 1936, FPF.

59. Mrs. Don Zuhlke to Clements, January 20, 1938, FPF.

60. Braecklein to Trowbridge, May 3, 1948, Spiro Mounds Collection, HTRL.

61. Hamilton to Brown, February 15, 1964, Spiro Correspondence Folder, SNOM.

62. Hamilton to Orr, May 16, 1946, Orr Correspondence Folder, Spiro Collection, SNOM.

63. Hamilton to Brown, February 25, 1965, Spiro Correspondence Folder, SNOM. Another author believed the McDannald Collection contained fake pipes. In a typed note attached to stories about pipes in Hobbies, an unknown author wrote, "The pipes from the McDannald Collection are fakes that were sold as original stone effigy pipes from the Spiro Mound site." "Masterpiece of the Mound Builders," Hobbies, June 1942, 102; "Mound Builders' Pipes," Hobbies, August 1942, 96. Photocopies and typed notes found in Spiro Collection, SNOM.

64. All these museums realized and admitted they were fakes. Personal communication with the author.

65. Headley, "Experiences of a Collector," 98–99.

66. Robbins, "The Art of Restoring Indian Relics," 101–102.

67. Daniel, "Fakes—Around the Mound," 96.

68. Braecklein to Trowbridge, May 3, 1948, Spiro Folder, Spiro Mounds Collection, HTRL.

69. Ibid.

70. Pfalzgraf to Phillips, September 14, 1936, FPF.

71. Secretary to Pfalzgraf, December 23, 1936, FPF.

72. Hamilton to Brown, February 25, 1965, Spiro Correspondence Folder, SNOM.

73. Mrs. Don Zuhlke to Clements, January 20, 1938, FPF.

Chapter 9

1. Clements to Phillips, November 4, 1938, FPF.

2. Orr, "The Archaeological Situation at Spiro," 228, note 2.

3. Orr to Dr. J. Willis Stovall, December 18, 1944 in Current Work Report by Dan Rogers, November 1979, Spiro Collection, SNOM.

4. Preliminary General Report on Archaeological Work in Oklahoma, August 1938, "Le Flore County," folder 1, box 1, minor box I-21, W.P.A. Archaeological Survey Project File.

5. Newkumet, August 21, 1939, WPA Field Diary, May 1939 to July 1940.

6. Orr, Instructions to WPA Foremen, c. 1938, Spiro Collection, SNOM.

7. Newkumet, May 12, 1939, WPA Field Diary; "List of Men on the WPA Work Crews in Le Flore County," Field Notebook of Harry H. Atkinson, U of A School of Medicine, Junior, no. 5, July 1936, SNOM [Note: This date might be a typo for 1938].

8. List of Spiro excavators, From Survey Notes Daily Log Record, Le Flore County, February 12, 1938, Spiro Collection, SNOM.

9. Newkumet, November 13, 1939, WPA Field Diary; Mr. and Mrs. Edison Barnes, interview, March 15, 1979, Spiro Collection, SNOM.

10. J. Daniel Rogers, "Federally Sponsored Archeological Work in Oklahoma before World War II," December 12, 1978, presented to Dr. Robert E. Bell, Inventory Book, WPA Archaeological Survey Project Files Iva Mayhar Chelf, interview, March 16, 1979, Spiro Collection, SNOM.

11. Spiro Mound Views, Clark Field Papers.

12. Iva Mayhar Chelf, interview, March 16, 1979.

13. Cornelious Shoates, interview, March 15, 1979, Spiro Collection, SNOM.

14. Brown, *Spiro Ceremonial Center*, 1:60.

15. Ibid., 1:60 (quotation), 105; Phillips and Brown, *Pre-Columbian Shell Engravings*, 1:8.

16. Rogers, "Federally Sponsored Archaeological Work"; "They've Dug Into the Middle Ages in an East Oklahoma Indian Mound."

17. Phillips and Brown, *Pre-Columbian Shell Engravings*, 1:8; Peterson, "A History of Excavations," 116–17; Brown to Orr, September 14, 1964, Spiro Correspondence Folder, SNOM.

18. Photos, October 1936, Spiro Mound Views, Clark Field Papers; Cornelious Shoates, interview, March 15, 1979; Iva Mayhar Chelf, interview, March 16, 1979; Clements to Trowbridge, February 25, 1937, Archaeology-Oklahoma Folder, Spiro Mounds Collection, HTRL.

19. Clements to Mrs. Don Zuhlke, March 24, 1938, FPF.

20. Clements to Phillips, November 29, 1939, FPF.

21. "Called Meeting of the Board of Directors," 411.

22. Newkumet, August 8, 1939, WPA Field Diary; Groves, NAIRCA Report, 4.

23. Newkumet, July 6, 1939, WPA Field Diary.

24. Clements to Trowbridge, February 25, 1937, Archaeology—Oklahoma Folder, Trowbridge Collection, HTRL.

25. Phillips and Brown, *Pre-Columbian Shell Engravings*, 1:8.

26. Photos, October 1936, Spiro Mound Views, Clark Field Papers.

27. Newkumet, August 18, 1939, WPA Field Diary.

28. Newkumet, August 17, 1939, WPA Field Diary.

29. Newkumet, August 18, 1939, WPA Field Diary.

30. Cornelious Shoates, interview, March 15, 1979, Spiro Collection, SNOM.

31. George Baxter biography, Spiro Collection, SNOM.

32. Mr. and Mrs. Edison Barnes, interview, March 15, 1979.

33. Iva Mayhar Chelf, interview, March 16, 1979.

34. Newkumet, January 12 and 13, 1939, WPA Field Diary; Mr. and Mrs. Edison Barnes, interview, March 15, 1979.

35. Bruner, "They Found Oklahoma's Greatest Treasure," 12.

36. Cornelious Shoates, interview, March 15, 1979; Iva Mayhar Chelf, interview, March 16, 1979.

37. Photos, October 1936 and April 1937, Spiro Mound Views, Clark Field Papers; *Tulsa Daily World*, October 20, 1936, Spiro Mound Views, Clark Field Papers; Cornelious Shoates, interview, March 15, 1979; Minutes of the Oklahoma State Archaeological Society, April 29, 1939, folder 3, minor box 48, Bell Collection.

38. Mrs. Don Zuhlke to Clements, October 12, 1938, FPF; Clements to Phillips, December 11, 1938, FPF.

39. Cornelious Shoates, interview, March 15, 1979.

40. Clements to Phillips, December 11, 1938; Clements to Brown, March 5, 1965, Spiro Correspondence Folder, SNOM.

41. George Baxter biography, Spiro Collection, SNOM.

42. Orr, "Field Notes," microfilm, University of Chicago, 1950, Spiro Collection, SNOM.

43. Preliminary General Report on Archaeological Work in Oklahoma, August 1938, WPA Archaeological Survey Project Files; Brown, *Spiro Ceremonial Center*, 1:105.

44. Newkumet, April 23, 1938, Field Notes, 1938, Spiro Collection, SNOM.

45. Brown, *Spiro Ceremonial Center*, 1:123.

46. Newkumet, November 26, 1939, WPA Field Diary.

47. Newkumet, April 19, 1938, Field Notes; Newkumet, August 17, 1939, WPA Field Diary.

48. Newkumet, May 8, 1938, WPA Field Diary.

49. Newkumet, November 26, 1939, WPA Field Diary.

50. Newkumet, December 18, 1939, WPA Field Diary.

51. Newkumet, December 4, 1939, WPA Field Diary.

52. Newkumet, March 17, 1939, WPA Field Diary.

53. Newkumet biography, Spiro Collection, SNOM.

54. Zadoc T. Harrison interview, 28:175, IPH.

55. Newkumet, May 12, 1939, WPA Field Diary.

56. Iva Mayhar Chelf, interview, March 16, 1979.

57. Ibid.

58. Cornelious Shoates, interview, March 15, 1979.

59. Ibid.

60. Ibid.; Mr. and Mrs. Edison Barnes, interview, March 15, 1979; Newkumet biography, Spiro Collection, SNOM.

61. Mr. and Mrs. Edison Barnes, interview, March 15, 1979.

62. Newkumet, November 14, 1939, WPA Field Diary.

63. Newkumet, December 31, 1939, January 17, 1940, WPA Field Diary.

64. Brown, *Spiro Ceremonial Center*, 1:60; Peterson, "A History of Excavations," 116–17.

Chapter 10

1. "They've Dug into Middle Ages in an East Oklahoma Indian Mound.".

2. "Where 'Mound Men' Dwelt," *Christian Science Monitor*, August 31, 1938, photocopied clipping, Spiro Collection, SNOM.

3. Macdonald, "'King Tut' Tomb."

4. "Traces Pipe to Mayans: Beloit Expert Reports on Relic Found in Oklahoma Mound," *New York Times*, April 11, 1936.

5. Groves, NAIRCA Report, 10.

6. "Lost Civilization in Oklahoma May Be Related to the Mayas," *Kansas City Star*, October 10, 1938, Spiro Folder, Spiro Mounds Collection, HTRL.

7. Jennings, *The Founders of America*, 62.

8. "Scientists Buy Right to Explore." Photocopied clipping, unknown newspaper, May 8 (c. 1936), Spiro Collection, SNOM.

9. "Spiro Indian Mounds Yield Archaeological Treasure," *Southwest-Times Record*, May 9, 1937, typed copy in Spiro Collections, SNOM.

10. Peck, *Le Flore County*, 6–7; "Rune Expert Visits Area," *Poteau Daily News and Sun*, June 3, 1992, Spiro Folder, RSKM.

11. Trowbridge to Albert F. Ganier, July 17, 1948, Spiro Folder, Spiro Mounds Collection, HTRL.

12. Phillips and Brown, *Pre-Columbian Shell Engravings*, 1:7.

13. Ibid.; "Scientists Buy Right to Explore"; "Spiro Indian Mounds Yield Archaeological Treasure."

14. Clements, "Historical Sketch," 59–60.

15. Letter to the Editor, "Mormon Biblical History," Charles B. Woodstock, *Kansas City Star*, December 22, 1935, Spiro Folder, Spiro Mounds Collection, HTRL.

16. Farley, "The Spiro Stone Tablet," 155–56.

17. Orr to Stovall, December 18, 1944, in Current Work Report by Dan Rogers, November 1979, Spiro Collection, SNOM.

18. Ibid.

19. "EM Gets $1,900 Award to Conduct Research Among Oklahoma Indians," clipping, n.d., unknown newspaper, c. 1945, Orr Notes Folder, SNOM.

20. Wyckoff, "Transcripts," 25; Schambach "Spiro and the Tunica," 188.

21. Orr, "Archaeological Situation at Spiro," 254–55; Orr, "Field Notes," 32–35.

22. Wyckoff, "Transcripts," 28–30; La Vere, *Caddo Chiefdoms*, 29; Peterson, "A History of Excavations," 119; Brown, *Spiro Ceremonial Center*, 1:33–34; Thomas, *Exploring Ancient Native America*, 169–70; Brown, "Arkansas Valley Caddoan."

23. Brown, *Spiro Ceremonial Center*, 1:31–32; Wyckoff, "Transcripts," 26–27.

24. Wyckoff, "Transcripts," 28–30.

25. Thomas, *Exploring Ancient Native America*, 169–70; Peterson, "A History of Excavations," 119; Peterson, "Mounds Magic"; Brown, *Spiro Ceremonial Center*, 1:32, 38; "Introduction to the Arkansas Basin Caddoans;" Wyckoff and Peterson, "Spiro Mounds," transcript for Spiro video, Spiro Mounds Archaeological Park, N.d., no publisher.

26. "Museum, Indian Nations in Quandary Over Who Gets Artifacts," *The Sunday Oklahoman*, April 22, 1990, Spiro Folder, RSKM.

27. Schambach, "Spiro and the Tunica," 169, 189–90.
28. Ibid.
29. Ibid., 180–83, 193–99.
30. Hamilton, "Spiro Mound," 17–88.
31. Cecil to Brown, September 8, 1964, Spiro Correspondence Folder, SNOM.
32. Bruner, "They Found Oklahoma's Greatest Treasure," 15; W. M. DeGeer to Brown, May 4, 1965, Brown to DeGeer, May 17, 1965, Spiro Correspondence Folder, SNOM; "Oklahoma Works to Preserve Spiro Ruins," *Southwest Times-Record*, September 4, 1993, Spiro Folder, RSKM.
33. Brown to Rucker G. Blankenship, August 17, 1965, Spiro Correspondence Folder, SNOM.
34. Brain, "Great Mound Robbery," 22–23.
35. "'Spiro Mounds' Study Undertaken by Stovall," *Daily Oklahoman*, March 11, 1964, photocopy in Spiro Collection, SNOM; "Six Anthropologists Examine Spiro India [sic] Buriel [sic] Mound," *Daily Oklahoman*, May 9, 1964, photocopy in Spiro Collection, SNOM.
36. Peterson, "A History of Excavations," 117. See the bibliography for some of James A. Brown's publications.
37. Brain, "Great Mound Robbery," 22–23.
38. Current Work Report by Dan Rogers, November 1979, Spiro Collection, SNOM; Wyckoff, "Spiro," 58; Peterson, "A History of Excavations," 117; "Spiro Mounds Offers Change to Watch Digs," *Spiro Graphic*, n.d. (c. 1980), clipping in Spiro Folder, RSKM; "Study Resumes at Spiro Mounds," *Spiro Graphic*, n.d. (c. 1980), clipping in Spiro Folder, RSKM.
39. "Radar 'Unearths' Ruins," *Southwest Times-Record*, September 4, 1993, clipping in Spiro Folder, RSKM.
40. "Spiro Mounds Stalemate Poses $300,000 Threat." *Le Flore County Sun*, October 14, 1973, clipping in Spiro Folder, RSKM.
41. Ibid.
42. Ibid.
43. Bruner, "They Found Oklahoma's Greatest Treasure," 15; Peterson, "A History of Excavations," 117.
44. "Spiro Mounds house Due Restoration by OU Students," *Le Flore County Sun*, June 1, 1980, clipping in Spiro Folder, RSKM.
45. "Graphic Letters," *Spiro Graphic*, n.d. (c. 1990), clipping in Spiro Folder, RSKM.
46. "A Memorable Event," photo, *Poteau Daily News*, November 8, 1988, clipping in Spiro Folder, RSKM; "Nickles Speaks at Spiro Banquet," *Southwest Times-Record*, April 9, 1989, clipping in Spiro Folder,

RSKM; "Spiro Mounds Gets $5,500 Gift," *Spiro Graphic*, February 10, 1993, clipping in Spiro Folder, RSKM.

47. "Plans Submitted for Spiro Mounds Projects," *Spiro Graphic*, March 28, 1991, Spiro Folder, RSKM; "Spiro Mounds in New Hands," *Daily Oklahoman*, July 7, 1991, Section X, Spiro Mounds, OHS.

48. "Spiro Mounds in New Hands."

49. Exhibit display card information at the Robert S. Kerr Museum, Poteau, Oklahoma; Jewel Costner [curator] to workshop coordinator, November 14, 1980, Correspondence, Inquiries and Appreciative Letters Folder, RSKM; Rogers, Moore, and Stanley, "Some Additional Artifacts from Craig Mound," 33–50.

50. Guinn Cooper obituary, n.d., unknown newspaper, clipping in Correspondence, Inquiries and Appreciative Letters Folder, RSKM; Walter Guinn Cooper to Joy, November 13, 1974, Spiro Folder, RSKM.

51. "Retired Teacher Gives Museum Rare Spiro Mounds Collection," *Le Flore County Sun*, January 26, 1975, clipping in Spiro Folder, RSKM; "This N That," *Poteau Daily News and Sun*, August 22, 1990 in William Beach Folder, Spiro Folder, RSKM.

52. "Retired Teacher Gives Museum Rare Spiro Mounds Collection."

53. "Indian Relics Still Gone," *Kansas City Star*, November 25, 1938, clipping in Spiro Folder, Spiro Mounds Collection, Spiro Mounds Collection, HTRL.

54. Greg H. Perino to Jim [Brown], February 24, 1965, Spiro Correspondence Folder, SNOM.

55. Robert O. Fay to Robert E. Bell, January 3, 1966, Robert E. Bell to Robert O. Fay, January 4, 1966, Spiro Correspondence Folder, SNOM.

56. Items Missing from Various Displays at Kerr Museum, Terry L. Smith, January 27, 1992, Conch Shell Folder, Spiro Folder, RSKM; Gloria Farley to curator, North American artifacts, Peabody Museum, January 30, 1992, Spiro Folder, RSKM.

57. Farley to curator, North American artifacts, Peabody Museum, January 30, 1992, RSKM.

58. Laird King to Le Flore County Sheriff's Office, May 22, 1992, Conch Shell Folder, RSKM.

59. Laird King to James Brown, April 30, 1992, Conch Shell Folder, RSKM; handwritten notes, Conch Shell Folder, RSKM.

60. Handwritten notes.

61. Laird King to Le Flore County Sheriff's Office, May 22, 1992; handwritten notes; *Heavener Ledger*, April 15, 1993, photocopy in Conch Shell Folder, RSKM.

62. *Heavener Ledger*, April 15, 1993; handwritten notes; Laird King to John Campbell, April 30, 1992, Conch Shell Folder, RSKM.

Epilogue

1. "Mounds Magic," *Spiro Graphic*, October 27, 1988, November 17, 1988, clippings in Spiro Folder, RSKM; "Spiro Mounds in New Hands," *Daily Oklahoman*, July 7, 1991, clipping in Section X, Spiro Mounds; "Third Annual Kite Flite Day Set at Mounds," *Spiro Graphic*, February 15, 1990, clipping in Spiro Folder, RSKM.

2. James H. Kellar to Jim Brown, November 21, 1964, Spiro Correspondence Folder, SNOM.

3. See Deloria, Jr., *Red Earth, White Lies*.

Bibliography

Archival Sources

Balloun, Joe. Collection. Harry Trowbridge Collection, Harry Trowbridge Research Library, Wyandotte County Historical Society and Museum, Bonner Springs, Kans.

Bell, Robert E. Collection. Western History Collection, University of Oklahoma Libraries, Norman, Okla.

Braecklein, J. G. Collection. Spiro Mound Information and Photographs Box, Gilcrease Museum, Tulsa, Okla.

Field, Clark. Papers. 1934–1937, Spiro Mound Information and Photographs Box, Gilcrease Museum, Tulsa, Okla.

Indian-Pioneer Histories. 112 volumes. Indian Archives, Oklahoma Historical Society, Oklahoma City, Okla.

Melrose Collection. Cammie G. Henry Research Room, Eugene Watson Library, Northwestern State University, Natchitoches, La.

Oklahoma Archaeological Survey, Norman, Okla.

Spiro Mound Information and Photographs Box, Gilcrease Museum, Tulsa, Okla.

Phillips Foundation, Frank. Woolaroc Museum, Bartlesville, Oklahoma.

Spiro Collection. Site Documents Archives, Archaeology Collection, Sam Noble Oklahoma Museum of Natural History, University of Oklahoma, Norman, Okla.

Spiro Folder. Robert S. Kerr Museum, Poteau, Okla.

Spiro Mounds Collection. Harry Trowbridge Collection, Harry Trowbridge Research Library, Wyandotte County Historical Society and Museum, Bonner Springs, Kans.

Spiro Mounds. Indian Archives, Oklahoma Historical Society, Oklahoma City, Okla.

Spring, Otto F. Collection. Western History Collection, University of Oklahoma, Norman, Okla.

Trowbridge, Harry. Collection. Harry Trowbridge Research Library, Wyandotte County Historical Society and Museum, Bonner Springs, Kans.

WPA Archaeological Survey Project Files for Oklahoma, Western History Collections, University of Oklahoma, Norman, Okla.

Books, Periodicals, and Papers

Barreis, David A. "The Southern Cult and the Spiro Ceremonial Complex." *Bulletin of Oklahoma Anthropological Society* 5 (1957): 23–38.

Bell, Robert E. "Trade Materials at Spiro Mounds as Indicated by Artifacts." *American Antiquity* 12 (1947): 181–84.

Brain, Jeffrey P., "The Great Mound Robbery." *Archaeology* 41 (May/June 1988): 18–25.

Brose, David S. "From the Southeastern Ceremonial Complex to the Southern Cult: 'You Can't Tell the Players without a Program.'" In *The Southeastern Ceremonial Complex: Artifacts and Analysis, the Cottonlandia Conference,* edited by Patricia Galloway, 27–37. Lincoln: University of Nebraska Press, 1989.

Brown, James A. "Arkansas Valley Caddoan: The Spiro Phase." In *Prehistory of Oklahoma,* edited by Robert E. Bell, 241–63. New York: Academic Press, 1984.

———. "Exchange and Interaction until 1500." In *Handbook of North American Indians: Southeast,* vol. 14, edited by William C. Sturtevant and Raymond D. Fogelson, 677–85. Washington D.C.: Smithsonian Institution, 2004.

———. "Spiro Art and Its Mortuary Contexts." In *Death and the Afterlife in Pre-Columbian America,* edited by Elizabeth P. Benson, 1–32. Washington D.C.: Dumbarton Oaks Research Library and Collections, 1975.

———. *The Spiro Ceremonial Center: The Archaeology of Arkansas Valley Caddoan Culture in Eastern Oklahoma.* Memoirs of the Museum of Anthropology 29. 2 volumes. Ann Arbor: University of Michigan, 1996.

"Called Meeting of the Board of Directors of the Oklahoma Historical Society, December 1940." *Chronicles of Oklahoma* 18 (1940): 411.

Clements, Forrest E. "Historical Sketch of the Spiro Mound." In *Contributions from the Museum of the American Indian Heye Foundation,* vol. 14, 48–68. New York: Museum of the American Indian Heye Foundation, 1945.

Collins, Steve. "'On Land Where the Indians Lived,' Harry Martin Trowbridge: A Wyandotte County Avocationalist." *Society for American Archaeology Bulletin* 17 (November 1999): 1–6. http://www.saa.org/publications/saabulletin/17-/saa13.html (accessed April 24, 2002).

Cooper, Lola Person. *Lest We Forget*. Russellville, Ark.: privately printed, 1972.

Creel, Darrell. "Bison Hides in the Late Prehistoric Exchange in the Southern Plains." *American Antiquity* 56 (1991): 40–49.

Crosby, Alfred W. *The Columbian Exchange: Biological and Cultural Consequences of 1492*. Westport, Conn.: Greenwood Publishing, 1972.

Daniel, H. T. "Fakes—Around the Mound." *Hobbies*, December 1935, 96.

Debo, Angie. *The Rise and Fall of the Choctaw Republic*. 1934. Norman: University of Oklahoma Press, 1961.

Deloria, Vine, Jr. *Red Earth, White Lies: Native Americans and the Myth of Scientific Fact*. New York: Scribner, 1995.

De Mézières, Athanase. *Athanase De Mézières and the Louisiana-Texas Frontier, 1768–1780*. 2 vols. Edited by Herbert Bolton. 1914. New York: Kraus, 1970.

DePratter, Chester. *Late Prehistoric and Early Historic Chiefdoms in the Southeastern United States*. New York: Garland Press, 1991.

Derrick, Sharon McCormick, and Diane Wilson, "Cranial Modeling as an Ethnic Marker among the Prehistoric Caddo." *Bulletin of the Texas Archeological Society* 68 (1997): 139–46.

Dillehay, Tom D. "Disease Ecology and Initial Human Migration." In *The First Americans: Search and Research*, edited by Tom D. Dillehay and David J. Meltzer, 231–64. Boca Raton, Fla.: CRC Press, 1991.

Duffield, Lathel F. "The Oklahoma Craig Mound: Another Look at an Old Problem." *Bulletin of the Oklahoma Anthropological Society* 22 (1973): 1–10.

Dunham, Will. "Climate Drove Southwest Native Cultural Changes." *Daily News, Yahoo.com*, October 5, 2001. http://dailynews.yahoo.com/htx/nm/20022004/sc/science_stalagmites_dc_1.htm.

Early, Ann M. "Prehistory of the Western Interior After 500 B.C." In *Handbook of North American Indians: Southeast*, vol. 14, edited by William C. Sturtevant and Raymond D. Fogelson, 561–73. Washington, D.C.: Smithsonian Institution, 2004.

Emerson, Thomas E., Randall E. Hughes, Mary R. Hynes, and Sarah U. Wisseman. "The Sourcing and Interpretations of Cahokia-Style Figurines in the Trans-Mississippi South and Southeast." *American Antiquity* 68 (2003): 287–313.

Faiman-Silva, Sandra. *Choctaws at the Crossroads: The Political Economy of Class and Culture in the Oklahoma Timber Region*. Lincoln: University of Nebraska Press, 1997.

Farley, Gloria. "The Spiro Stone Tablet." *The Epigraphic Society* 12 (June 1984): 149–57.

Fiedel, Stuart J. *Prehistory of the Americas.* New York: Cambridge University Press, 1987.

Ford, James A., and Gordon R. Wiley. "An Interpretation of the Prehistory of the Eastern United States." *American Anthropologist* 43 (1941): 325–63.

Foreman, Grant. *The Five Civilized Tribes: Cherokee, Chickasaw, Choctaw, Creek, Seminole.* Norman: University of Oklahoma Press, 1934.

Fundaburk, Emma Lila. *Sun Circles and Human Hands: The Southeastern Indians Art and Industries.* Luverne, Ala.: privately printed, 1957.

Gibson, Jon L. *The Ancient Mounds of Poverty Point: Place of Rings.* Gainesville: University of Florida Press, 2000.

Groves, Glen. I. "The North American Indian Relic Collectors Association Report on the Great Temple Mound in Le Flore, Co., Oklahoma." *North American Indian Relic Collectors Association* 1 (March 1936): 3–10.

Gunning, I. C. *Prehistoric People of Oklahoma and Their Culture.* Poteau: Eastern Oklahoma Historical Society, 1974.

Hamilton, Henry W. "The Spiro Mound." *Missouri Archaeologist* 14 (October 1952): 17–88.

Harrington, M. R. "A Pot-Hunter's Paradise." In *Indian Notes and Monographs,* vol. 1, no. 2, 84–90. New York: Museum of the American Indian, Heye Foundation, 1924.

Headley, O. T. "Experiences of a Collector." *Hobbies,* April 1935, 98–99.

Hester, Thomas R. "The Prehistory of South Texas." In *The Prehistory of Texas,* edited by Timothy K. Perttula, 127–51. College Station: Texas A&M University Press, 2004.

Hodge, Frederick. *Spanish Explorers in the Southern United States.* 1907. New York: Barnes and Noble, 1971.

Holmes, Mary Ann, and Marsha Hill. *The Spiro Mounds Site.* Norman: University of Oklahoma Stovall Museum, 1976.

Hoving, Thomas. *King of the Confessors.* New York: Simon and Schuster, 1981.

Hudson, Charles. *The Southeastern Indians.* Knoxville: University of Tennessee Press, 1976.

Hultkrantz, Ake. *Native Religions of North America: The Power of Visions and Fertility.* San Francisco: Harper and Row, 1987.

Jennings, Francis. *The Founders of America: From the Earliest Migrations to the Present.* New York: W. W. Norton and Company, 1993.

Joutel, Henri. *The La Salle Expedition to Texas: The Journal of Henri Joutel, 1684–1687.* Edited by William C. Foster. Translated by Johanna S. Warren. Austin: Texas State Historical Association, 1998.

Kniffen, Fred B., Hiram F. Gregory, and George A. Stokes. *The Historic Indians Tribes of Louisiana: From 1542 to the Present.* Baton Rouge: Louisiana State University Press, 1987.

Knight, Vernon James, Jr. "The Institutional Organization of Mississippian Religion." *American Antiquity,* 51 (1986): 675–87.

Krieger, Alex D. *Cultural Complexes and Chronology in Northern Texas.* Austin: University of Texas Publication, 1946.

———. "The Eastward Extension of Puebloan Datings Toward Cultures of the Mississippi Valley." *American Antiquity* 12 (January 1947): 141–48.

———. "The First Symposium on the Caddoan Archaeological Area." *American Antiquity* 12 (January 1947): 198–207.

Kupperman, Karen Ordahl. *Roanoke: The Abandoned Colony.* Lanham, Md.: Rowan and Littlefield Publishers, 1984.

La Vere, David. *The Caddo Chiefdoms: Caddo Economics and Politics, 700–1835.* Lincoln: University of Nebraska Press, 1998.

———. *The Texas Indians.* College Station: Texas A&M University Press, 2004.

Lawson, John. *A New Voyage to Carolina.* Edited By Hugh Talmage Lefler. 1701. Chapel Hill: University of North Carolina Press, 1967.

Lintz, Christopher. "Texas Panhandle–Pueblo Interactions from the Thirteenth through the Sixteenth Century." In *Farmers, Hunters, and Colonists: Interaction between the Southwest and the Southern Plains,* edited by Katherine A. Spielmann, 89–106. Tucson: University of Arizona Press, 1991.

Martin, Susan R. *Wonderful Power: The Story of Ancient Copper Working in the Lake Superior Basin.* Detroit: Wayne State University Press, 1999.

Miles, Charles. "Indian Relics: Mounds." *Hobbies,* May 1960, 112.

Moorehead, Warren King. *Archaeology of the Arkansas River Valley.* New Haven, Conn.: Yale University Press, 1931.

Morris, John W., Charles R. Goins, and Edwin C. McReynolds. *Historical Atlas of Oklahoma.* 1965. Norman: University of Oklahoma Press, 1986.

"Naturally Speaking." *Newsletter of the Dallas Museum of Natural History* 10 (January–March 2001): 3.

Newcomb, W. W., Jr. *The Rock Art of Texas Indians.* Austin: University of Texas Press, 1967.

Orr, Kenneth Gordon, "The Archaeological Situation at Spiro, Oklahoma; A Preliminary Report." *American Antiquity* 11 (1946): 228–56.

———. "The Eufaula Mound: Contributions to the Spiro Focus." *The Oklahoma Prehistorian* 4 (September 1941): 2–15.

Pauketat, Timothy R. *Ancient Cahokia and the Mississippians.* Cambridge: Cambridge University Press, 2004.

———. *The Ascent of Chiefs: Cahokia and Mississippian Politics in Native North America.* Tuscaloosa: University of Alabama Press, 1994.

Peck, Henry L. *The Proud Heritage of Le Flore County: A History of an Oklahoma County.* Van Buren, Ark.: The Press Argus, 1963.

Peebles, Christopher S., and Susan M. Kus. "Some Archaeological Correlates of Ranked Societies." *American Antiquity* 42 (July 1977): 421–48.

Peterson, Dennis A. "A History of Excavations and Interpretations of Artifacts from the Spiro Mounds Site." *The Southeastern Ceremonial Complex: Artifacts and Analysis, the Cottonlandia Conference,* edited by Patricia Galloway, 114–21. Lincoln: University of Nebraska Press, 1989.

Peterson, Dennis A., J. Daniel Rogers, Don G. Wyckoff, and Karen Dohm. *An Archeological Survey of the Spiro Vicinity, Le Flore County, Oklahoma.* Report 37. Norman: Oklahoma Archeological Survey, 1993.

Phillips, Philip, and James A. Brown. *Pre-Columbian Shell Engravings from the Craig Mound at Spiro, Oklahoma.* 6 vols. Cambridge, Mass.: Peabody Museum Press, 1978.

Pilquist, G. E. "Along the Arkansas." *Hobbies,* April 1935, 101–102.

Prentice, Guy. "Marine Shells as Wealth Items in Mississippian Societies." *Midcontinental Journal of Archaeology* 12 (1987): 193–223.

Robbins, Maurice. "The Art of Restoring Indian Relics." *Hobbies,* May 1935, 101–102.

Rogers, J. Daniel, Mike Moore, and John Stanley, "Some Additional Artifacts from Craig Mound." *Bulletin of the Oklahoma Anthropological Society* 30 (1981): 33–50.

Schambach, Frank F. "Osage Orange Bows, Indian Horses, and the Blackland Prairie of Northeast Texas." In *Blackland Prairies of the Gulf Coastal Plain: Nature, Culture and Sustainability,* edited by E. Peacock and T. Shauwecker, 212–36. Tuscaloosa: University of Alabama Press, 2003.

———. "The Significance of the Sanders Site in the Culture History of the Mississippi Period Southeast and the Southern Plains." In *The 1931 Excavations at the Sanders Site, Lamar County, Texas: Notes on the Fieldwork, Human Osteology, and Ceramics,* edited by A. T. Jackson, Marcus S. Goldstein, and Alex D. Krieger, 1–7. Austin: University of Texas, 2000.

———. "Spiro and the Tunica: A New Interpretation of the Role of the Tunica in the Culture History of the Southeast and the Southern Plains, A.D. 1100–1750." In *Arkansas Archaeology: Essays in Honor of Dan and Phyllis Morse,* edited by Robert C. Mainfort, Jr., and Marvin D. Jeter, 169–224. Fayetteville: University of Arkansas Press, 1999.

———. "Spiroan Traders, the Sanders Site, and the Plains Interaction Sphere: A Reply to Bruseth, Wilson, and Perttula." *Plains Anthropologist* 45 (2002): 7–27.

Shaffer, Lynda Norene. *Native Americans before 1492: The Moundbuilding Centers of the Eastern Woodlands.* Armonk, N.Y.: M. E. Sharpe, 1992.

Sibley, John. "Historical Sketches of the Several Indian Tribes in Louisiana, south of the Arkansa [*sic*] River, and between the Mississippi and River Grand." In *Travels in the Interior Parts of America.* Edited by Thomas Jefferson. London: J. G. Barnard, 1807.

Smith, Marvin T. *Archaeology of Aboriginal Culture Change in the Interior Southeast: Depopulation during the Early Historic Period.* Gainesville: University Press of Florida, 1987.

Swanton, John R. *Indian Tribes of the Lower Mississippi Valley and Adjacent Coast of the Gulf of Mexico.* Smithsonian Institution, Bureau of American Ethnology, Bulletin 43. Washington: Government Printing Office, 1911.

Tallant, Montague. "The 'Bug' of Archaeology." *Hobbies,* July 1935, 101.

Thoburn, Joseph B. "The Prehistoric Cultures of Oklahoma." *Chronicles of Oklahoma* 7 (1929): 211–41.

Thomas, David Hurst. *Exploring Ancient Native America: An Archaeological Guide.* New York: Macmillan, 1994.

———. *Skull Wars: Kennewick Man, Archaeology, and the Battle for Native American Identity.* New York: Basic Books, 2000.

Trowbridge, H. M. "Analysis of Spiro Mound Textiles." *American Antiquity* 4 (1938–39): 51–53.

Turpin, Solveig A., Maciej Henneberg, and David H. Riskind. "Late Archaic Mortuary Practices of the Lower Pecos River Region, Southwest Texas." *Plains Anthropologist* 31 (November 1986): 295–315.

Webb, Malcolm C. "Functional and Historical Parallelisms between Mesoamerican and Mississippian Cultures." In *The Southeastern Ceremonial Complex: Artifacts and Analysis, the Cottonlandia Conference,* edited by Patricia Galloway, 279–93. Lincoln: University of Nebraska Press, 1989.

Wyckoff, Don G. "Spiro: Native American Trade a Millennium Ago." *Gilcrease Journal* 9 (Winter 2001): 49–63.

Wyckoff, Don, and Dennis Peterson. "Spiro Mounds: Prehistoric Gateway . . . Present-Day Enigma." Transcript for Spiro video, Spiro Mounds Archaeological Park: n.p., n.d.

Acknowledgments

Though authors get the credit, books are never really written by one person. In making this project a reality, I received help from people around the country. I am indebted to so many and I thank each and every one of them. They should know that they share in any success this book might receive, but for any mistakes in it, I'll shoulder those alone.

At the Sam Noble Oklahoma Museum of Natural History, Don Wyckoff, Peggy Rubenstein, Bernard Schriever, and Julie Dokes graciously allowed me to go through their archives and cheerfully put up with me asking to see this or copy that. At the University of Arkansas Collections, Mary Suter and Jane-Ellen Murphy took time away from their work to show me through the university's magnificent holdings of Spiro artifacts. At the University of Arkansas's Special Collection Library, Anne Prichard, Andrea Cantrell, and Angela Hand went out of their way to help me find information on Sam Dellinger's Spiro connections. In Bonner Springs, Kansas, at the Wyandotte County Historical Society and Museum, Patricia Schurkamp and Joel Thornton were invaluable in assisting me through Harry Trowbridge's records. Carol A. Spindle, at the Robert S. Kerr Museum in Poteau, Oklahoma, gave much of her time to help me go through the museum's files, show me their Spiro artifacts, and even put me in contact with former museum curator Laird King.

Other people in the general Spiro area who gave much of their knowledge and time to me are Katie Murdoch at the Pope County Public Library, Russellville, Arkansas; Melba Wadsworth at the Poteau Valley Genealogical Society Research Library, Poteau; Sara Erwin at the Gilcrease Museum, Tulsa; Phyllis Adams and Terry Zinn at the Oklahoma Historical Society, Oklahoma City; Jennifer Rano, Twila Camp, and Jaymie Lang at the Western History Collection on the University of Oklahoma campus in Norman; Richard Drass, Bob Brooks, and Lisa Stambeck at the Oklahoma Archaeological Survey, Norman; and Kenneth D. Meek at the Woolaroc Museum in Bartlesville, Oklahoma.

Several people went above and beyond their duties. I wound up spending a considerable amount of time with them discussing Spiro and sharing ideas about this mysterious city. Dennis Peterson, site manager at the Spiro Archaeological Park, loves his job and loves Spiro. I spent days following him around the site, asking questions about the mounds, their history, and his interpretation. And he patiently answered them all. He might recognize much in this book. Frank Schambach at Southern Arkansas University not only spent hours with me discussing Spiroan trade, cranial deformation, and their connection to the Tunica, but he ensured I had copies of his articles and letters. Then there is Phil Newkumet, who had actually worked on the Craig Mound in its heyday. I spent many an evening at Phil's home in Norman, drinking coffee and talking way into the night about his Spiro adventures. His insight and the insights of all these men were invaluable to me.

There were also friends who were incredibly hospitable to me during my Spiro travels. First and foremost are Terri Baker, her husband, Tom, and their son, Charles. Terry and I are old friends from way back, and they put me up at their home in Tahlequah for several days while I did my research. They are warm, wonderful friends, and I owe them much. Also, I need to thank the people of the Caddo Indian Tribe in Binger, Oklahoma. They long ago adopted me, and I them. I never go to Oklahoma without visiting them, and they always treat me like a long-lost son. Bobby Gonzalez, Robert Cast, Cecile Carter, and a host of others provided me with their interpretations of Spiro. Also, my hat goes off to Jim Bruner, first manager of the Spiro Archaeological Park. Though I've never met him, I appreciate that he was able to interview some of the old Pocola Mining Company partners and leave a record of it.

At my home at the University of North Carolina Wilmington, I am also indebted to many people. Kathleen Berkeley, former chair of the Department of History, encouraged my writing and always put up with my travels. Current chair Sue McCaffray does the same, and I thank her for it. Mark Spaulding and Jo Ann Seiple, former dean of the College of Arts and Sciences, both helped me get a semester research reassignment. Will Moore and his wife, Charlotte, listened to my descriptions of Spiro art and provided me with books and information to clarify my ideas. Eleanor Reber, an archaeologist at UNCW, provided valuable insights on Cahokia and Mississippian archaeology. And last, but never least, Sophie Williams, Madeleine Bombeld, Mary Corcoran, Cleta Mosley, and Daren Dean at UNCW Inter-Library Loan always delivered even the most obscure title I wanted. They do great work! And there are just a host of friends and relatives who always provided their support. Thanks go to my mother, Ann, and sisters, Tracy and Rhonda. But many thanks also go to such friends as Kevin Sands, Jack and Carol Mills, Buddy Ebron, Raoul Sosa, David Fann, and Patrick "La Gaule" Arnold, who made it a point to drag me away from my writing every now and again. But most thanks go to Caryn Mills La Vere, who loves me and made my Spiro writing possible. To all these people, I say thank you.

Index